ARLEEN PATRICIA MERCORELLA

A Matter of Survival

THE STORY OF FRANCES

SPRINGTIME PRESS
LELAND, NORTH CAROLINA

Copyright © 2014 Arleen Patricia Mercorella
All rights reserved.
ISBN: 0615993605
ISBN 13: 9780615993607
Library of Congress Control Number: 2014905642
Springtime Press, Leland, North Carolina
Cover Design: Pat Marriott
Author's Photo: John Domoney of JDI Photography, Inc.

Dedication

To Uncle Ralph for his inspiration and encouragement,
which led to this book becoming a reality.

Acknowledgements

My sincerest thanks go to my cousins Grace, Loretta, and Donna Jean for their support, encouragement and validation of family information. A very special thanks to my husband, Ralph, for his reassurance and untiring support.
Thanks also go to the fine folks of CreateSpace who helped bring this book to life.

Prologue

Does it seem too hard to cope with life's challenges and hardships? Some of us might find life's difficulties too much to handle and may indulge in self-pity, looking to others to feel sorry for us or worse yet, seek unconventional methods of coping. I hope anyone who may be facing life's hardships and difficulties will read this story and receive reassurance and inspiration from it.

This is the story of Frances, my mother. A story one may think is unbelievable, although I can assure you this story was based on true facts. It is one woman's illustration of how she coped even in the most adverse of times.

As the author of this book, I did much research, going back several generations of family who lived before me and realizing the influence they have had on my own life. In doing so, I recognized that if my ancestors had chosen to make different decisions in their life, or had taken a different path, I would not be the person I am today, nor would I even be living here in this great country. While many family values were instilled in me, I had taken these values for granted.

This book is a personal reflection of stories my mother told me about her life as well as my having lived a part of it. The validation of family lore from the little family I have left has made me recognize that Frances exhibited extraordinary strength and courage and managed to survive it all. It astonishes me how she remained so sweet and kind and demonstrated no bitterness because of the many difficulties she encountered. She set a remarkable example, persevering through so many challenges while still keeping her faith in God. Maybe as a child I didn't quite understand how difficult it must have been for her as a single parent, considering the many obstacles she faced, but years later, when raising my own family, I tried to follow her example and came to realize this inspirational story needed to be told. Hence, this novel was created.

Contents

		Page Number
Chapter 1:	Where Am I?	1
Chapter 2:	A Life Before	12
Chapter 3:	Moving from Italy	15
Chapter 4:	Dolores	22
Chapter 5:	Life Gets Harder	35
Chapter 6:	Living in the Home	37
Chapter 7:	Growing Up	43
Chapter 8:	Three Years to Go	47
Chapter 9:	A New Life Begins	62
Chapter 10:	The Search	71
Chapter 11:	Kay	73
Chapter 12:	Long-Lost Family Relatives	80
Chapter 13:	The Meeting	88
Chapter 14:	Summer Fun	96
Chapter 15:	Now That's an Attractive Young Man	98
Chapter 16:	Meeting His Family	112
Chapter 17:	Courting	117
Chapter 18:	The Wedding	122
Chapter 19:	Married Life	133
Chapter 20:	The Next Phase	142
Chapter 21:	A Big Surprise	150
Chapter 22:	A New Family	158
Chapter 23:	Life Changes	164
Chapter 24:	The End Is Near	181

Chapter 25:	The Plan	196
Chapter 26:	The Start of a New Life	207
Chapter 27:	A New Start Again	217
Chapter 28:	A Time to Celebrate	224
Chapter 29:	Making Changes	230
Chapter 30:	We're Looking for Your Husband	234
Chapter 31:	A New Christmas Season	242
Chapter 32:	Frances Meets Her Brother	254
Chapter 33:	Introducing the New Man	263
Chapter 34:	The New Arrival	268
Chapter 35:	Decisions, Decisions	277
Chapter 36:	Life with Mother	281
Chapter 37:	Making It All Work	292
Chapter 38:	Another Coincidence	297
Chapter 39:	When All Is Going Well, Look Out	301
Chapter 40:	Road to Recovery	309
Chapter 41:	Unforeseen Opposition	313
Chapter 42:	The Honeymoon Is Over	317
Chapter 43:	A Thanksgiving Not to Be Forgotten	322
Chapter 44:	Approaching the Sunset Years	329
Chapter 45:	…Until Death Do You Part	352
Epilogue:		361

One

Where Am I?

The year was 1923.

As Frances sat at the bottom of the gigantic staircase, tears rolled down her tiny face in silence. If the truth was really to be known, her weeping was silent due to her fear of being heard. She was little for her age, six years, and she was so frightened, so very frightened. The strange lady, dressed in black, had ordered her to clean all the cobwebs on the stairs and the ceiling above it. But what were cobwebs? What was she doing here? Who was this strange person? Where was her mommy? Where was her brother, Peter, and why had he and her daddy disappeared?

She sat there trembling with her eyes shut tight. She was afraid to look around because she was so engulfed with terror. Suddenly she felt a hand being placed softly on her shoulder, and, almost afraid to look up, she heard a gentle voice ask if she could help.

"Hi," she said. "My name is Melody. What is your name? Can I help you? I live here too."

Trying desperately not to show the older girl her tears, Frances replied, telling Melody her name and saying with deep, gasping sobs, "Sister Mary Gerard brought me to these stairs just after I came to this awful place. She acted so mean and told me I had to clean the cobwebs on the staircase." The little girl continued through her tears. "But, Melody, I don't know what cobwebs are. She said she is coming back later to inspect the work that I am to do for her, but I'm not even sure what she wants. She kept telling me that 'cleanliness is next to godliness,' whatever that means."

Melody told Frances that she had been living here since she was five years old. She said she just turned fifteen, and in one year she would be leaving this place to start a new life to live on her own.

Melody wiped Frances's tears with the hem of her meager dress and covered her with a warm hug.

"First, let me tell you what Sister wants you to do. Frances, cobwebs are spiderwebs," the young girl explained.

"Oh," Frances said, almost with a little giggle. "I know what spiderwebs are, but I never heard of the name that Sister called them. Why didn't she just say that?"

Melody sat next to the little girl on the step. She took her hand into hers and explained that there were many, many young girls who lived together in this building and Frances was just the newest addition. Each girl had chores to do. The Sisters were very strict and constantly inspected their work.

"Melody, how am I ever going to reach the ceiling? It's too far away."

Melody got up and told Frances to follow her. She showed the little girl a closet at the top of the staircase. Inside there were all sorts of mops, brooms, and rags and an assortment of other things placed neatly together.

"Frances, let me show you what Sister wants you to do." Melody took two aprons out of the closet; one was small and the other was larger. Both aprons looked somewhat frayed and old, but still they appeared to be very clean. She then instructed the little girl to first put on the smaller apron. Taking two additional cloths from the closet, Melody showed Frances how to fold one in half like a triangle and place it on her head, tying it under her hair. Then, reaching back into the closet, Melody handed Frances the biggest mop she had ever seen. "Watch me. Just hold your mop straight up and drag it over the ceiling above the steps. When this is finished, you must then go over all the steps with the mop. When all has been cleaned, we will take the mop outside and shake it until no more dust comes out of it."

Frances wiped her face several times with the bottom of her apron. She was grateful she'd found a friend, even though she was so much older than herself. Could she really trust her? She didn't say much to Melody, but she was thankful to have her next to her.

Frances tried to hold the large mop straight up, but she had a difficult time trying to balance the big stick in the air.

"Melody, I am never going to learn to do this. The ceiling is too high, and this mop is too big," she pleaded.

Melody replied, telling her to "Keep working and try to do your best, because you will probably have to do this work often."

As she tried to reach the ceiling, Frances lost her balance one or two times and almost fell backward down the stairs. Luckily, the railing saved her from tumbling down the many steps.

When the work was done, the two girls went outside. Melody showed Frances how to shake all the dust out of the mop, telling Frances they had to make sure the mop was just as clean as when they'd taken it from the closet. They then placed the mop, aprons, and head scarves back neatly in the closet. She and Frances sat on the top step in silence. Melody was hoping Frances would speak first.

Finally, after a long stillness, Frances looked up at her new friend and asked, "Melody, when am I going to be able to go home?"

Frances thought surely her mother would be looking for her, and she probably didn't know where she was.

"Oh Frances, you poor little child," the older girl said sadly. "I also remember that strange and frightening feeling of being left alone here. Frances, you are here to stay, to live here with the rest of us."

"Oh no," Frances replied. "I have my suitcase packed, and I am leaving as soon as I can."

The sun was now peeking through the large window, casting sunbeams up and down the staircase. It was strange—even though the stairs were the biggest she had ever seen, the sunrays seemed to make it a warm and secure place. Suddenly she felt very tired. She cuddled up to Melody and fell fast asleep.

After a few minutes, Melody heard the sound of strong wooden heels coming down from the upper stairs. She was frightened, but she didn't know what to do with Frances. She simply wasn't strong enough to carry the little one down to find a safe place to hide.

"And what is this?" the woman in black said sternly. "Is this what we call sleeping on the job? It's time for me to inspect the work she was to do, and if it's not satisfactory, I will take a switch to her."

Sister Mary Gerard then swept her hand over a step; thank goodness she didn't get dust on it. Then she did it again and again.

"All right," she said. "Melody, take her downstairs to the dormitory with her suitcase and ask the Sister there to show you where she will sleep. Then you go to where you're supposed to be and leave her! If you don't listen to me, then you will be the one to get the switch."

"Yes, Sister," Melody replied.

Melody realized the little girl was exhausted, not only because of the work they had accomplished, but because of the fright she must have felt. Melody gently called to wake her up and told her they must find a place to put her things and get her a place to sleep. Frances rose quickly to her feet, all the time staring at the fierce-looking lady in black. Somehow she managed to cling to Melody as if she was going to be the only safe and kind person she would find in this place. They walked down the big staircase and then down a very long hallway. Finally, they came to a doorway, and Frances saw another nun sitting at a desk. Melody spoke first to Sister Mary Joseph, telling her Sister Mary Gerard had sent her down to the unit so that Frances could be assigned a place to sleep. The Sister looked exhausted and shook her head, mumbling sadly that there was so little room and so many girls; she didn't know where she was going to put her new charge. Finally, after some time, the Sister managed to squeeze yet another bed and another little night table into the large room. It was near the end of an aisle, and Sister Mary Joseph directed the girls to make Frances's bed. She had placed a set of sheets, a pillow, and a thin blanket on top of what appeared to be a clean, but very worn-out mattress. The Sister also left a little gray dress that looked as if it might fit the newest member of her ward. Melody told Frances the dress was a uniform, and they all had to wear it. After helping her make the bed, she assured Frances she would be okay now as long as she listened to whatever she was being told to do. Frances was so frightened, because she knew that Melody was now going to leave her. Even though she was young, she thanked the older girl for being so nice to her. She then asked if she would see her again. Melody said that she would visit her the next day after breakfast.

A Matter of Survival

Frances replied, "Gee, I don't think I'll be here after breakfast. I'm sure I will be going home!"

After Melody left, Frances opened her small, battered suitcase, and inside was the most precious thing she had—her rag doll. Frances squeezed the doll tighter than she ever had. The tattered doll offered her the only sense of security in this strange new place. She then quickly put a pair of underwear, a faded cotton dress, and one pair of socks in the night table's drawer. She didn't want to put down her precious doll, but suddenly a loud bell rang, which Frances discovered was the announcement of dinner. With much hesitation, she placed the doll carefully with her other belongings in the drawer. All the girls lined up in front of their beds, and Frances followed, doing the same. Then they all marched out of the large room, down again into the hallway, and finally turned into a very large room lined with tables. All the girls were seated according to their age group. It seemed like there were an awful lot of girls at her table. At each seat there was a metal plate, a fork, knife, spoon and a tin cup. Everyone stood in back of a chair, and no one made a sound.

Then one of the other Sisters came into the room and announced, "Grace will be said by the leader at table twelve."

After the young girl said some words of prayer, Frances heard a strange sound, like a toy "clicker." Everyone immediately sat down into the chair that was in front of them. Frances almost let out a giggle, because the girls looked just like the toy soldiers she had watched her brother play with. She looked around and saw that no one was laughing. They all sat at the tables in silence. Suddenly, the doors to the kitchen opened, and, almost as if it was a parade, many other Sisters came from the kitchen holding big pots and ladles. They were wearing large white aprons that covered most of their long, black dresses. The Sisters reminded Frances of a time when she had visited the zoo and watched the penguins running around.

The nuns ladled something that didn't look too good onto their tin plates. Frances was so tired and hungry; she didn't care what the food looked like. She was grateful for whatever she was given. She tried to talk to the girl next to her but was hushed up. She quickly learned that talking was not allowed during dinner. Frances had started to pick at her food when all of a sudden, a little girl at the end of her table started to cry, saying she didn't like the food. One of the Sisters came over to her, and without saying a word, she pinched the little one's nose and dropped the food into her mouth. Frances learned very early not to cause any kind of fuss that might upset the Sisters. She didn't want this to happen to her!

After dinner, each girl took her plate and eating utensils to a large table just outside the kitchen. Then it was announced they would be now be allowed to enter the recreation rooms for one hour of free time.

Frances followed the other young girls she had been sitting with into a large room. It seemed the first four tables of girls had all marched together and entered the room. The room had chairs, tables, books, and even a large radio. The room looked very neat and very clean, even with so many young people in it.

One of the little girls approached Frances and asked her name. She said Frances could sit by her if she liked. She said her name was Theresa, and she was seven years old. She had been living in this place for as long as she could remember. She told Frances she was not so frightened anymore, but then whispered, confessing she was only scared of the Sisters.

"Frances, whatever they tell you to do, do it, and you will be fine."

"Oh, I will try to be a good girl, but I'm sure I will be leaving first thing tomorrow morning."

Frances was grateful that she had made a friend in Theresa. They stayed together for the rest of the hour. There was some pleasant music playing on the radio, and Theresa showed Frances some little paper dolls they were allowed to play with. Theresa said when the first warning bell rang, they would have to return them to the cabinet. Suddenly a loud bell rang. Theresa told her it was now time to put the paper dolls away, and maybe tomorrow night, they could play with them again.

But Frances replied, "I'm sure I won't be here tomorrow, but thank you anyway."

All the young girls lined up, and when another loud bell rang, they all marched back to the dormitory. They were told to line up in front of their beds, and the first section would be allowed to go into the bathroom to wash up and brush their teeth before bedtime. The routine continued until all the girls had had a chance to go into the bathroom to wash up. Luckily, Theresa slept next to Frances's bed. The girls smiled at each other, happy to have made friends. Then Sister, using her "clicker," said they all were to kneel beside their beds to say their nighttime prayers together, and then it was lights out. Frances closed her eyes and fell fast asleep. This day had been so exhausting for her.

It seemed that she had been asleep for just a short time when a loud bell rang, startling her awake. It was still dark outside, but all the lights went on in the dormitory, lighting up the enormous room. Everyone awoke, knelt down, and recited their morning prayers together. Immediately after their prayers, they made their beds. Frances also rose quickly and tried to follow the routine of the others. She pulled her suitcase from under the bed and put her meager possessions into it. She somewhat made the bed, washed up, tried to comb her hair, and then sat on the bed with her suitcase under her arm. She was sure her mother would be coming this morning to take her home. She waited and waited, but no one called her name to tell her that her mother was here.

Instead another bell rang, and all the girls marched out of the dormitory down the hall to the doors that led outside. There was a church across the street, which Frances learned later was St. Michael's Roman Catholic Church. Despite the chill in the air, all the girls walked through the darkness to it in silence and entered the church. After they were all seated in the church, a priest came out to say Mass for the girls. Frances thought the church appeared to be an endless sea of young girls dressed in the same ugly uniform. She noticed there were also many Sisters sitting at the end of various pews throughout the building. As an adult, when Frances reflected back, she thought if one didn't know better, they looked more like prison guards than religious nuns.

To Frances it looked as if the church couldn't fit even one more person into it. One of the Sisters indicated again, with the noise of a "clicker," that all the girls were to kneel up straight in the place where they were. Each girl not only had to kneel with their back straight, but also had to place their hands so that they were touching together with fingers pointing straight up in prayer. No one dared to lean back or move their hands. They all stayed this way for a very long time until the priest left the altar.

Frances felt like she was going to pass out. She was tired and hungry, and it was still dark outside. Finally they were told they may proceed and march to the dining hall to have breakfast. Even though Frances was hungry, she didn't want to have breakfast—she wanted to go home.

When Frances lived with her mother, she would help herself to whatever was available for breakfast. Normally, she would go into the kitchen hoping to find juice or milk in the ice box and if she was lucky, she might even find corn flakes in the cabinet. If not, she would make do with what she could scrounge.

After saying grace they all sat quietly. Again the Sisters came out with their pots and ladles. They dropped lumpy stuff—oatmeal—into their dishes. Frances remembered from the night before to eat very quickly and to eat in silence.

When the girls finished breakfast, it was announced which group of girls would have kitchen duty to help the Sisters to wash what must have been hundreds of dishes. Everyone else placed their dishes on the long tables, just as they'd done the night before. Groups of four tables were then brought to an assembly area. It was at this time they were given their assignments for the week. Some would be assigned to wash sheets and towels, sweep floors, clean rooms, wash windows, and on and on. The list of chores seemed to be endless. She tried but was not allowed to go back to her bed to get her suitcase. How would her mother find her? When could she please go home?

It seemed as if everyone had been given their weekly assignments except Frances, and one by one they left the room. Frances sat on a bench, waiting for whatever was to come next, and after a very long time, she was the only one left in the room. Finally, her name was called. She was so excited, because she knew it was time to leave. Surely her mother was here. Frances ran back to the dormitory, grabbed her suitcase, and running to the front desk, she said, "Sister, Sister, I'm Frances. You called me."

"Yes, I did call your name," the Sister replied, "because you have not been assigned to your classroom. You will join the other girls your age in your assigned room and start your lessons. After your lessons are over today, you will then return to me, and I will assign chores for you to attend to this week."

Little Frances could not believe it. How and when was she going to leave this place? She hated it here! But, she was an obedient child and followed the instructions that were given to her by the Sister very carefully.

Melody did come by to see her as promised. She told Frances, she would try to come to visit as much as possible, but that it was very difficult for her to leave her assigned area.

Day after day the routine was always the same; she would get up, repack, and get ready to leave this awful place. She would tell her little rag doll today was the day they would be leaving. She would even say good-bye to Theresa and a few other new friends and wait for her mommy to come. But Mommy never came for her.

Finally, after several weeks of doing the same thing every morning, Frances was starting to get very discouraged and was constantly on the verge of tears. As promised, Melody came again to visit her. She looked at Frances, thinking, *Frances always seems to be so sad.* Melody decided it was time. She sat on Frances's bed next to her. Putting her arm around Frances's little shoulders, she took a deep breath.

"Frances, you must listen very carefully to what I am about to tell you. Your mother will not be coming for you. Not today, not tomorrow. You are going to be here for a very long time. This is now your home. You must just get used to it."

She continued as Frances looked up at her in disbelief with tears rolling down her cheeks. She didn't want to live here. Frances could no longer cry in silence. She threw herself down on the bed, and loud sobs came from deep inside her. Melody put her hand on Frances's back, stroking her ever so softly, remembering when she too had gone through the terrible realization that this was now home.

"Frances, try to accept what I am saying, and please try to make the best of it. I know how you feel, because I also went through this. Keep busy and ask God and his saints to help you. Sometimes it actually seems okay. I've made many friends here, and I know you will also. Remember, I will always come to visit you if you need me. Just ask one of the Sisters, and I promise I will be there for you."

After some time, Frances stopped crying because in her heart, she feared Melody was telling her the truth. Her mother hadn't come, and she had no idea where her father and little brother were.

Once she reluctantly resigned herself to what Melody had told her, things seemed to get a little better. The routine of day-to-day living took hold. The hardest thing was getting up so early every day, which Frances discovered was five o'clock in the morning. It was so difficult to get dressed and then go to Mass in what seemed like the middle of the night. She was always on the verge of passing out in the pew where she knelt. Frances found this routine to be very difficult. They were told they had to practice to be good Catholic girls. Eventually the time would come for them to receive Holy Communion; this was the reason why none of them were allowed to eat anything before receiving the daily host. This type of discipline must be observed. Each day Frances didn't know how she was going to make it through the Mass; she always felt as if she was going to pass out from hunger. The girls were never given a great deal of food—just enough.

Assignments were given out to the girls on a regular basis, and one of them Frances liked a lot. She was assigned to bring Father Reilly his breakfast after he said Mass. She would get a tray, which had been prepared by the Sisters in the kitchen, and bring it to him into the sacristy of the church every morning. She would then return later to pick up the tray when he was finished. He never ate the entire breakfast and always left toast or something else on the tray. Each day before bringing the tray back to the kitchen, Frances would hide in one of the church doorways and finish Father Reilly's breakfast. That was the best part of the day! When the Sisters wanted to give this assignment to someone else, she would plead with them, saying she liked spending extra time in the church, and begged them to let her continue this chore. It was, of course, the extra food she wanted to gulp down before anyone discovered her secret.

Years later, when Frances was an adult, she thought back to those days and was certain Father Reilly deliberately left something on his tray so that she would get a little something extra.

As part of her religious training, every Saturday each girl had to go to confession and confess her "sins" to the priest so that she would someday be able to receive the sacrament of Holy Communion. Frances would go to confession and make up sins, because she really couldn't think of anything she did that was bad, except maybe for finishing Father Reilly's breakfast.

A Matter of Survival

It seemed now the days ran into weeks, and the weeks ran into almost a year. Frances discovered that Christmas was a very special time at the home. At dinner on Christmas Eve, each girl had an orange placed on her plate. How special this seemed to her. She could not recall ever seeing one before. One of the other girls had to show her how to eat this sweet treat. She ate it ever so slowly because she wanted the sweetness to last for as long as it could.

The biggest surprise of all was on Christmas morning. After going to Mass and after finishing breakfast, the girls were told there would be no chores on this day and that they were to go straight to their recreation rooms. The rooms had been decorated with greenery the Sisters had taken from outside and strung across the room in a very pretty way. There was even a tree, which had been donated to the home from people who lived in the nearby town. When Frances and the other young girls entered the room, they were each given a package by the Sisters. Hers had brightly colored red-and-green paper wrapped around it, and Frances couldn't imagine what could possibly be in it. She could not believe that she was actually being given a present. The excitement that arose inside her could hardly be contained. She carefully unwrapped the package, and much to her delight, she discovered a pair of roller skates. Her friend, Theresa, opened her package, and there was a pretty doll in her box. What fun this was today!

She started to feel a little more comfortable with the other girls and, of course, Melody still came to visit her. She grew to love Melody and her visits. The only thing that still troubled her was a recurring dream she had.

Two

A LIFE BEFORE

Frances had frequent recurring nightmares dreaming of her home and past life. Many nights she would wake up with fright and find she was screaming out loud. Upon waking she could remember another place—a large building where her mother, Dolores, her father, Frank, younger brother, Peter, and she were eating a meal at a large table. In the center of the table were pretty colored eggs, and she and her brother were each given a chocolate bunny to save for later in the day. Both she and her brother were wearing new clothes, and the family had gone to church all together that morning. She knew this was a special day. After church she and Peter had played together in their room, and a short time later, they were called to be seated at the table. At first it seemed quiet, but then her mother and her father started raising their voices and became so loud that she and her little brother, Peter, shook with fear. They sneakily left the table, and she took Peter with her to where they slept at night. The yelling continued. They both put their hands over their ears and closed their eyes. Suddenly it got very quiet. Then, unexpectedly, her father came into the room and, without saying a word, grabbed three-year-old Peter by his arm, opened the window, and took him down the fire escape. Frances watched from the window with horror. Peter was crying and screaming all the way down the metal ladders with his father pulling him harder and harder. *Why did her father take Peter out the window? Why did he only take Peter? Why did*

A Matter of Survival

he not speak to me? Where were they going? The sounds of Peter's cries could be heard less and less and finally faded into a silence that swept over the room. The quietness was a new kind of fear that she had never felt before. Frances sat on the floor under the window, bewildered at what she had just witnessed.

Abruptly the door to the room swung open. Her mother was standing there, enraged.

"Where are they?" She turned to Frances, but Frances was afraid to answer.

Her mother shook her hard. "Did you hear me? Where are they?"

Frances started to cry and pointed out the window. Her mother stuck her head out and looked up and down the street. Then panic set in. All at once, the most piercing scream came from her, followed by deep sobs. Her husband and beloved son were gone!

Several days passed, but still her little brother and father had not returned. Frances's mother seemed to be talking to herself all the time and mumbling something to the effect that there wouldn't be enough money to buy food or pay the rent. Frances didn't understand but tried to console her mother with soft caresses while her mother mostly ignored her. She didn't seem interested in her young daughter's affections at all.

Dolores was ultimately forced to get a job working in a factory and decided to leave Frances alone in the apartment when she went to work. She warned the child not to let anyone in while she was gone. This routine continued for two weeks. Six-year-old Frances stayed alone each day in the apartment and tried not to let the solitude frighten her, but she was terrified. The only companion she had was a rag doll, which she always carried with her. There were days when her mother would forget to leave food for her, and Frances would search through the kitchen cupboards, hoping to find crackers or anything else she could eat. Suspicious neighbors watched Dolores leave each day and then reported her to the authorities for abandoning her child. The little girl was lonely and afraid to be by herself, so one day when the doorbell rang, she answered it. Two strangers, a lady and a man, were standing before her, demanding to know if she was alone. Frances nodded her head affirmatively. The lady walked past Frances and entered the apartment. Finding a small suitcase, she placed some of the child's clothes into it. Terrified at what she was witnessing, Frances quickly grabbed her rag doll as if the doll was going to offer her some sort of security. All of a sudden, the strangers were pulling at her, telling her she would have to come with them. Little Frances was panicked and desperate, belatedly remembering what her mother had told her about not answering the door. She didn't want to go with these people. She kicked, screamed, and cried for her mother, but the strangers overpowered her. They dragged her off, leaving a notice on the apartment door saying the child was now in the custody of protective services.

Frances continued screaming and kicking, even when they reached the street. The woman offered no comfort to the hysterical child, but rather told her to calm down. She was going to be better off than she was now, and she should stop giving them a hard time. Before she knew what was happening, she was shoved into a car, and after what seemed like a very long ride, they arrived at a large unfamiliar building.

A sign outside the building read, "St. Joseph's Home for Girls."

Three

MOVING FROM ITALY

During the latter part of the nineteenth century, farm laborers in Italy lived under extremely harsh conditions and were very poor. Landlords charged high rents for inadequate housing, and to make matters worse, disease had spread throughout farms in Italy, destroying crops, particularly grapevines. This resulted in an agricultural crisis; as such there was very little work for farm laborers. Those lucky enough to have found work were forced by landlords to live in harsh conditions, often residing in one-room houses with no plumbing or privacy. Landlords ruled the land, offering low pay and providing unsteady employment. In addition, many laborers were isolated due to the lack of roads in Italy. Because of dire hardships facing the Italian people, the Italian Government offered free passage to its citizens to leave Italy and go to the Americas. Thus, many Italians left Italy due to extreme poverty.

While some Italians migrated to the United States, a great many found their way to South America. They'd heard stories that in South America there was an abundance of farming land, low taxes, and good wages for laborers. They hoped if they moved to South America, it would only be temporary and dreamed that someday they could return to Italy with enough money to buy land of their own.

So in 1897 Frances's grandparents, Pietro and Rosa, together with their child, Maria (Mary), migrated to Rio de Janeiro, Brazil, where many other

Italian farm laborers had settled. Work was supposed to be plentiful. They anticipated working as farm laborers on coffee plantations. However, shortly after arriving in Rio de Janeiro, they discovered that yes, work was plentiful, but the new Italian laborers were not treated well by the plantation owners, who were seeking cheap labor and expected the new immigrants to work exceedingly long, hard hours for low wages. Getting adapted to this new land was not what they'd expected or hoped it would be. It didn't take long to discover that they did not like living in Brazil.

Pietro felt sure the move to South America had been a big mistake. Despite Rosa's pleas to stay and settle there, or even worse, go back to Italy, he decided Brazil should now be thought of as an interim move. Certainly going back to Italy without funds was simply not an option. He had a friend, Giuseppe, who wrote to him regularly, and after reading his many letters, he was determined the family should try now to get to America. He was a strong-willed individual, and since he felt he was the head, as well as the ruler, of his family, he expected his wife to go along with any decision he made.

Giuseppe had moved from Italy to Rio a few years before, and he too, found it not to his liking, and moved on to New York. He wrote telling Pietro that in America Italians were able to find work, not as farm laborers, but could earn good wages working in construction, and it was easier for them to support their families and at the same time save money. He wrote of the many opportunities that were plentiful, as there was new construction everywhere. Many new buildings, roads, bridges, and tunnels were being constructed, especially in New York. Laborers were needed for these numerous construction jobs, which made it much easier to obtain steady work. The work was hard, but the pay was good. He also heard other stories telling of Italian immigrants who had left Italy before them and gone directly to New York, and were now becoming rich. He decided New York was the place to go.

Shortly after arriving in Rio, a second daughter was born, who they named Dolores, followed by six more children. However, one child died at birth, another child drowned at the age of six, and still another died from smallpox. They scrimped and saved with a plan that someday they would move to America. After twelve hard years, the family had saved enough

A Matter of Survival

money for steamboat passage. In 1909 they again set sail, but this time for America, heading to New York.

When they arrived and finally entered New York Harbor, a deep silence fell across the crowd. As the poorest of poor stood next to the boat's railing, they viewed the welcoming sight of the Statue of Liberty and had the feeling they had made a good decision to come to this new land. This was a new beginning. When the ship docked, the new immigrants were required to pass through Ellis Island to obtain the proper documents clearing them to enter into the United States. Finally after many hours of waiting and nervous anticipation, they were approved to enter the United States via New York City.

The family, carrying all their worldly possessions, stepped out onto the streets of New York. Pietro pulled a letter from Giuseppe from his jacket pocket containing directions to where many Italian immigrants had settled in New York's Lower East Side. He wrote often, telling Pietro of the great success he had achieved.

New York was crowded with people everywhere. As the family walked with their children in tow, they found an area where horses and carriages were waiting for passengers. Pietro handed the letter to the horseman, showing an address on Mulberry Street. Finally, after several miles that proved to be a long, uncomfortable, and vile-smelling ride, they arrived at their destination. Along the way, they'd observed streets littered with garbage and congested with pushcarts as well as people. The noise level was very loud with people shouting and speaking in all different languages. The pushcart merchants seemed to be haggling with residents over fresh vegetables and other items while ignoring the filth in the street. The entire atmosphere made them feel very uneasy thinking that this area might even be dangerous and unsafe. As they got closer to their destination, they saw shops and pushcart signs they could understand, as now the spoken language was Italian, which, at last, was familiar to them. Finally they reached a building with the number on it that they were seeking. Surprisingly, the building appeared to be not one of great wealth as they'd anticipated, but rather, it was an old, dirty, and dilapidated five-story walk-up tenement building. Fire escapes adorned each floor, which also had clotheslines hanging from them. People were everywhere, and the noise level was deafening!

Pietro exited the wagon and climbed a stoop of stairs, leaving his family below. The family, too, got out of the wagon and waited with great eagerness to meet their old friends. Looking at the mailboxes, Pietro located the name of his friend. He rang the bell where his friend's name appeared, but there was no answer. He rang again, but still no answer. Finally, somewhat disappointed, he went back down to the street and he, his wife, and family sat on the concrete steps for quite some time. The family was exhausted from their long journey. The children were now getting hungry and restless. Rosa tried to discipline her children, but without much success. Suddenly, coming through the crowd of people in the street, Pietro spotted his friend walking through the busy maze.

"Giuseppe," he called, "I'm here."

The men exchanged greetings and a warm embrace. Finally, the wife and children were acknowledged. Giuseppe had remembered the wife as a young, nice-looking woman, but now he observed only a tired and somewhat aged woman. The years in Rio apparently had taken a toll on her. These days, the hardships they'd all endured had taken a toll on them all.

Giuseppe invited the new immigrants to spend the night with his family, and in the morning he would introduce Pietro to the *padrone* who could help his friend find work and a place of their own to live. Giuseppe explained the *padrone* was the person new immigrants went to; he was considered the "boss" or "middleman." Since he had been living in America for quite some time, he had connections with American employers.

Giuseppe guided them to his small apartment, which turned out to be on the fifth floor. The climb seemed to take an eternity. Rosa was drained. She'd endured the long and exhausting trip of getting to New York, the anxiety of waiting to satisfy the authorities to pass inspection at Ellis Island, and then the difficult wagon ride to find Giuseppe's address. Now the strenuous climb to Giuseppe's apartment, together with the stench of sickening smells throughout this tenement building, nauseated Rosa to a great extent. She felt the day's journey was all too much for her and had to talk herself into not passing out. The living conditions seemed intolerable to her, but Giuseppe explained later that this was only to be a temporary home. They could live here inexpensively and return to Italy with enough money to buy their own land.

A Matter of Survival

As they reached his flat, Giuseppe's wife, Anna, appeared. She had been on the roof of the building, retrieving the day's wash, and was carrying baskets that contained small mountains of garments. After many trips from the roof to their flat, she would finally be able to start preparing the evening meal.

Entering the flat they observed a meager sitting room, which contained a small sofa as well as a table and several chairs. Adjacent to the sitting room, there was another room that housed two beds and a crib. Rosa, not daring to question her husband, thought, *How are we all going to fit into such a small place?* The family who was providing for them also had three young children, who were playing near their mother. Anna seemed to be a kind woman who at one time was very pretty, but she too had aged much faster than her years with the hardships she endured. She did not appear to be upset about making dinner for all these extra people. She prepared a delicious-smelling sauce, which was to be accompanied by spaghetti. The woman's preparation of familiar food certainly touched the senses with an appetizing aroma from the tiny cooking area. Her cooking seemed to drown out the horrific smell of the tenement. She smiled, greeted them in Italian, and beckoned for them to sit down. Rosa wanted to help, but the journey had been too much for her. She was so tired; she thought if she were to sit down, she would surely fall asleep. The kind woman who was providing for them understood this. She remembered only too well what it had been like when they arrived a few years before. But she was happy with their decision, and even though there was definitely an absence of luxury, it was a good feeling knowing they were living and working in America. Anna believed their dream of returning to Italy with enough money to buy land of their own was becoming a close reality.

The new arrivals sat down and appreciated their dinner with their American friends. Mother, Father, and the five children were totally exhausted, but somehow there was still an air of excitement in starting their new life in America. Even the little ones had sensed there was something better.

After dinner the men discussed how other new immigrants had been able to find work. Giuseppe told his friend that he wanted to be called by his American name now, which was simply "Joe." He said it was easier for him to get work, since the employers remembered him better by his new name. Now that he had "Americanized" his name, he decided he actually liked it better. He told his old friend many new shops were always looking for helpers, but he advised that construction was the best way to find work. Roads were continuously being built, and new buildings were going up all over. The city was rapidly expanding, and new construction was essential to keep up with the influx of immigrants from Europe and South America.

Pietro, with the help of the *padrone,* found work on one of the many construction projects building new uptown city streets. The work was hard, but it paid the rent and put food on the table. The family settled near their friends on the Lower East Side of Manhattan.

The years passed, and Rosa had another child. Dolores, who was now a teenager, was given the responsibility of caring for several little children.

As time went on, the idea of returning to Italy seemed to be a forgotten dream.

Sometimes on an occasional Sunday, her father would take the family on an outing. They would journey to Queens, taking several different trolley lines to reach their destination. They loved visiting the "country," and eventually he decided to move the family to where the air was cleaner and the world was greener. They moved to a small town in Queens called Corona where many other Italian immigrants had settled. Eventually he found work constructing new homes in Queens. Queens was rapidly changing, as more and more city people were moving there. He stopped working at five each day and then would walk about a mile to where they now lived.

Life was not easy for the family. Days were long and hard for all, including the children. It was not unusual for Rosa, together with all the children, to walk a mile or more to buy fresh groceries, especially if it meant saving a few extra pennies for the evening meal. Her husband demanded that dinner be on the table by six. There was no coddling or softness with the children. Discipline was strictly enforced. Rosa missed the city life, but dared not to complain. She accepted the move because it was what her husband wanted. All the children attended a local school but had to leave by the third grade to help with household responsibilities.

However, it was Dolores who gave the most worry and aggravation to her parents. Now, at seventeen, she was the dreamer of the six children. She had

A Matter of Survival

visions of grandeur. Dolores would start her delegated chores, but somehow always got lost in her fantasy of becoming a great actress when she grew up. She imagined wearing beautiful clothes and jewels while performing before adoring audiences. Once, while walking with her mother to buy groceries, she spotted a fashion magazine that had been dumped in someone's trash. Trailing behind her, she quickly grabbed it and put it under her shabby sweater. She knew her mother would not let her keep such a frivolous publication.

That night, after dinner and the cleanup was completed, Dolores went to her bed and pulled the magazine from under the flimsy mattress. She took the magazine outside and hid in the back of the building to look at it. Dolores loved viewing the beautiful dresses and the ladies who posed in them. She enjoyed reading about the latest fashions of 1914 depicting dresses with their long narrow hobble skirts and tunic tops. The magazine also had an article about her favorite movie star, Mary Pickford, who was modeling many of these styles. Her mother's anger and temper would not be appeased with such outrageous delusions. Little did she know Dolores was feeding her fantasy with feelings of splendor and magnificence from the publication she had found. Only "loose" women would ever consider theatrical work, or worse yet, pose for magazines. Girls were meant to marry, and have families of their own and take care of their husband and children. Sometimes Dolores's mother would catch her daydreaming and scold her for it. Her brothers and sisters would snicker and laugh at their silly sister. They made fun of her constantly.

Their father took pleasure in owning his new home in Corona, as it gave him a feeling of accomplishment. He decided, as a tribute to his ownership, he would build a grape arbor in the backyard. He worked on this project diligently whenever time would allow. When it was finished, grapevines were planted, and when the grapes were harvested, wine would be made for his enjoyment in the cold winter months. Dolores loved the arbor. Sometimes she would stand under the arbor and pretend she was a great actress appearing on a stage, performing for the wealthy people in New York.

Then it happened. Her mother discovered the magazine. She used the magazine to give Dolores a swift slap on her head, then yanked her hair so hard that Dolores was sure her mother had pulled a fistful out of her head. She screamed at her, saying she would not tolerate such evil nonsense.

Four

DOLORES

Dolores's parents became more furious with her as her silly daydreaming continued, and as such, it was not uncommon for Dolores to receive several beatings weekly. Her superstitious parents thought surely she had an evil spell cast upon her. Or maybe she had been born with an evil spirit inside her. Or maybe even someone had placed a curse on her. Her behavior was so odd, and yet she still continued her daydreaming, no matter how much she was disciplined. Her mother questioned why Dolores was so unlike the other children. She tried to tell herself what this child needed was simply more punishments. However, she became more and more frustrated, because even the most severe discipline never seemed to curtail Dolores's fantasizing.

When Dolores was approaching her nineteenth birthday, her parents decided the best thing to do with her was to marry her off, and they arranged a meeting with a friend of her father's whose son, Frank, was ten years older than Dolores. Dolores learned Frank was working as a house painter. She considered him to be a good-looking man, and the few times they met, he seemed to speak to her nicely. Of course, the family was pleased that he would be able to provide for his new bride, as young Frank always seemed to have steady work. Dolores's parents were just happy to be rid of this child who caused them so much grief.

Arrangements were made by both families, and their children were married in 1916 in a simple ceremony. Dolores's mother had given her daughter a pretty new dress to be married in. Dolores loved the dress, and when she looked in the mirror, she saw the great actress she was supposed to be. Dolores, for the first time, felt happy with the thought of getting married; at last it was a way of getting away from her parents. She couldn't stand how they were always angry with her. Now maybe she could get on with becoming an actress.

With all parents present, they went to the local church, and the priest proceeded with the marriage. After a short ceremony, Dolores and her new husband returned to her parents' home, where her mother had prepared a special meal for them all.

Much to Dolores's shock, and at Frank's insistence, she learned they were moving away to the Belmont section of the Bronx. The new area was completely foreign to her. She found the area home to many apartment buildings, and it appeared to be very congested, not at all like living in the "country" that she'd grown to like so much. Before long Dolores found she was not only lonely for Queens, but surprisingly her family as well. What was even more of a shock, she found Frank did not treat her nicely. He drank, stayed out late playing cards with his cronies, and came home whenever he pleased. If she questioned him, it was not unusual for him to strike out at her, sometimes striking her so hard that Dolores would fall back, hitting the floor. Even after coming home late and reeking of liquor, he would expect Dolores to perform her wifely duties for him. She hated married life and wished she had the nerve to leave him, but then thought, *Where could I go? How could I disgrace my family, and what would I do for money?* There were never any answers for her.

After just a few months of marriage, Dolores found she was expecting a child. She was not happy at all. Actually, she was not happy with the life her parents had chosen for her. Now that she was with child, how was she ever going to be an actress? Needless to say, the idea of pregnancy literally nauseated her.

She hated the fact that her once-lovely figure was now rapidly changing. She was quickly losing her waistline and getting fatter every day, not to mention how sick she always felt. Even though she was several months pregnant, her husband was not particularly kind to her. He would reprimand her if dinner was not served on time, and he was always finding fault with the apartment, saying she didn't keep it clean to his liking. It was not unusual for him to slap her across the face if he felt she was not performing the duties a good wife was supposed to do.

Dolores hated being married. She not only hated the life her parents had chosen for her, but she also resented this baby growing inside of her and wanted it out of her life. Dolores was still determined to become an actress after the baby was born. Her resentment of the child growing inside her became overwhelming. She didn't want it.

Dolores found the perfect escape. Sometimes she was able to hide a little bit of her house money and go to the movie theater. Then afterward she would have to rush to go to the market and hastily buy whatever was needed for dinner and hurry home. Frank never suspected his wife was spending his money on such foolishness.

She would look in awe at the large screen and imagine herself in the part of the heroine. Yes, this was what she wanted to do with her life. She hadn't figured out quite yet as to how she was going to take care of this baby when it was born and get on with her life as an actress. She would much rather forget who she really was and pretend she was someone else. At twenty years old, she sometimes felt her life was already over, and she would not get the chance she needed to become a famous actress. No, she must not conform. She would sit in front of the mirror, combing her long black hair and sometimes piling it high on top of her head, just like the women she saw in the movies. She would look into the mirror, believing she was on the screen, and would repeat the lines she had read on the theatre screen. In her head she would act out the part of the heroine.

Frank became increasingly upset with her. The only thing he seemed to be interested in when it came to her was eating the dinner she prepared and then at night demanding she come to bed so that he could be satisfied. He never asked how she was feeling, nor would he offer to help her in any way. He, as well, did not seem to relish the fact that she was expecting their first child. When he made reference to it, he said he would like it only if it was a boy.

A Matter of Survival

She never let on that she spent days on end at the movies. She didn't care if the house was not clean enough to his liking, or if dinner was served on time. But what did upset her was the possibility he would beat her if he was not happy with his home life. As each day passed, she resented more and more the upcoming birth of her child and the responsibilities that went along with it. She remembered how her mother was so old-looking and never seemed to have a kind word for her daughter. She wanted the freedom to come and go as she pleased. But then who would take care of her, support her?

Months passed quickly, and she grudgingly prepared for the birth of this child. At night she would sew little clothes. She, too, hoped it would a boy. Summer came, and it was an extremely hot one. Summers in the Bronx could be unbearable, and as if the hot air wasn't bad enough, smells from the other apartments would make her even sicker. Their little place seemed to have no air. Even when she was just sitting and doing nothing, she would feel beads of perspiration running down her face and the drops stinging her eyes. Dolores believed she might pass out from it all. She would go to the window and put her head outside, trying to breathe. Life was not supposed to be this hard. She had read stories about the movie stars who lived in gorgeous homes and had servants to clean and wait on them for their every need. This was the life she was supposed to have. It all seemed too much for her to bear. She would bury her head in her arms and sob, but she never felt any different. Her tears, she thought, would only make her look older, and she certainly was sure never to cry in front of Frank. They were barely talking these days, and she would never tell him how unhappy she really was.

They lived just two blocks from the doctor who would be delivering her child. His name was Dr. Abbott, and he seemed to visit everyone who needed him, no matter what time of day or night it might be. Even though he was just a short distance from her home, she visited Dr. Abbott only one time before, to discuss the necessary arrangements. He would come to her meager flat when her time was due, which he guessed would be about mid-July. Up until now, no one had given her any guidance as what to expect—not even the doctor.

Arleen Patricia Mercorella

Dolores didn't speak very much to the people who lived near her, but late in June she approached one of the woman neighbors they called Nellie. Nellie lived in the downstairs apartment. Dolores couldn't stand watching this woman tend to her motherly chores. She would watch her carry heavy loads of washed laundry to the stairwell and bend out the window, pinning up the never-ending basket of clothes to dry in the hot, sticky air. The sight of the many laundry lines extending from one side of the building to the other looked almost comical to Dolores. The lines appeared as if they were holding up the building, and if one line was to come down, surely the building would also fall. Later in the day, near dinnertime, she would again watch Nellie pull the dry garments in and pile them up into the now heavy basket. Nellie had several children. Actually, Dolores couldn't keep track of just how many there really were. One day while they were talking about their day-to-day routines, Dolores gathered enough nerve to ask Nellie what it was like to give birth and how she would know when it was time. The woman giggled and told her when it was time, she would know it. She explained to her that the pain would become increasingly unbearable, and water would flow from her body. When this happened to Dolores, they agreed she was to call Nellie. She would help her and send one of the older children to summon the doctor.

Then late one very hot night in July, Dolores started to feel sharp pains in the lower region of her body. *Is this supposed to be it? Is this what Nellie was talking about?* Suddenly she felt a gush of warm liquid run down her legs onto the floor, and she nervously felt somehow she must clean up the mess for fear that Frank would strike out at her. She was alone in the apartment. Frank was out playing cards with his cronies and, as usual, he offered no support or help to his wife. After her somewhat poor attempt to clean up, Dolores was barely able to crawl to the door. The pain was getting greater and greater. Finally she reached the stairwell and shouted for Nellie. Nellie came to the stairs, and a look of fright came over her. She quickly turned to one of the young boys and told him to get Dr. Abbott and hurry. Nellie tried to remain calm, but she wasn't sure how long it would be before the baby arrived. After taking a deep breath and observing the situation before her, she realized there probably would be enough time since this was Dolores's first time giving birth, but still she was concerned.

A Matter of Survival

Nellie convinced herself she must remain calm, if not for Dolores's sake, but her own as well. Quickly she took hold of the situation and put her plan into action. She was hardly able to help Dolores get back into her bed. She placed her hand on Dolores's and offered a few kind words of comfort to her. She then gathered clean towels and started to boil water on the old wood stove in preparation for the doctor's arrival. Dolores was only vaguely aware of what Nellie was doing for her, but still she was grateful to have her nearby. As Nellie was giving comfort to Dolores and awaiting the doctor's arrival, she was shocked at the words coming from this woman.

"I don't want to be a mother; I want to be an actress."

"There, there," Nellie said, "you are going to have a beautiful baby. I'm sure you don't realize what you are saying."

Just then Dr. Abbott arrived. He didn't say much, except to shout quick orders to Nellie, telling her to fetch more towels and get boiling water for him to sterilize his instruments. Dr. Abbott observed it probably would be some time before the baby arrived. He told Nellie and Dolores he would have to leave to attend to another patient who was quite ill with fever and said he would return as soon as he was able. He then whispered to Nellie she should stay with the expectant mother and for her to stay calm. All signs indicated Dolores would have a normal birth, and he said he would return before the actual birth.

Nellie was quite anxious, but she never let on to Dolores. She just gave her as much comfort as she could summon within her. After all, she had given birth so many times before, she should be well experienced at this, but still, she had to stifle the panic within.

Finally, after several hours Dr. Abbott did return as promised. The birth appeared to be progressing normally, and except for the frequent screams of pain coming from Dolores, he felt there wasn't anything unusual about this birth. Finally, Dolores was almost at the point of exhaustion and passing out when Dr. Abbott told the two women that the baby's head was starting to appear. He firmly instructed Dolores to push, assuring her all the while that she and the baby would be fine.

Dr. Abbott was extremely professional as he helped aid Dolores in the birthing process. Nellie was relieved at the baby's pending arrival, which would be any minute now. She then took a moment to observe that this familiar man, who had delivered all her children—all seven of them—was aging ever so very much and looked extremely tired. Tired to the point of collapsing, but still he continued. Nellie's mind began to wander to the last time she gave birth, remembering that the ending was not so happy. Her last child was dead when it was born, and the sad memories of this birth came quickly back to her. At that time Dr. Abbott had told her she was lucky to be alive and she should be grateful for not losing her life. Otherwise, there would be seven children who would grow up fending for themselves with no mother to care for them. Nellie's eyes started to well up with tears as her mind went back to that unhappy birth last year. It was a heartbreaking outcome that she had never expounded upon with Dolores in their many conversations regarding childbirth. Unlike Dolores, she had a husband who was a hardworking man, but more importantly, a good family man who idolized his wife and children. She was lost in her thoughts when suddenly she was brought back to reality by the loud crying of the new arrival. At last, now after many hours of unbearable pain, Dolores gave birth to a healthy baby girl. Dr. Abbott placed the little baby on Dolores's abdomen and shouted to Nellie to wrap the new child in the clean towel he'd placed earlier at the bottom of the bed. He proceeded to cut the cord and then with Nellie's assistance they both cleaned this new little life. In doing so Dr. Abbott diligently checked over the little baby girl and told the mother her baby was perfect.

Dolores was worn out from what she had just experienced. She was barely able to speak and started to cry. She didn't want a girl. *Oh no,* she thought. *Frank will be furious with me for not having a boy, the son he wanted.*

Nellie handed the new life to Dolores to hold, but she seemed too exhausted to hold the little one. Nellie then placed the new infant in the little basket near the bed, wrapped her in a new diaper and shirt, and covered her with the blanket her mother had made while waiting for the birth of her child.

Dolores dozed off, and Dr. Abbott told Nellie he was due at yet another home where the father had taken gravely ill. He asked Nellie to take care of cleaning up the birthing remains and to tend to Dolores's needs if she needed help. Just as Dr. Abbott was starting to gather his instruments, putting them into the battered medical bag, Frank abruptly appeared at the door.

A Matter of Survival

Frank was surprised to see a baby had been delivered. It was obvious to both Dr. Abbott and Nellie he had been drinking and could hardly stand straight. Frank quickly surveyed the situation and immediately tried to sober himself up, realizing that he had not been available when his wife needed him, and also he was not making the best impression on the two people who stood before him.

He didn't pay too much attention to his wife, but immediately he asked what "it" was, adding, "It's a boy, I assume."

"No," Dr. Abbott replied, "you have a healthy and beautiful baby girl."

"Oh God, what a disappointment this is," Frank uttered.

Dr. Abbott glanced at Nellie, who looked helpless as she tried to find the right words. She was glad that Dolores was now sleeping soundly, and unable to see her husband's disappointment. Dr. Abbott made no further comment and left the small flat. Nellie quickly cleaned up and told Frank she was also leaving. She said if he needed her, he could come downstairs and call on her. Nellie was also exhausted and couldn't wait to join her sleeping husband in their bed.

Frank was tired, drunk, and disappointed. All he wanted was to flop into bed. He never changed his clothes, but just fell onto the bed next to his sleeping wife. He didn't look at his new daughter. Just before passing out, he mumbled something to the effect that he guessed it might be good to have an extra pair of hands to help out around their flat.

When morning came, surprisingly Dolores realized that this little helpless child had done nothing to her, and she started to sense a genuine love for the new little baby.

Dolores decided to name her "Frances"; she had seen the name on the front of the movie theatre. *She'll be proud of me someday when I'm a famous movie star*, she thought.

As Dolores slowly healed, she accepted the fact that being an actress just might not happen right now. Instead she was surprised at herself, because she found that she liked her little daughter more than she'd ever imagined. She looked forward to feeding the infant and offering her breast to her. It was a closeness she didn't expect to find within her, but it all seemed so natural. She realized she had never loved anyone this much before. This was all very new to her.

As time passed Dolores realized how foolish she had been not to want this child. Sometimes, even Frank was nicer to her and, even more surprisingly, he seemed to occasionally show a fondness toward his daughter.

Two and a half years passed, and little Frances was growing prettier and nicer with each passing day. She was a very good girl and listened to her mother. Dolores recognized there seemed to be an innate sense within this little girl to always remain docile and not cry out for attention. She taught her little girl how to help, giving her small chores, even at her tender age. She would help carry clothes from the window, where her mother hung them out to dry, and then help carry them back into their meager apartment. She already knew to place the clean clothes on the bed for her mother.

As the child grew first into a toddler and then into a little girl of three years, Dolores discovered she could sing and dance before the little one. Little Frances would laugh and clap in amusement. She enjoyed this little one more and more, but lately Dolores noticed her husband never seemed to want to hold or acknowledge his child. All he ever did was complain that there was another mouth to feed and that he worked too hard. He was mean to Dolores and now also to their daughter. He didn't offer her any affection or consideration of any kind.

These days Dolores was not feeling well and noticed she wasn't as strong as she once was. In the morning an acute sense of illness would come over her, and before long she realized she was expecting another child. Her dream of being a famous actress was not as frequent as it once had been. Sometimes when the apartment was quiet, she would lie in bed, and a tinge of longing would invade her mind. She wondered what ever happened to the pretty young woman who had those very, very strong ambitions. The young woman who was chastised by her mother, ignored by her father, and laughed at by her siblings for her foolish thoughts.

It was now March, and Dolores was faced with the many months of pregnancy ahead. She hated to tell her husband that a new little person was growing inside her. After about three months into her second pregnancy, Frank came right out and asked her if she was carrying another child. When she confirmed his suspicions, he muttered something to the effect that he hoped she would do better this time. And just like that, he left her to meet up with his cronies.

A Matter of Survival

Winter turned to spring and then into a blistering hot summer. The heat of the summer became unbearable. There were many times she felt she was going to pass out. Somehow she held on, if only for the sake of her little Frances, who always remained at her feet or played nearby. Sometimes she would take Frances and they would visit her only friend, Nellie. Nellie was a big source of comfort to Dolores. Little Frances would play with Nellie's children while the women would sip something cool and dream about the future. Nellie told Dolores her husband worked very hard building new roadways to the other boroughs, and he wanted to someday leave the Bronx and move to a place where the air was cleaner, maybe Queens. Dolores had found that Nellie was a real friend, and she could hardly bear the prospect of losing her to another location. Sometimes she had to admit, if only to herself, that she was a little envious of her friend. Nellie's husband always seemed concerned about his wife and obviously loved her and their children—be they boy or girl.

Dolores did all she could to try to take care of her home and her small child, and now another one was on the way. It all became too much for her. It wasn't long before young Frances received little or sometimes no attention at all. She was lucky if her mother remembered to feed her. Now the young mother would stare blankly and didn't care how she or her daughter looked. Even Nellie was becoming concerned at her friend's changing attitude, but she already had enough to worry about in just taking care of her own family.

The summer months finally passed, and now the cool breezes would touch her face as she leaned out the apartment window to get air. Dr. Abbott had told her the baby would probably come in October. Apparently he felt he didn't have to give her any more information than that since she had already experienced childbirth. Now Dolores found it increasingly more difficult to clean the apartment and do the washing and ironing and so many other household chores. It became increasingly hard for her to carry the wash to the stairwell window and hang it outside. She would take little Frances with her, and she taught the young child to hand her the pins, making it easier for her to hang the household laundry. Her belly was becoming so huge that it became almost impossible for her to lean out the window.

Almost daily, she would take Frances to buy food for that night's supper. She longed to go into the theatre when she passed it by.

There was always so much to do in her little home, and if it was not done by the time Frank arrived in the evening, she would have to bear his wrath. He didn't seem to care that she was carrying another child. He was certain she would probably have another girl, and since she failed him the last time, he didn't want to be around her company.

Sometimes Dolores would exit their flat, leaving little Frances alone in her crib. When she eventually returned home, she would find that Frances was just fine. After a while her absences became longer and longer and more frequent. She would even sneak out to go to the movie theatre and leave the little one behind in the flat.

Occasionally Dolores would feel guilty about leaving her little daughter alone, and she would take her outside for a carriage ride and walk for as long as she was able. The city streets were amusing to her. She would look at all the people and wonder what their lives were like. She assumed they all must have better lives than her.

The autumn air entered the windows of the flat and gave much relief from the heat of the summer. Dolores liked her time alone, just taking in the fresh air. She hated the responsibility of taking care of a child, and now with another on the way, she would just let her mind escape to another place. She just wanted to be left alone and not do anything.

One night, about three o'clock in the morning, she started to feel great pains in her lower body. She had to wake her husband, and this time he went to get the doctor. He had resigned himself to another girl being born. After a few hours and much to his surprise, the doctor announced to Frank he now had a healthy little baby boy.

"At last, my own son," he said. He immediately went into the bedroom and took the baby from Dolores's arms and held him and welcomed him into the world. He decided he was going name this boy Peter.

There were many nights when Frank didn't come home at all. The truth was he disliked his wife and reveled in the company of many other women. Many times he would come home after work, wash up, and then leave, not to return again until one or two nights later. Habitually, he would then start to pick a fight with his wife. It was not unusual for Dolores to question her

A Matter of Survival

husband's whereabouts, but when she questioned him, he would get very nasty and strike out at her. She learned to ignore him and was just grateful when he gave her the money for rent and food. Dolores found herself alone most of the time with just her children for company. Even the children seemed to take care of themselves. This arrangement was just fine for her now.

As the years passed, she became very proud of her son. Little Peter was now three years old and was the most adorable little child any mother could hope for.

As Peter grew, he and Frances would play together and were good companions for each other. In the evening when their father did come home, he always went right to his son, picking him up and caressing him. He barely looked at Frances.

There were times when Dolores actually did take pleasure in her children and even felt a great sense of love for them, especially for this little baby boy.

Her fantasy of becoming a great actress was again put on hold. What with taking care of two children, cleaning, cooking, and whatever else there was to do, it just didn't seem possible to run away to become an actress. Winter came, and it was a bitterly cold one. The flat never seemed warm enough, and Dolores always felt chilled. She found it increasingly difficult to keep both children with her as she performed her household chores or shopped for the night's dinner. She did try, but she kept telling herself it was all just too much for her. Her mind started playing tricks on her, to where she believed someone else was taking care of her children when actually they were in the next room with little Frances taking care of her brother.

Finally spring arrived. All the snow had melted, and birds were singing loudly in the trees in front of the flat. Dolores felt great relief to finally feel some warmth in her body. She was trying more and more to please her husband, but he didn't seem interested or want anything from her.

While out one afternoon with her children, Dolores noticed the shops and carts in the neighborhood were preparing for the arrival of Easter. Even though Frank was a difficult man to please, she decided she would try to make a joyous celebration for him and their children. She went to great pains to plan a festive family dinner. She asked her husband to please be home. Perhaps they could all go together to their local church and then come home for a family dinner. At first he balked at her request, but after thinking about it, he decided it might be good for the neighbors to see him as a devoted husband and a good father, no matter what his reputation was. Yes, he finally agreed. For the first time in a very long time, she was happy and planned to make it a very special day. Easter came—it was a beautiful Sunday, and everyone was dressed in what they considered to be their best outfits, no matter how poor they really were. It had been a very long time since they had been to church as a family. In the past sometimes Dolores would take the children, but Frank never came with them. She felt a feeling of warmth, glad that they were finally a complete family. After Mass she smiled to herself as they all walked home together, even if was in silence.

Dolores had managed to color eggs for the children, and she had saved a small amount of money to buy them little chocolate bunnies. She had also planned a special meal for her family. She was excited that after all this time, maybe she could actually please her husband. The children were delighted to find the bunnies and to see the colored eggs. Much to her horror, when they sat at the table, her husband did not appreciate any of it. He scolded her for her foolishness with the colored eggs as well as for spending too much on this one meal. Their voices rose louder and louder. Dolores was screaming, saying that she hated him, and she told him she knew he was seeing other women. Furthermore, he did not appreciate all the sacrifices she had made for him. She had given up her life's ambition for him, and he appreciated nothing. As the words rose into thunderous sounds, they never noticed the children running from the table. At one point Dolores feared she might have said too much and was afraid he might strike out at her. She ran from the flat down the street to a nearby park with tears stinging her eyes. After about fifteen minutes, when Frank didn't come after her, she decided to return to the flat, feeling upset that her children had been exposed to this terrible scene on a day that was supposed to be so special.

When she entered her humble home, there was a stillness, which she didn't expect. She heard nothing. No blaring words from her husband, no crying from the children. She wasn't sure what she was about to encounter, but a sense of horror filled her very core.

That was when she learned her husband had taken their son out the window and down the fire escape, to a destination unknown to her.

Five

LIFE GETS HARDER

Dolores never saw her husband again.
Even though Frances was only six years old, she sensed something was very wrong. She noticed her mother seemed to be talking to herself all the time and mumbling something to the effect that there wouldn't be enough money to buy food or pay the rent. Other times she kept incoherently mumbling her son was gone and she wasn't able to find him. Frances didn't understand. She tried to console her mother with soft caresses, but her mother didn't seem interested in her affections.

Dolores was left to fend for herself. One week passed, then two weeks, and Dolores realized she was running out of food. She had nowhere to turn. It was unthinkable to turn to her family for help. They would only blame her for not being a good wife.

She decided she would try to find some kind of work so that she could support them both. Neighbors knew she was alone and yet offered no help. Her only friend, Nellie, had since moved to Queens. She was truly alone.

Finally, she was able to get a job in a factory. She decided she would leave little Frances alone for now, telling her to wait in the apartment for her return. After a few days, one of the neighbors decided to spy on Dolores. It had occurred to her that the little six-year-old child was being left by herself and she reported this to the police.

When Dolores came home, there was a note posted on the door. Her child had been taken from her and was being placed in the care of social services. Dolores's heart sank. First she had lost the son she adored, the financial support of her unkind husband, and now her daughter. She fell to the ground and let out great sobs that actually could be heard throughout the entire neighborhood.

The next day she went to the address that appeared on the posted notice to get her daughter back. She found it wasn't going to be easy. She pleaded for her daughter, but they only asked many questions, none of which Dolores could answer to their satisfaction. They informed her that her child was going to be taken away from her and placed in a home for girls. If she could show them that she was going to receive some sort of financial support for herself and child, the child would be returned to her. They told her Frances had been placed in a Catholic home for girls somewhere in Queens and that maybe someday, if social services deemed it appropriate, they might allow her to get her child back.

All Dolores's problems would manifest themselves in her mind to such an extent that she would mentally escape from it all. She could actually shut down her mind and turn all the horrors away when she wanted to do so, and now she wanted to do so. She started mumbling without making sense as she walked the streets. People would just stare and avoid her as much as possible.

Six

LIVING IN THE HOME

Many months in the orphanage passed. The months grew into more than a year, and at this point Frances accepted her life at the home with difficulty. Unhappily she now believed she would never see her family again. She was curious as to what she could have possibly done wrong to be placed in this home for girls. Some nights she would lay awake in bed, thinking of what she might have done differently so that maybe her mother would have kept her. Could she have been a better girl? Could she have been more helpful? Loving?

Sometimes the girls would talk about their previous lives. One of the little girls said both her parents had died, and then there were girls who, like Frances, just didn't know what had happened to their parents. When they did discuss their pasts, and now their present, they resolved they had no choice but to accept it—they were all here to stay, and they accepted the fact that they were now labeled "orphans." Orphaned children no one wanted. They all felt saddened by this, but somehow they realized they were in it together and vowed to remain friends even when they grew up and left the home.

One day the Sisters told the girls they were being prepared to receive their "First Holy Communion" and repeatedly emphasized to them they must be as godly as possible. After their chores were completed, they were told they must learn the prayers of the Catholic Church, and they would have to recite them perfectly to the Sisters. If they did not learn them flawlessly, they would be punished. There would be no free time in the evening. They would learn to recite the prayers over and over until they finally got them right. Once these prayers were learned, each girl was excused and would now be allowed to enter the recreation room. When the day finally came for the girls to receive their First Holy Communion, each girl was given a white veil to wear with her uniform, a little white prayer book, and a pair of rosary beads. Frances could hardly wait as excitement built up inside her for this special day. It was emphasized by the Sisters that this sacrament was very important in their young lives. They told the girls that all of their training and discipline was to prepare them for a life devoted to God. When they were finally ready, the day came. All the communicants attended a special Mass. They lined up perfectly, at first standing at the altar railing, then, with the clicking of the Sister's signal, they simultaneously knelt down and waited for the priest to place the wafer on their tongue. What a special day this was! At long last and after all their hard work and devotion, they received the sacrament of First Holy Communion.

Frances didn't appreciate it at the time, but she was actually receiving an extraordinarily well-rounded education. Not only was she being strongly educated in the basics of reading, writing, and arithmetic, but she was also learning responsibilities in a very hard way. She had no idea that all this would become very helpful to her in the future. Someday Frances would realize she probably had received a far superior education than if she had been left to grow up on the streets of the Bronx.

Each day the girls would attend to their lessons, then go to their rooms, put on their work clothes, and perform their assigned chore for the week.

One of Frances's favorite assignments was when she got to help in the kitchen. Actually, it was now her most cherished assignment. There were also many other girls assigned to the Sisters in this very large room and she not only liked the company of them, she found she enjoyed watching the preparation of the food. She would watch in awe when she saw the enormous pots and utensils all clanking in the room. Before long, as if by some kind of magical accomplishment, a meal was prepared for the many girls that lived here. Then there were also the times when no one was looking, and she was able to steal a dirty carrot or potato and bite into it. It didn't

A Matter of Survival

even matter to her that the vegetable still had mud on it. She knew she would have to take this sin to confession, but she was always so hungry that she just couldn't help herself. Her hunger justified the sin.

The grandest time she had was when Sister Mary Clair asked her to go into the large refrigerator to get some milk. When Frances entered the cold chamber, her eyes opened wider than ever before. She could hardly believe it. Her discovery was the largest bowl of Jell-O she had ever seen. This treasure was just too much for her to ignore; the temptation was far too great. It was very cold in the large box, and she shook with the lowered temperature, but she just couldn't resist. Even without the possession of a spoon, Frances got carried away. She simply swept through it with her hands.

Finally, when Sister Mary Clair came back from her immediate distraction, she realized her helper had disappeared. *Oh no,* she thought. *I better find her myself.* She did, and when she discovered her whereabouts, Frances looked so guilty with Jell-O all over herself that even the Sister had a hard time trying not to laugh. Frances assumed she was going to get it, but was surprised the Sister chose not to get angry with her. A stomachache followed that night, but Frances felt it was well worth it. In reflecting back, Frances realized that maybe the Sisters tried to act stern, but actually they were very human and did the best that they could. One thing she did know—this experience taught her she could no longer stand the sight of Jell-O, even after growing into adulthood!

Melody, who was her dearest friend, kept her promise and came to see her as often as possible. Today Melody came for a visit, but this day it was quite different. What a sad day this turned out to be for Frances. Melody told Frances she was going to leave the home in a few days. Her sixteenth birthday was approaching. The Sisters had been good to Melody and prepared her well to start a new life. They arranged for her to live with a family, and soon after she would start a job. Frances started to cry with the agonizing realization that she could no longer look forward to visits from Melody.

"Melody, what am I going to do without you?" she cried.

"Frances, you have adjusted very well since the first time we met."

Then, taking the little girl's hand in hers, Melody said, "Don't be sad. I'm actually excited to start a life on my own, and maybe I'm a little scared too, but I want you to be happy for me. I know you don't realize it now, but time will go fast for you just as it did for me, and then you will be leaving here as well."

Melody spoke to the sad child further in a very soft and loving tone. "Frances, I promise as soon as I'm able, I will come back to visit you and tell you all about my new life. It's time now that I live on my own."

Frances thanked Melody for coming to see her and said she would look forward to hearing her stories of the world beyond the big fence that surrounded their home. The girls hugged each other very tightly, and without saying another word, Melody left.

A month had passed since Melody's departure. Frances was absorbed in her schooling and chores in the home when one of the Sisters from the office came to her and said she had a visitor. *Oh,* Frances thought, *Melody has come back as she promised.* She was so happy and excited. Without any hesitation and barely waiting for the Sister to give her any further details, she ran down the hall and down the stairs.

"I can't wait to see Melody," she said out loud. In her exhilaration she combed her little fingers through her hair, trying to make herself look pretty for her friend, and ran to the office where visitors waited. She quickly entered the room and breathlessly announced to the Sister who was sitting at a very large desk that her friend Melody had returned to see her. The Sister simply pointed to the visiting room, a room Frances had never entered before.

When Frances hastily entered the room, her knees suddenly went weak and she couldn't believe the sight before her eyes. It was not Melody who was before her, but rather a woman who appeared to be old, disheveled, shabbily dressed, and not very pretty. It was her mother! Frances froze, not understanding what was happening. Her mother spoke first.

"Frances, come here and let me look at you."

Frances didn't move. She took deep breaths, trying to hold back the tears from her eyes. She couldn't believe her mother had finally come to see her. She had been at the home for more than a year, and out of nowhere her mother had appeared. Little Frances was momentarily lost in her thoughts as she reflected back to all the nights she'd cried herself to sleep, frightened and alone.

"Aren't you happy to see me?" the woman asked.

The woman then got up from the chair and took Frances by the hand. Frances still hesitated to come near her.

"I guess you must be wondering what happened to me?" she said. Frances simply nodded her head in an affirmative way, still unable to speak.

"Life has been very hard for me. I miss you and your brother. You do remember your brother, don't you?"

Frances again nodded her head in an affirmative manner.

"I don't live in the Bronx anymore. Do you remember the Bronx?" this stranger asked.

The little girl now shrugged her shoulders, not knowing how to answer this woman.

"I now live in Queens. As a matter of fact, I live here in Flushing. I live not too far from this place. You see, I'm still trying to be an actress, but no one will let me perform for them," the peculiar woman continued. "So today I decided I would come by and see how you are doing. You look very nice."

Finally, the little girl asked in a cracking voice, almost afraid to receive the answer, "Am I going home with you now?"

"Oh heavens no," the woman replied. "How would I ever take care of you? Sometimes I help people clean their homes and I'm able to make a little money, but not enough to take care of us both...and then I need to get acting lessons. Maybe you would like me to sing and dance for you?"

Little Frances just shrugged her shoulders and noticed her mother didn't wait for an answer as she proceeded to prance around the room. She abruptly stopped, and raising her voice angrily, she said, "You have your father to thank for this mess."

The little girl started to panic, thinking, *I don't want to be with this lady. Could this woman really be my mother?* Her mind was racing; her heart was pounding so loudly she was sure the woman could hear it. Suddenly she was interrupted by the woman's ranting.

"I've been told by other people that he took your brother to Italy—that's very far away—and left him there just to spite me. Huh. I have no way of seeing or finding my dear little son, your brother, imagine that! I hate that man!"

Now Frances was really frightened by this woman. Not only was the woman rambling on and on, saying things that didn't seem to make sense to the young child, but her mannerisms were not like anything or anyone she had seen before. Frances became terrified. She tried to leave the room, backing out so very carefully, trying to look for the security of the Sister she'd left sitting at the desk. But the lady grabbed her arm in a hurtful way and yelled she must not leave her. Their visit wasn't over yet.

"Come, give your mommy a hug and kiss. I need to feel you still love me. Tell me you love me!" the odd woman demanded.

The little girl answered, "Yes, I love you, but now I must go to continue the work I was doing for the good Sisters."

With that the little one backed into the doorway, and the Sister sitting at the desk realized maybe this child wasn't so happy with her visit. She announced to the lady that their visit would have to be over, as the girls had to start their preparations for dinner.

"All right, I will leave now." Not taking her eyes from Frances, she continued, "But I promise, I will be back soon."

With that she left in a rather dramatic fashion.

Frances was visibly shaken. The Sister asked if she would like to stay with her in the office for a while, but she simply shook her head and said, "No, thank you." She proceeded to return to the area where she had come from earlier and when she reached the stairs, she sat for a moment, feeling familiar tears swelling in her eyes and sliding down her cheeks. The visitor she had waited so long to see had finally come, and the disappointment was almost too much to bear. It was the realization that she was afraid of her very own mother!

Seven

GROWING UP

Frances ran past the office, down the hall, up the stairs, and instead of returning to the chores at hand, she ran to the large room that contained her bed. She threw herself down and almost uncontrollably sobbed and cried as though her little heart was breaking. The one person she had wanted to see for such a long time had turned out to be a terrible disappointment. She was only almost eight years old, but she knew that something was wrong with the woman who had come to visit her. Her previous fantasies of her mother coming for her and removing her from this home were just that, fantasies. How could this have happened? The woman who had come to visit looked awful. She was not the pretty woman she remembered, and her ranting had frightened the little girl.

While her head was buried in her pillow, she felt a hand on her back, and much to her surprise, it was Sister Mary Gerard, the very nun she feared the most. Instead of scolding Frances, she turned her around and took the little girl in her arms and held her ever so close until she finally calmed down. Sister Mary Gerard had seen this scene so often before. Girls were left in the home, and when the parents finally showed up and did not take them, the disappointment was too much for the girls to bear. Sister spoke very softly to Frances, telling her that she understood what she was going through. Sister had witnessed this many times; usually it was best to let the little ones cry it out, but somehow Sister Mary Gerard knew that all Frances really needed was comforting. After a while she spoke softly to Frances, telling her, "Sometimes we change bad situations in our minds into believing they are good situations. Just like fairy tales." Sister stroked Frances's head and consoled her, telling her to make her mind up once and for all that this was her home, that she might even like living here. After all, it really wasn't that bad, and while she probably didn't believe it, the Sisters really did love the girls they took care of. Once Frances had calmed down, Sister told her to go back to her chores and put these bad feelings behind her.

Frances did as she was told and returned to her duties.

The years passed quickly, and Frances started to somewhat enjoy life in the home. She liked her lessons and was particularly fond of reading and arithmetic.

In all the years Frances was in the home, her mother came only two more times. Frances greeted her quietly and didn't say too much to her. She was always glad when her mother's visit was over and she left. On one of the visits, when Frances was twelve years old, she asked about her brother. Her mother told her she never saw her brother again, and as far as she knew, he was still living somewhere in Italy. She said she had heard from others that Frances's father did return to America, but without his son. At that point, she started to cry in front of her little girl.

Another time, Frances was called to the office; only this time Sister told her an uncle was here to see her. Frances couldn't remember having an uncle, and she was curious as to who it was. When she entered the visiting area, she was shocked to realize this man was not her uncle, but her father. He told her he was embarrassed to tell the Sisters he was her father since five years had passed and this was his first visit. As it turned out, in all Frances's years of growing up in the home, it was his only visit. No one had to tell Frances her father never cared about her. This she did remember. She remembered always the sense of rejection, being ignored, and sneered at. Frances had learned at a very early age that her father did not like her. He constantly expressed the hardships of having a daughter.

She could remember, however, the loving attitude he demonstrated toward her brother. Therefore, the first question she had for him was not about why he hadn't come sooner, but what had happened to her brother? He told his daughter her brother was being raised by relatives in Italy and was very happy. She tried to tell her father her mother had come to visit her, saying she seemed strange and she was afraid of her. His reply was not very comforting. He said she was not a good wife or mother and had always been strange. He was never happy with his parents' choice for him, but he believed Frances was probably too young to understand. Frances thought her father seemed to be very well-groomed and quite handsome, but he was still very distant and showed her no affection. Frank kept his visit quite brief as he found there was really nothing to talk about with her. So he said he had to leave and would visit her again, which he never did.

One day in 1929, Frances and the other girls discovered something terrible must have happened in the outside world. For reasons the girls didn't quite understand, people had lost their money, and the charitable donations that had always been given to the home were going to come to an end. The wonderful Christmas presents were going to stop also, because the wealthy people who had always provided gifts to the home were no longer able to do so. It was after this time that the Sisters would take their old truck, along with a good number of girls, and ride out to Long Island, where they would visit the farmers and beg for food to feed their charges. What the girls didn't know was just how hard it was for the Sisters to run the home with the absence of donations.

Occasionally, Melody did come to visit Frances and tell her what it was like on the outside. She had gotten a job cleaning homes for wealthy people, but recently she had been asked by most of them not to return to their homes, since they had lost their money. Fortunately, she was still living with the same people she had been placed with and was able to clean and cook for them and their two children. The people she lived with were good to Melody, and she was happy to have this job. Frances was happy to learn Melody was doing well. Most times Melody would bring Frances a little treat, be it a piece of candy or a small toy. Frances was always grateful to see her and looked forward to her visits. On one such visit Frances confided in Melody, telling her just as she'd predicted, she had grown to accept life in the orphanage, and it didn't seem so bad after all. Melody was glad to hear that Frances had adjusted just as everyone else had. There really was no choice but to accept things as they were.

Life at the home continued as normal, but then one afternoon, while playing on the outside playground, Frances felt a sticky, wet feeling in her underwear. She went into the bathroom only to discover blood coming from her body. *Oh my,* she thought. *I must have injured myself while on the slide. I better tell Sister quickly.* She ran from the bathroom and spoke to the Sister in charge of the play area.

"Sister, Sister. I must have done something terrible to myself, because I am bleeding in my underwear, and the bleeding doesn't seem to want to stop."

Sister told her to immediately go to the infirmary and tell the Sister there what had happened to her. Frances was frightened and couldn't imagine what she had done to herself. She ran as quickly as she could, and when she reached the infirmary, she was so out of breath that she could hardly speak to the Sister in charge. When she finally did speak, the Sister couldn't understand what she was saying, but she had a good idea of just what this was about. Finally, Frances blurted out very dramatically that she was bleeding to death and she didn't think she had much more time to live. The good Sister must have had a difficult time trying to conceal her smile while listening to Frances. She reassured her, telling her she wasn't going to die, and then she explained that this was something that would be happening to her each and every month. She took out two rags from the closet and wrote her first initial and last name in bold black ink across each one. She told Frances she was to fold each rag and place it in her underwear, and when one became full with the blood, she was to wash it out and hang it outside to dry. She would then be able to replace it with the other. Frances quickly discovered that when she was menstruating, everyone else knew it also. The clothesline was like a built-in communication system.

Eight

THREE YEARS TO GO

The next three years passed quickly, and now Frances was approaching sixteen and preparing for her graduation. She was excited, although somewhat apprehensive, at the prospect, like Melody, of starting life on her own. The Sisters explained to the girls that upon graduation, those girls who did not have parents would be placed in homes where they would be able to work for their room and board. In Frances's case, however, she would go back to live with her mother. They also explained that even though they would be receiving a diploma from the home, they would have to continue for one more year at the local high school to receive a diploma recognized by the state.

Since Frances had only seen her mother three times in all the years she lived in the home, she was somewhat uneasy but also eager to finally be able to live with her. She had so many questions in her mind, but she assumed that once she graduated, all her questions would be answered. She was excited as graduation day approached. Unfortunately, neither of her parents came to see her graduate on this special day. Her mother never showed up and neither did her father, even though they had been notified by the home. Not only did Frances receive her diploma, she received the Best Conduct Award. The only person who came to her graduation was Melody, and Frances was very grateful she did. Melody was always so kind to her, and today on this special day she was there again.

The Sisters had prepared refreshments in honor of the graduates. They made lovely cookies and a punch in celebration of this particular occasion. Frances sat with Melody, and while they were enjoying their punch, Melody gave a prettily wrapped gift to Frances. Frances could never remember anyone giving her a gift like this. She was speechless. Melody encouraged her to open it, and when she did, Frances discovered it was a little gold cross and chain. Frances was delighted with this fantastic gift, and Melody placed the cross around her neck and secured it in place. Frances hugged Melody tightly and couldn't stop thanking her. The afternoon was wonderful.

Frances stayed in the home one additional week, waiting for her mother to claim her so she could start her grown-up life. Finally, her mother showed up. She had very little to say to the Sisters, but Frances thanked and hugged them all, one by one. She reflected back to when she had first arrived at the home and how very frightened she was. She remembered how she didn't want to stay there from the start. Now she was sorry the time had come and she had to leave. It was hard to believe ten years had passed.

Frances's mother looked very strange to her and said very little except to tell her they would be taking a bus to where she lived. The bus ride took about twenty minutes, and when they got off the bus, they walked about five long blocks to an older-looking brick home in a nice residential neighborhood. Her mother told her she had an apartment on the second floor and this was where they were going to spend their time together. Once they entered the apartment, Dolores told her daughter she had to go to work the next day and Frances would have to clean the apartment as well as prepare something for them to eat for dinner. Frances sensed something was wrong; her mother appeared to be agitated that her daughter was now living with her. She didn't understand what it was that was bothering her mother when suddenly Dolores slapped Frances across the face, saying she was the reason she was never able to become an actress. Frances was stunned. She felt a sharp stinging pain not only on her face, but it seemed to encompass her entire body as well. In all the years of living in the home, she could never remember anyone hitting her. Frances could not believe her mother's actions. She was too frightened to speak back to this madwoman whom she hardly knew.

A Matter of Survival

Dolores told Frances she would have to sleep on the couch as there was only one bed, and it belonged to her. Frances tried to sleep, but she was still upset at the display of anger her mother had demonstrated. Sometime in the middle of the night she must have fallen asleep, because the next thing she knew, her mother was shaking and pulling her to get up and make something for her to eat before she went to work. Frances obediently got up, washed quickly, and went into the little kitchen area to prepare something for her mother. She found some bread, jam, and juice and put everything on a plate for her mother. Her mother ate it and told Frances to have something prepared for dinner when she got home. She left her no money and did not even tell her what to prepare.

When Dolores left, Frances quickly and nervously looked around the tiny apartment, surveying what needed to be done. There were a few clothes that required washing, so she decided to tend to that chore first. She then looked around and found only a little bit of food in the small ice box. She looked in the pantry and found some canned soup and crackers and decided this would be dinner. She dusted the apartment and swept the floor. She also decided to wash the curtains that were hung on a rather dingy-looking window. Frances then cleaned the window, and when the curtains were dry, she hung them back on the window. She generally neatened the area as best as possible and was satisfied at the work she had accomplished, hoping her mother would be pleased. The place looked very clean, maybe not as clean as the home she left, but clean just the same.

When Dolores arrived home in the late afternoon, she looked around and said the apartment was not clean enough to her liking, and again she struck out at Frances, only this time she actually knocked her to the ground. Frances was stunned and flabbergasted. When she tried to get up, her mother kicked her back down again. Pain consumed her entire body.

"You think because you went to that fancy home, you're better than me; I'll teach you a thing or two," Dolores screamed.

Frances was petrified and shaking not just from the pain, but from the immense fear she felt within. She didn't understand this woman who was acting out like no one she had seen before. She barely got to her feet, went to the corner to sit in a chair, and out of terror said nothing to this wild woman.

The following days all seemed to be the same. She would get up and fix something for her mother to eat. She would stay in all day cleaning the apartment and then waited for her mother to come home. It seemed that no matter what she did, she could never please her. Her mother would attack her, slapping and kicking her while blaming her for the hard life she was living. Frances was getting very discouraged, and finally after two weeks, she got an idea. She remembered passing the local high school when they got off the bus upon her arrival to this new area. She decided she was going to speak to someone there about enrolling in the school, hoping she could have some kind of a normal life.

Frances showed the dean of admissions her papers from the home, and the woman seemed impressed with Frances's accomplishments. She said Frances could start the next day, but her parent would have to sign the necessary papers.

That evening Frances was very quiet when her mother came home. She didn't quite know how to tell her what had transpired that day. Finally, her mother sat down on the chair in silence when Frances approached her.

"Mother, I went to the high school today, and I'm eligible to go there for a year to complete my education. I would very much like to attend this school." She continued, "They have asked that you sign papers saying you approve of my decision."

Her mother looked piercingly at her. "How will you get your work done if you are going to school?"

Frances replied, "I promise I will do everything you want. Please, please sign the papers."

At first there was a deafening silence and finally she spoke.

"I'll sign the papers, but you better not disappoint me around here. Understand?" Dolores signed the papers, at the same time laughing at her daughter, mocking her for wanting to go to school.

Frances was excited to start school the next day. She loved her first day and was thrilled to start classes. She hurried home afterward to quickly clean the apartment, find something to fix for dinner, and start her homework. When Dolores returned home, Frances could see her mother was upset but didn't question her.

A Matter of Survival

All at once Dolores reached over to her daughter and tore off her beloved cross. She then started hitting Frances harder and harder, saying the devil must be inside her. Frances tried desperately to keep her arms and hands above her head to protect her face, but the woman hit her harder and harder. The rest of the night she sat in silence, not wanting to irritate the woman who was supposed to be her loving mother. Frances was really upset about the cross Melody had given her, and she wanted it back. The next day before she left for school she looked around, but her cross was nowhere to be found.

The days ran into weeks, and each day Frances was glad to go to school. She loved learning but kept very much to herself. Then one day she met a girl who she liked a lot. Her name was Kay, and they had a number of classes together. Kay made a real effort to make friends with Frances. After a short time of knowing each other, Kay asked if Frances would come to her home after school. At first she was reluctant, but she finally accepted the invitation. When they got to Kay's home, Frances was amazed at how nice it was and how nice Kay's mother was to her. Kay had several brothers and sisters, but most of them were not home from school yet. Kay went to the cupboard and then the refrigerator. She put two glasses on the kitchen table so they could feast on the cookies and milk that was placed before them. They laughed at things that happened at school that day. It was obvious to Kay's mother just how much they were enjoying each other's companionship.

Each day Frances would dread returning to her home. Her mother's beatings were becoming a regular event, and Frances could never figure out why. It was now four months since Frances had graduated from the home. She could hardly believe it, but now she missed not only the home, but the Sisters as well. She hated her life with her mother. The only thing she was happy about was going to the local high school and her new friend, Kay.

One afternoon Dolores came home earlier than usual, and she did not find Frances there. This infuriated her. Frances had stopped by her friend's house, and as usual, the girls were talking and laughing over the day's events. She liked visiting Kay's home after school. The two girls had now become close friends and would spend many afternoons doing their homework together and relished the many snacks Kay's mother prepared for them. Kay had asked Frances about her home and her mother, but quickly sensed this was not a topic for discussion. She had noticed several bruises on Frances, but when she asked about them, Frances said she had fallen. When further pressed for an explanation, she simply said she didn't want to discuss it.

While at Kay's home, Frances realized it was getting late and she better hurry home. She had cleaned the apartment before school, but remembered she hadn't planned something for the evening meal. She told Kay she had to go, quickly gathered her belongings, and started to rush home.

The autumn weather was now turning colder. Frances did not have a warm coat but rather a threadbare sweater that was old and quite worn. Nevertheless it was something, and she was grateful to have it. She wrapped the sweater tightly around her and headed for the apartment. When she arrived home, she was on time and actually in a rather happy mood. She usually was in a good mood after spending the afternoon with Kay and her mother.

Much to Frances's surprise, when she reached the door, it was already unlocked. Something told her to enter the apartment very cautiously. Upon entering, she saw her mother with arms folded against her chest and a belt hanging from her right hand.

"Where have you been?" Dolores asked the shaking young girl.

Frances tried to answer respectfully, explaining that she and a classmate had been doing homework together.

"Well, that will be the end of that," Dolores screamed at her. "Now you will not be returning to that high and mighty school of yours. I am taking you out of it. You have caused me nothing but grief, and I have had the most miserable life all because of you."

Frances was visibly shaken and started to cry. She knew her mother would and could do this to her.

"Please, please," she begged, "don't do this to me. I am doing good work at school and will make you proud of me, I promise."

The tears started to roll down her face, and the more she cried the more her mother laughed, and then all at once, she started beating her with the belt.

She said, "I promise there will be no more school for you now. You will have to get a job and start supporting yourself."

A Matter of Survival

Frances pleaded with her mother to stop hitting her, but with each plea, she just hit harder and harder. Frances couldn't take it anymore and darted out of the apartment into the evening's cold air. She didn't know where she was going, but all she knew was she had to leave this place she called her home. She found herself running to Kay's house.

When Kay answered the door, she was horrified. There were big welts and bruises starting to appear on Frances's face and hands. Frances asked Kay not to ask any questions, but could she please lend her carfare so that she could take the bus and go back to the home where she was raised? Frances also begged Kay not to tell her mother that she was in trouble. Kay respected her plea but was quite upset at her friend's insistence. She tried to tell Frances her mother would help her, but Frances was adamant. She just wanted to go back to St. Joseph's Home. She needed comfort from the good Sisters.

It was now getting late, approaching eight o'clock. She ran to the bus stop and waited in the cold chill for the bus to come. Finally, after about a half hour, the bus came. She got on it, avoiding the stares of the driver and other passengers. All she could think about was how much she wanted to go back to St. Joseph's.

At last, the bus stopped within one block of the home. Frances got off and started crying again, but this time with deep sobs. She approached the large iron fence that surrounded the familiar building; she opened the front gate and ran up to the main entrance. Once she reached it, she pounded and pounded on the large wooden door, at the same time pressing the bell beside it.

After what seemed like an eternity, one of the sisters came to the door and was taken aback at the view before her. Frances immediately recognized Sister Mary Theresa and practically fell into her arms.

"What is it, my child?" she asked.

Frances was so uncontrollably upset that she couldn't speak. The Sister took her by the hand, still managing to keep her arm around the young girl, and led her into the infirmary so that the Sister on duty there could look at Frances. The two Sisters observed this frightened young girl and looked at each other in disbelief. They made Frances sit down and then started asking her questions.

"What happened to you, my dear? Please tell us. Did someone attack you in the street? What happened to you? Does your mother know where you are?"

With horror, Frances responded, "Please, please don't tell her where I am. I'm sure she will kill me this time."

The two Sisters looked at each other again, only this time in astonishment.

"Frances, you may stay here tonight, but we will have to contact your mother. She must be very worried about you."

The good Sisters decided not to question Frances any further that night. It was obvious they were not going to get straight answers anyway. Instead they made up a bed in the infirmary and told Frances she was welcome to sleep there for now. The Sister in charge of the infirmary found a nightgown and gave it to Frances. She also gave her a towel, a washcloth, and a toothbrush. She then gently helped her to wash her face. She saw not only the swelling of new bruises appearing on Frances's face and arms but also noticed several more bruises on her body, but she made no further mention of them. She dressed the wounds and helped Frances wash up for the night. Both Sisters helped tuck the frightened girl into bed and covered her with a worn, but clean, blanket. Sister Mary Theresa then placed a medal of the Virgin Mary tightly in Frances's hand and whispered that the blessed mother would take care of her. Frances was exhausted from all that she had been though and it wasn't long before she fell fast and deeply to sleep, feeling the comfort and safety of the home she loved so much.

The Sisters quietly left the room and closed the door behind them. They started to discuss what had transpired before them this evening. They both had known Frances while she was growing up and knew she was not the type to disobey her mother. They were quite baffled as to what had happened to this girl.

Sister Mary Theresa was certain that even though it was very late, she would need to report this incident to the Mother Superior. She knew the Mother Superior would decide how to handle this situation.

After hearing the details of what had happened, the Mother Superior became very quiet and said she would like to speak with Frances in the morning. She told Sister Mary Theresa to let Frances sleep as long as the

A Matter of Survival

young girl needed, and after she had breakfast, she should bring the girl to her office. She would then decide how to best handle this new problem at hand. The Mother Superior was well experienced in handling problems. Overseeing a home that housed five hundred girls was never without problems, but this one might be a little different.

Frances slept until almost nine o'clock and was thankful to wake up in the familiar place where she felt comfort and a sense of security. Frances was instructed to get washed and dressed and go to the dining hall. The morning meal was simple, as it usually was, consisting of a watered-down orange drink and a small amount of oatmeal topped with the usual watery powdered milk. Frances didn't care what she ate; she was just grateful to be there. After getting her breakfast tray, she returned to the dining room, sat down, proceeded to eat, and wondered what was going to happen next.

One of the Sisters came over to Frances and whispered for her to eat quickly, as the Mother Superior was waiting in her office and wanted to speak to her. Frances gulped down the small amount of food, brought her dishes back into the kitchen, and then headed for the office.

When Frances entered, she noticed Mother Superior had been joined with two others, Sister Mary Gerard and Sister Mary Katherine. They all sat in silence for a few minutes. The Mother Superior beckoned to Frances to sit down. She began, "Let's discuss what is going on in your life now, Frances. Can you tell me what brought you back to St. Joseph's?"

Frances stirred uneasily in her seat. It was obvious to the women that this young girl was uncomfortable, but still they waited for a response. Frances, holding back tears as best as she could, started to speak.

"Sister, ever since I left here and went to live with my mother, things have been very difficult for me."

The Mother Superior spoke. "Difficult? What do you mean by 'difficult'?"

Frances hated to tell the nuns what her life had been like since she left the home. Maybe this was the way it was supposed to be on the outside for some families. Finally, Frances started to speak again.

"Sister, my mother hits me all the time. No matter what I do, or how hard I try to please her, she hits me so hard that I am very afraid of her."

She continued, "When I first went to live with my mother, after a few weeks, I pleaded with her to let me go to the local high school. She finally said that as long as I promised to continue to do my chores, she would agree to this. When Mother came home early yesterday and discovered I was not home, she was furious. I still got home about the same time I usually did, but she was so angry that she started hitting me with a belt. She hit me so hard that I was afraid she was going to kill me. All the time she was hitting me, she was saying she was not going to let me continue with school."

Tears started to roll down Frances's face as she went on with her story.

"Mother said the school was evil and the people who ran the school were also evil. Sister, I was doing well in school, and I even made a friend. I am so afraid of my own mother that I didn't know what else to do. I ran as fast as I could to my friend to ask for bus money, and then I came straight back here last night."

Mother Superior and the two other nuns sat in silence, staring in disbelief at the young girl sitting before them. Finally, the Mother Superior spoke.

"Frances, as you know, when you reached sixteen, you were required to leave here. According to laws of the state, and because you have a mother, it was necessary that you get placed in her care. We cannot keep you with us, as you now have reached this age. We can no longer provide for you. I think your mother may be strict, and you are probably exaggerating about her 'beating' you. Today in these hard times, many parents discipline their children severely. Maybe your mother just got a little overzealous, because you are now living at home and she has the added responsibility of a daughter. I'm sorry, but you cannot stay here. You must be returned to her. Frances, we sent for your mother earlier this morning. We will speak with her, but be prepared, she will be here shortly to take you home."

Frances became horrified. "Sister, please, I beg you; don't send me back to her. She will beat me again. Please, please, don't do this to me."

Even though Frances was visibly shaken, she was instructed to wait in the outside room.

The room seemed somewhat bare and cold. It contained only a few pieces of old, scarred furniture: a desk and chair, a file cabinet, and the wooden bench that Frances was sitting on. There was also a statue in the room. It was a statue of Saint Anthony holding the little baby Jesus in his arms. The walls in the room were a faded green, but in spite of it needing a painting, the room was very clean. Frances also noticed a clock on the wall above the bench where she was sitting. The clock read eleven twenty-five. Suddenly panic started to set in. *How could the good Sisters send me back to live with my mother? Don't they care what would happen to me?* Frances decided she would pray as hard as she could. "Please, God," she prayed. "Don't let them send me back, don't let them send me back to her." She sat there in silence for what seemed to be a very long time. Suddenly, the door opened, and now Frances saw the reality of what was to be. Accompanied by one of the Sisters, her mother entered the room. No words were spoken by any of them. The Sister knocked on the Mother Superior's adjoining office and announced the arrival of Frances's mother. The Mother Superior requested that Frances join them in her office. She then summoned Sister Mary Gerard and Sister Mary Katherine to join them. Finally, with all five of them together, the Mother Superior spoke first.

"Mrs. Antenelli, we asked you here today so that you may take Frances back home with you. Frances came to us late last night, saying that you hit her all the time. She also tells us that you want to take her out of the school she is attending. We realize Frances may be having a difficult time adjusting to the outside world, but we know she really belongs with family. She may be finding discipline on the outside different than the kind of discipline we have here at the home. We would like to hear what you have to say about Frances's coming here last night."

Frances's eyes widened. The fear of returning to her mother sickened her. It might not have been visible, but she was shaking inside with panic.

At last Frances's mother spoke. Looking directly at her daughter, she said, "Oh Frances, how could you paint such a terrible picture of me to these good Sisters. You know how much I love you. I would never hurt you. I'm sure after living in this marvelous place, having to move to a tiny apartment with me was difficult for you, but we always made the best of it. How could you tell the Sisters that I was going to take you out of school? I am so proud of what you are doing. I love and need you with me."

She continued, now directing herself to the Mother Superior. "Sister, I love my daughter and would never hurt her. Please, do let me take her back home where we will be able to work things out and be happy together."

The Mother Superior had a gentle smile on her face and replied to the older lady who sat before her. "I'm so glad you really love your daughter and you want her to continue to live with you. I know you will be able to work things out together. I'm sure this was just one big misunderstanding. I think it would be wise to let mother and daughter have some private time alone. Please take some time to talk to each other about whatever problems you are having. We are going to leave you here in my office, and you can discuss whatever you need to discuss. Make yourselves comfortable and take all the time you think necessary. We will be in the outer office, and when you are finished, just call us."

Dolores thanked the good Sisters for their kindness to her and expressed her gratitude to them for granting her time alone with her dear beloved daughter.

The Mother Superior indicated for the other Sisters to leave the room with her and let Frances and her mother work things out.

Frances's mother smiled and thanked them again and said she was sure they wouldn't be too long in using her office. She then gently took her daughter's hand in hers and started patting it ever so gently. She then proceeded to stroke Frances's hair in a loving and very caring way. Frances felt relieved that her mother was being so kind to her. Maybe she really did love her, she thought.

The Sisters left the room and gently closed the door behind them.

Once the door was closed, Frances saw her mother's expression change from one of a gentle, caring lady to a horrid, mean, and growling woman.

"How dare you embarrass me like this?" she said angrily. "When I get you home, you'll be lucky if I ever let you out. You will get a beating that you will never forget. I'll tie you to the kitchen sink if I have to. You better keep your mouth shut if you know what's good for you, you little ungrateful brat. I can't wait to get my hands on you. I'll teach you a good lesson once and for all!"

Frances's eyes filled with tears. "Oh no, Mother—please, please, don't hurt me."

A Matter of Survival

Just then the office door swung open, and the Mother Superior and the two other Sisters entered the room. Frances's mother was now the one who was shocked and horrified. Fortunately for the young girl, the Sisters had left the office but continued to listen in on the conversation between mother and daughter.

"Mrs. Antenelli, you will now have to leave the office and this home. We will see to it that you are escorted out of St. Joseph's, and please do not try to come back again. Frances was a very good child while she was here, and we are very fond of her." Frances's mother stormed out of the office looking livid that the nuns had tricked her.

Once Frances's mother was gone, the Mother Superior put her arms out to the young girl, and Frances immediately got up. She was grateful for the comfort that the Mother Superior gave her. "Frances, you may stay here for a short time, but we will have to make other arrangements for you. I will speak to you about them when plans become finalized. In the meantime, you may sleep with the older girls, and I will discuss your future with you in a day or two. Right now I would like you to go and help out in the kitchen."

As Frances opened the office door, she turned to the Mother Superior and said, "Thank you, Sister."

The Mother Superior simply looked at her and said, "May God always bless you."

Over the next few days, Frances went about the home, doing chores and feeling relieved to be back at St. Joseph's. Even though she knew she would not be able to stay, she was happy for the feeling of security this place gave her.

After three days Frances was summoned to the Mother Superior's office. She immediately tried to fix her appearance to look as neat as possible. She was very anxious to hear what the Mother Superior had to say.

Frances knocked on the Mother Superior's door, and when her knock was acknowledged, she entered the large office. Mother Superior put out her hand, indicating for the young woman to sit before her. After a brief pause, she spoke to Frances.

"Frances, we have always enjoyed having you here, but as we explained to you before, the state will simply not let us keep you since they consider you old enough to be on your own. I am so sorry that things didn't work out with your mother, but I'm sure that as you become older, you may understand more and maybe even forgive her for her actions. I don't believe she is responsible for herself, let alone able to take care of you. The world had been very hard on many people for such a long time now, and obviously it was particularly hard for your mother. Sometimes people can't cope with problems and change into someone other than their real self. Although we don't quite understand it ourselves, but hopefully you will someday understand, Frances, your mother is mentally ill. Mental illness is a subject that no one talks about. No one really knows or understands what makes people act the way they do. We realize there is no reasoning with or changing individuals such as your mother, so we think it best to make other living arrangements for you. I think you will be pleased with them." Frances didn't quite understand the words "mental illness." It was a term she had never heard before, but she was curious and anxious to hear more.

"Now you are going to put all these problems behind you; we will not discuss them again, but rather I want you to look forward to the future, your future," the Mother Superior continued. "We have found a good family for you to live with. You will be required to help them out by doing chores, but mostly you will help them to raise their children. In return for your help, you will have a nice room and be provided with meals. You will also receive a small amount of money each week. They live in a lovely area in North Flushing, not too far from here. I met these people several weeks ago and have also visited their home. They came here to St. Joseph's seeking one of our older girls. The children happen to be a four-year-old boy and two-year-old twin girls. I think you might be very well suited for this position, Frances. Now, what do you think about all this?" she asked.

Frances smiled. She was very grateful to the Mother Superior for making these arrangements and giving her so much to look forward to.

"When will I get to meet them?" Frances asked anxiously.

"She wanted you to start as soon as possible. In two days, we will provide you their address and give you bus fare to their home. We will also provide you with a letter of introduction, and then you will be well on your way to making a new life for yourself. Sister Mary Gerard will give you all the details tomorrow.

"One more thing, Frances—I am also providing you with some names of people who are actually part of your extended family. We have the names and address of your grandparents, as well as one or two aunts and uncles who no doubt have a few cousins for you to meet. We also have the last known address of your father. Someday you may want to contact your relatives, but that will be up to you. Frances, let us hear from you from time to time so that we will know how you are doing."

She put her arms around the young girl and said, "God bless you, my child, and may God always protect and keep you."

Frances responded, "I will always love and treasure you for helping me. I will be grateful to you and St. Joseph's for as long as I live, Sister. Thank you so very much."

When their embrace broke, Frances wasn't sure but she thought the Mother Superior turned to look away so that she could avoid looking at Frances. As stern and demanding as the nuns tried to appear to their young charges, there were moments, such as now, when their eyes would well up with tears for the heartbreak these young girls had to endure. With that, the Mother Superior indicated by a swish of her hand that Frances should now leave her office. Once Frances left and closed the door behind her, the Mother Superior pulled a handkerchief from her pocket and wiped her eyes as tears now rolled down her face.

Nine

A New Life Begins

Frances joined the other girls in attending morning Mass and then proceeded to the dining hall for breakfast.

Now the time had come. It was a bright and clear autumn morning, and Sister Mary Gerard summoned Frances to the office. When she walked into the office, she noticed the sun was streaming brightly through the large windows, as if to indicate there was a bright new world waiting on the outside for her. She knew today was the day she was to be given all her instructions, and she was anxious to discover what would lie ahead of her. Firstly, Sister handed her a paper bag that contained a uniform skirt, blouse, and set of underwear. She was also given the old nightgown she had been wearing as well as the toothbrush she was given on the night she had fled back to the home.

Sister also provided Frances the list of her family members. This made Frances very curious. Thoughts raced quickly through her mind: *I have relatives, I really have relatives.* She wondered what they were like and what reaction they would have when they heard about her. *Why didn't anyone ever visit me? What happened to my father, and why did he only come to see me one time?* But the most important question she had was, where was her brother? She could remember as little children they had been very close and loved each other very much. Unfortunately, none of the information that was provided to her contained anything regarding her brother. Frances found herself getting lost deep in her own private thoughts when suddenly Sister Mary Gerard called to her.

"Frances, Frances—are you listening to me? Are you listening to what I am telling you? I will give you these instructions only one time, so pay attention."

This brought Frances immediately back to the present.

Sister continued, "You are going to live with Dr. and Mrs. O'Neill, where I am sure you will no doubt appreciate the comforts of their lovely home. As previously explained to you, Mrs. O'Neill will expect you to help out with household chores and with taking care of the children. She is expecting you today. We told her you would be at their home probably sometime before noon. I have written out traveling instructions for you. As you will see, it is necessary for you to walk nine blocks to Northern Boulevard, and there on the corner you will see a bus stop. Take either bus number Q28 or Q13 and get off at 162nd Street. You can ask the driver of the bus to let you know when your stop is approaching. Once you get off the bus, cross the large boulevard and walk three blocks up on 162nd Street. After three blocks you will see a large white house on a hill with the address I have written on this paper. As I said, Mrs. O'Neill will be expecting you."

Frances was a little intimidated. She had never actually traveled alone and had no idea what to expect on the unfamiliar streets, but she decided she would do exactly as Sister had instructed her to do and hope for the best.

After gathering all of her belongings, she said her good-byes to the good Sister as they walked together to the front door. Sister told her she would pray for her and wished her well. Now at last Frances headed to Northern Boulevard. While walking the nine blocks, Frances was surprised at the chill in the air. The sun was bright, but she didn't expect it to be so cold. Her worn sweater offered very little comfort. She decided to cross the street and walk in the sunlight. It wasn't much warmer, but it seemed better. Thinking of what was ahead of her did offer her some comfort. She was anxious to meet the people the Mother Superior had spoken so highly of.

At last Frances reached Northern Boulevard and arrived at the bus stop. Much to her surprise, people were everywhere. Everyone rushed around and seemed determined to arrive at their destination as quickly as possible.

Arleen Patricia Mercorella

Most of the men, she noticed, were well-dressed and appeared to be very handsome. What struck her the most were the ladies, who were apparently out shopping or running their necessary errands. They all looked so pretty. They all seemed to be stylishly dressed and wearing fashionable hats. The world seemed so different now. The only ladies Frances ever really knew were the nuns, except, of course, Kay's mother. Frances suddenly thought of Kay, longing for her good friend. She made a mental note to write to her, and hoped they would meet again someday.

People started to line up in front of the bus stop sign, and Frances did the same. It wasn't too long before the Q28 arrived. Frances watched the others deposit their nickels into the box near the driver and proceed to take a seat. She did the same. In a way, this was very exciting for her. She suddenly felt very grown-up. As she deposited her carfare into the box, she shyly asked the driver to let her know when they reached 162nd Street. After a short time, she noted that passengers would pull an overhead wire, evidently notifying the driver they wanted to get off at the next stop. She thought, *Someday, when I know where I am going, I too will learn when to pull the wire!*

She sat there with her nose almost touching the window, staring at all the activity that was now surrounding the bus. There were many more shops than she thought was possible. She saw food stores of every kind selling meat, vegetables, and groceries. She also noted many furniture stores, as well as many other stores selling household goods and kitchenware, but what interested her most were the clothing stores she observed. She thought it would be nice to enter one of the shops to see what was being sold.

Her thoughts were suddenly broken by the stopping of the bus and the driver calling out 162nd Street. When the driver repeated this again a second time, Frances realized he was calling out to her. She got up quickly and exited the bus, thanking the driver for helping her. She had obviously forgotten to pay attention to the street signs.

Okay. Now she was on the street again, looking around at the unfamiliar neighborhood. *Here goes nothing,* she thought. She crossed Northern Boulevard and started walking up 162nd Street. Frances noticed the street contained many trees, which were turning lovely colors of autumn. The street itself had a continuous blanket of leaves, which must have been dropping for weeks now; sometimes the colored blanket even reached the top of her ankles as she walked through them. She loved the sound of the crisp leaves.

Frances counted each very long block, and when she reached the third block she saw it—a very large, magnificent white house on the corner. She couldn't believe her eyes, and just to be sure, she glanced down to recheck the address that was written on the piece of paper in her hand. Yes, this was the address that had been given to her.

There was a very impressive stone wall she estimated to be about three feet tall that surrounded the house and seemed to go on forever. As she walked up the path leading to this very extraordinary house, she had to stop to admire the fall flowers surrounding the path. As she ascended the stairs leading to the double doors, she noticed a shingle hanging on a pole in the front yard that read, "Lawrence O'Neill, MD." Once she reached the entrance, she observed two large stone containers of amber and yellow flowers. In front of the flowers were several pumpkins and other autumnal items; items which she had never seen before. Frances could hardly believe how pretty everything was.

As she approached the front door, she hesitated for a moment, thinking *What if they don't like me?* She tried to put these negative feelings out of her head and summoned enough courage to finally press the doorbell. She waited for a few moments, and the door opened. There standing before her was a very pretty lady in a lovely brown-and-white dress. Frances found herself tongue-tied. The woman spoke first.

"You must be Frances, the girl from St. Joseph's. I'm Mrs. O'Neill. I've been expecting you. I hope you didn't have too much difficulty finding our home."

Frances felt a shyness that she hadn't felt before, and finally she said yes, she was the girl, and presented the letter of introduction provided by the Mother Superior.

"I have been so looking forward to meeting you, Frances, as the Mother Superior spoke very highly of you," Mrs. O'Neill said. "Why don't you put your package down here in the hall?" As she walked, she added, "Maybe we could get to know each other over lunch. I've prepared some sandwiches for us, and we can also have a nice cup of hot tea. Do you like tea?"

Frances couldn't actually remember ever having tea, but she said to Mrs. O'Neill that tea would be fine.

Frances followed Mrs. O'Neill into the bright kitchen. It was a very clean and pretty room with white cabinets and blue accessories. There was a large bay window at the end of the room, and the kitchen table and chairs were arranged in front of it. The curtains on the window were also white, and it was obvious they too were starched and ironed to perfection. The table was simply set for their lunch, and still it looked lovely. It had a white cloth and yellow checkered napkins and a small pretty pot of autumn-colored flowers sat in the center. Frances thought, *I wonder if Mrs. O'Neill was raised at St. Joseph's.* Everything to Frances looked to be very neat and clean, just as it was in the home.

Mrs. O'Neill put a kettle of water on the stove, and after a few minutes, she poured the hot water from the steaming kettle into a teapot that matched the dishes on the table.

"Now then," Mrs. O'Neill said. "Let's have some lunch."

With that she passed a plate of sandwiches to Frances. Frances had never before seen a table set as this one was, nor could she remember seeing so many sandwich halves prepared for just two people. When Mrs. O'Neill passed the plate to her, she took whatever was the closest. When the tea was poured, she tasted it, and the warmth of it felt good inside her.

Then Mrs. O'Neill got down to the business at hand.

"Frances, I would like to discuss your duties with you. I will be needing your help mostly with the children. As I do a great deal of charity work, you will have the responsibility of overseeing the children and oftentimes will be required to prepare their breakfast and lunch. I understand that you helped out in the kitchen at St. Joseph's, so I don't think it will be difficult for you to adjust to the kitchen. We also do a great deal of entertaining, and I will need your help in preparing the food and may need your help as well in serving our guests. I will from time to time also require you to do some shopping and some light housekeeping. I do have a cleaning lady who comes in twice a week, but I may require you to also help out when needed. My husband has his office attached to our home, but many times he is not there. Right now he is probably on his way home from the hospital. That is the reason why I have extra sandwiches prepared. It may be necessary for

A Matter of Survival

you to bring my husband's lunch into his office. If we don't do this, he'll surely forget to eat." She laughed.

Mrs. O'Neill continued, "Today I asked my mother to take the children out to the park so that we may have time together. She lives nearby and is always happy to help out. You will be meeting her and the children a little later."

Frances listened to Mrs. O'Neill very carefully. She wanted to be sure she understood everything that was required of her.

"Well, Frances, how does all this sound to you so far?" Mrs. O'Neill asked her. Frances finally answered the lady, saying she was sure she could handle the duties that would be entrusted to her and she would do her very best to please her. She was looking forward to helping her and anxious to start her new assignment.

For the first time since meeting Mrs. O'Neill, Frances actually smiled and appeared to be happy with her new surroundings.

"That's wonderful," the woman said. "After we clean up the kitchen, I will show you your room, and if you have any questions, I will try to answer them for you."

They started to clear the table together.

"All your meals will be provided by us, and I will also ask you to feed the children their dinner here in the kitchen unless you are told otherwise. You will have every Monday off to do as you please. Because we will be providing you with room and board, we will be paying you only a small amount of money each week, which will be five dollars."

Frances just smiled and nodded her head affirmatively.

Mrs. O'Neill continued, "Frances, our four-year-old boy, Timmy, has his own room at the top of the stairs, and the two-year-old twin girls, Jessie and Sara, share the room next to his. When the children come home today, I would like you to bring them upstairs and keep an eye on them until their dinner is ready. Is everything I have said acceptable to you so far?"

Frances nodded her head again. "Yes."

As they continued cleaning up the kitchen together, Mrs. O'Neill told Frances about the area. She told her where the bus stops were, the stores, the local park, and, of course, the closest Catholic church. Frances was excited about working here and wanted very much to please Mrs. O'Neill.

When the kitchen was cleaned and the dishes put away, Mrs. O'Neill told Frances to get her bag, as it was still in the hallway, and she would now show her the room that she would occupy. Frances retrieved the bag and proceeded to follow Mrs. O'Neill, who showed her a small but pleasant room located down a small hallway a short distance from the kitchen. There was a bathroom with a tub adjacent to the kitchen in the hallway. This would be the bathroom that Frances would use.

The room was pretty. It was done up in yellow and white. There was a nightstand with a lamp and a small clock, a small dresser with a mirror above it, and a white wicker chair in the corner with a little table beside it. She noticed there was a radio on the little table, and she instantly loved this luxury. Actually, Frances liked the room very much. It seemed like this was going to be her own special place, and for the first time in her life, she was happy to have a room of her own. She immediately thought of the Mother Superior and how very grateful she was to her for making such nice arrangements. Frances didn't care how hard she might have to work; she was thankful to be here and promised herself she wouldn't do anything to lose this.

Mrs. O'Neill asked, "Frances, do you like the room?"

Frances smiled, nodding, "Yes, I think it's very pretty."

Obviously, Mrs. O'Neill had no idea of the kind of life Frances had had before coming to her home.

All at once there was a noisy commotion coming from the front of the house. It was the children coming back from their outing. Mrs. O'Neill told Frances to come with her, and she would introduce her to the children and their grandmother. Frances followed Mrs. O'Neill out of the room. The three children looked flushed with the cold air still on their cheeks, and the grandmother looked tired. The children were all blondes with big eyes and were dressed very nicely.

"Frances, please take the children upstairs to their rooms. It looks like you can get them ready for a nap, and then change their clothes before dinner."

Frances took the children with her upstairs and helped them take off their outfits, putting them down in bed for a nap. She was surprised that neither the boy nor the twins gave her a hard time. They apparently were very well-behaved children. The children seemed perfect in this perfect house.

As the days went on, Frances learned to love the work she was doing and really liked Dr. and Mrs. O'Neill. They always seemed so happy and demonstrated their affection not only to their children, but each other as well. Frances thought it was wonderful to be part of this family. If she were to ever marry and have children, she would want her life to be exactly like this.

Mrs. O'Neill had given Frances a lovely gray tweed coat, saying she didn't want it anymore. Frances was thrilled. Mrs. O'Neill often gave her articles of clothing, always saying she didn't need or want them, but they seemed fantastic to Frances. All the clothes were quite nice, and Frances took very good care of them, just like she had been required to do when living at St. Joseph's.

Many days Frances would take the children to the local park. The little boy would ride his tricycle, and she would push the twins in their carriage. Things were working out for Frances, and she was very happy. She decided to write a note to the Mother Superior thanking her again and telling her how wonderful her new job was.

The Thanksgiving holiday came, and Frances was asked to help out with preparing the meal. She, Mrs. O'Neill, and Mrs. O'Neill's mother all worked together in the kitchen. She loved working with these ladies. Not only was she learning to cook, but there was a great deal of laughter among the three of them while they were working in the kitchen. Frances was invited to sit with the family in the dining room on this holiday. This was a very special treat.

Frances was a very shy girl. She never spoke to anyone outside the family, except for maybe a shopkeeper. On her Mondays off, she liked to explore the local shopping areas. Sometimes she would walk by the many stores in Flushing, and other times would go to Bayside just to walk along the main avenue. What made her even happier was, when traveling on the bus, she now knew when to pull the wire to alert the driver she wanted off at the next stop.

One day after several months of working for the O'Neill's, Frances and Mrs. O'Neill were in the kitchen together. Out of nowhere Mrs. O'Neill asked Frances if she had any family of her own. Frances responded by shaking her head no and then said, "I'm really not sure."

Mrs. O'Neill replied, simply saying, "Frances, everyone has relatives somewhere." Wise Mrs. O'Neill decided not to press the subject, but she did tell Frances that if she ever needed any help, she could certainly ask her.

That night, alone in her room, Mrs. O'Neill's inquiry triggered many unanswered questions in Frances's mind. She decided she was going to go through the papers that had been given to her by the Mother Superior. Now she had to admit, even if just to herself, she was more than a little curious regarding her relatives whose names were written on the official-looking papers. She knew these people were her relatives, but to her they were just names of people she did not know. She was particularly interested in contacting her father. She reflected back to the day when he'd visited her at the home, but told the nuns he was her uncle. *Why did he do this?* she wondered. This started Frances thinking back to memories that she didn't want to remember, but still they all came flooding back to her no matter how hard she tried to suppress them. After working and living with the O'Neill family, she questioned more and more what had gone wrong in her life. What could she have possibly done to deserve the treatment she received? She'd never heard from any of her so-called relatives, and she certainly couldn't understand the cruelty of her mother.

Then Frances started to cringe, remembering one event that she had pushed way back in her mind. It had happened shortly after she went to live with her mother. Her mother had come home, and as she did every day, had started yelling at her daughter and rambling on and on incoherently. Frances remembered only too well how the fear had quickly overtaken her. She'd started to leave the apartment when all a sudden, her mother struck out at her, hitting her so hard she had fallen down the stairs to the first landing. Pain had consumed her body, and when she looked up, her mother was laughing at her "stupid daughter." Frances didn't want to remember all these horrible events, but nonetheless the memories came flooding back to her no matter how hard she tried to forget them.

That night Frances cried herself to sleep, but at the same time she was glad not to be living with her mother.

Ten

The Search

A few days after Frances went through her papers, she decided to write to her good friend, Kay, thanking her for the bus fare. She asked Kay to forgive her for not writing sooner, but perhaps someday she would understand. She also told her that she missed her good friend a great deal and wrote her all about the family for whom she was working and living with now. At the end of her letter, she suggested to Kay that if she wanted, they could meet at a coffee shop one day soon to catch up on the events that had transpired in their lives since they last saw each other. She also mentioned she was off on Mondays.

Next was the big one—she decided it was time to write to her father. The last known address the home had for him was located somewhere in the Bronx. The address might have been in another state for all Frances knew. She had never been to the Bronx and wouldn't even know how to get there. She wrote to him, simply saying she was sure he would remember her. She told him once she reached her sixteenth birthday, she was required to leave the home and she had gone to live with her mother, but that didn't work out too well. She did not elaborate. However, she did tell him she was living with a wonderful family in Flushing. Frances said, if possible, she would like to see him again and asked him to please write back to her. She signed the letter, "Your Daughter, Frances."

One more letter to go—it was to a woman who was listed as her mother's sister. *This woman would be my aunt,* Frances thought. The woman lived somewhere in upstate New York, a town that again Frances didn't know, and furthermore, never even heard of. She was particularly curious to meet this woman with the hope of finding out what she might know about her mother and why her mother was so strange. Maybe this woman, Mary, would have the answers Frances so desperately needed to learn.

The next day, after taking the children to school, Frances walked to the post office, placed the proper postage on each letter, and one by one dropped them in the mail slot, hoping for the best.

Eleven

KAY

A week had passed since she'd mailed the letters, and Frances was busy doing chores. It was a sunny early spring day, and the trees and flowers were beginning to bud, shaking off winter's frost and getting ready to burst with blooms. Frances thought what an exceptional time of year this was. She was happy to be living in this beautiful home with this beautiful family. As she worked in the kitchen, Mrs. O'Neill came in with an envelope and a surprised look on her face.

"Frances," she said, "a letter came for you in this morning's mail."

Saying that Mrs. O'Neill looked very surprised was an understatement, as Frances had never received any mail before today. Frances's mind started to race as to who had been the first one to write back to her. She was hoping it was her father. She wanted to believe maybe he was anxious to see his long-lost daughter. Mrs. O'Neill handed the envelope to her, and when she glanced at the return address, she said to herself, *I might have known my good friend Kay would be the first to respond to my letters.*

Frances just smiled at Mrs. O'Neill and placed the letter in the pocket of the apron she was wearing. Even though she was very anxious to read its contents, she wanted to read the letter tonight in the privacy of her room. Frances couldn't wait for the end of the day.

Later in her room, she retrieved her nightgown and robe from the closet, took a quick bath, and then at last settled on her bed, propping the pillows behind her back.

She opened the envelope very carefully as if it contained some magic spell. The letter read:

Dear Frances,

You can't imagine how happy your letter made me. I was so very glad to hear from you and to find out that you are well. After that terrible night when you showed up at my door, I worried so much about you. I was hoping to see you at school the next day, but of course, you never did return to school. I miss you a lot and miss the good times we shared with each other.

I would like to meet with you very much. Please let me know what day is good for you, and I will make arrangements to meet you anywhere you want. Any day and place is good for me. Just let me know.

Love, your friend,

Kay

Frances, still sitting up on the bed, reread the letter from her good friend again. It made her feel warm and even loved. She would always cherish her friendship with her former schoolmate. That night she wrote back to Kay. The letter read:

Dear Kay,

How wonderful of you to reply so quickly. I am very much looking forward to seeing you. Perhaps we can meet next Monday in Bayside. There is a small ice cream shop in the little town where I stop often for a cool drink. It is called Betty's Ice Cream Shop. Since I'm off on Mondays, this would be the best day for me to meet you. I will be there at eleven o'clock. We can meet there at this time and perhaps have some lunch. I am so looking forward to seeing you.

Love,

Frances

When Frances finished writing to Kay, she looked over the letter she had just written. As she reread it, she thought back to the home and was thankful the nuns had prepared her so well for the outside world. Lessons in penmanship were very highly stressed. The nuns would require their students to repeat the exercises over and over, and now as she looked over the letter, she felt her hard work paid off as her handwriting was really very

A Matter of Survival

nice. With that, she sealed the envelope and put a stamp on it. She would drop the letter in a mailbox right after taking the children to school. As she looked at the sealed envelope, excitement was beginning to build with the anticipation of meeting her dear friend the following week.

With Frances's busy schedule, the days flew by and finally Monday was here. Frances got up early. She bathed and took extra time to dress. Frances wanted to look extra nice for her good friend. She decided to wear a pretty pink dress Mrs. O'Neill had given her. It had a matching jacket with white trim, and she loved the outfit. Then she added a cute little simple white hat that made her outfit complete. She was grateful to Mrs. O'Neill for giving her so many pretty clothes, often saying she was tired of them. *How can she get tired of them?* Frances thought. *They are all so nice and seem brand new.* Mrs. O'Neill always wore beautiful clothes. It was obvious she had a great sense of style. With Mrs. O'Neill's influence, Frances quickly discovered she also loved clothes. It didn't take long until Frances too developed her own sense of style and took great pride in her appearance. Frequently, after a day of shopping, Mrs. O'Neill would ask Frances to come up to her bedroom to see what she'd bought that day. She would try on new outfits, asking Frances her opinion as to how they looked on her. It was not unusual that after trying on the new clothes, she would look into her closet and give Frances outfits she didn't want anymore. Mrs. O'Neill always seemed so pleased that Frances loved whatever she gave her and that her young employee seemed so grateful to have them. Frances couldn't believe how lucky she was that Mrs. O'Neill was so good to her. Frances kept everything in perfect order. The nuns at the home had taught her well!

Shortly after moving into the O'Neill's home, Frances had opened a savings account at the local bank. As this was the mid-thirties, she was very cautious with her money and managed to save a little each week. She still couldn't afford to spend her savings on anything that might be considered a luxury, and this was the reason she would get genuinely excited each and every time Mrs. O'Neill would give her a new treasure. In her spare time, Frances would look through Mrs. O'Neill's fashion magazines to see the latest styles. Someday, she hoped she would be able to buy clothes like these.

Whenever Dr. and Mrs. O'Neill attended one of Mrs. O'Neill's charity events, Frances loved hearing about it the next day. She always wanted to know what the elegant ladies had worn to the affair. Sometimes a picture of them would even appear in the local newspaper, and all the ladies always looked stunning. Mrs. O'Neill and her friends were repeatedly praised in the papers for the marvelous charitable work they were doing for helping those less fortunate during the great depression.

Frances was now dressed and ready to meet her good friend, Kay. She glanced at the clock in her room; it read 9:45 a.m. Even though it was quite early and her destination was only a short bus ride into the town of Bayside, Frances didn't want to take a chance of being late. As she passed through the kitchen, Mrs. O'Neill appeared to be lingering over a second cup of coffee and reading the daily newspaper at the sunny kitchen table. She glanced up from the paper with an approving smile.

"You look lovely, Frances." Without actually asking, she continued, "You must have a special appointment."

Frances hesitated and then replied, "Yes, I am meeting one of my high school friends that I haven't seen for some time. We're going to catch up with each other and probably have a light lunch."

"Well, enjoy and have fun," Mrs. O'Neill said with a look of satisfaction. She was pleased to see her young employee finally going out to meet someone.

The bus came after a very short time and headed toward Bayside. When Frances knew her stop was approaching, she confidently pulled the wire above. The driver stopped, and Frances exited the bus. The ice cream shop was just a short distance away, and she walked into the shop at 10:35 a.m.

Betty, an older woman, always seemed to be working at the shop. She acknowledged Frances, as she had seen her many times before. As usual, she tried to engage Frances in conversation, but Frances, still being rather shy, just said hello and sat down in one of the booths.

Betty asked, "Do you want to see a menu?"

Frances said, "Thank you, but I am waiting for someone and will look over the menu when my friend gets here."

Betty looked surprised, because in all the times that Frances had entered her shop, she was always alone. "Fine then, I'll let you be. Just call if you need anything."

With that she busied herself behind the counter. The shop had very few people in it. There was a man reading the paper and sipping coffee and another woman at the far end of the counter eating alone. It was quiet.

All at once the entrance door opened, and there, as pretty as ever and exquisitely dressed, was Kay. In one quick glance, Kay saw Frances and rushed over to greet her. Frances immediately exited the booth and threw her arms around her good friend. They stood there for what seemed like an eternity, holding on to each other. Frances felt she was on the verge of tears at the sight of her good friend, only this time, they were happy tears. Betty, still working at the counter, was quite moved and knew this was a special day for both of these young women. Finally, they sat down. Kay was the first to speak.

"Frances, you have no idea how glad I was to receive your letter. I was so worried about you. Never hearing from you again, I didn't know what to think."

"I know," Frances replied. "I can't speak about what happened, because I find it is too upsetting, but I will tell you I'm happy now and I'm working for a wonderful family."

"Well, I can say one thing—you look really great!" Kay replied.

Kay was sincerely truthful. She was glad to see her good friend looking so well and wearing such a lovely outfit. In the past she remembered that Frances seemed to have a limited amount of clothes, and as the weather turned cooler, she felt Frances's sweater just hadn't been warm enough.

The girls ordered a light lunch and continued to talk and talk the entire time. The only thing that saddened Frances was when Kay told her she had graduated high school. Frances had so wanted to complete school, but unfortunately that just wasn't possible. Kay told her she was now working in the family business, so getting time off was never a real problem for her. They could meet whenever it was convenient for Frances. Kay said she would like it if they could get together often, and she invited her to come home to see her mother again. She told Frances her mother often mentioned her and wondered what she was doing with her life.

"My mother really liked you, Frances, and she was so happy to hear you had written me and that we were getting together today."

Frances told Kay all about the family she was living with and how good the O'Neill's were to her, particularly Mrs. O'Neill. She told her of her assignments and about the three well-behaved children she was responsible for. Kay told her how happy she was to finally be out of school and be a part of the family business. Before they realized it, two hours had passed. The ice cream shop now was almost full with patrons. Betty had observed the two sitting in the booth for so long, but she knew this was a special reunion and let them stay for as long as they wanted. The girls motioned to Betty for the check, paid the bill, and left the shop. Frances remembered to give Kay the bus fare she'd borrowed that horrible night, and even though Kay didn't want it, she insisted.

"Let's walk down the boulevard for a little bit. We can do some window shopping," Kay suggested.

The two walked, talked, and enjoyed window shopping. Frances admired the exquisite ladies' shops along the way. She had told Kay earlier how fantastic Mrs. O'Neill was to her, giving her such lovely clothes, and how much she liked her company.

The two young women walked along the boulevard among the busy lady shoppers who acted as if getting the just right groceries for that night's dinner was the most important thing in their lives, and it probably was. The girls did a considerable amount of stopping to look into the shop windows. They passed many more food stores, several pretty dress shops, and a millinery shop, where Kay discovered a hat that she just had to have. Both girls laughed as they tried on several hats, and Kay finally made her treasured selection. As they continued on their way, the girls were oblivious, but others in the street noted how attractive they were and how impeccably they were dressed. They had spent a delightful day together, and it was now approaching four thirty in the afternoon. Kay said she had to get home to help her mother, but she had had a fantastic time with her friend. They made arrangements to get together again the following week, only this time, they decided they would meet in Flushing on Main Street. Kay asked Frances if she knew where "The Clock" was, and Frances answered affirmatively as she often saw people waiting there. The girls proceeded to walk to their bus stops, and when they reached their destination, they looked at each other with a genuine

A Matter of Survival

sense of thankfulness they had had this day together. They hugged each other tightly, and both said they looked forward to the following week.

From then on Frances and Kay met regularly and continued to enjoy each other's company. Occasionally, Kay would ask Frances to meet her at her home. There they would spend time with Kay's mother, who would prepare them a delicious lunch. It was so good to have a best friend!

Frances didn't get back to the O'Neill's until almost six o'clock. Mrs. O'Neill greeted her warmly, asking if she had fun.

"It was a wonderful day. My friend and I had a great time," Frances replied. Mrs. O'Neill seemed genuinely happy for Frances and said "I have already given the children dinner and if you want something there is plenty left over and please, Frances, help yourself.

"Oh, by the way, Frances, another letter came for you today. I put it in your room on the dresser."

Twelve

LONG-LOST FAMILY RELATIVES

When Frances entered her room, she looked at the envelope on the dresser and was a little disappointed it was not from her father. Instead, it was from the woman that she only knew to be her aunt.

As before, she decided to take a bath and get into her night clothes first. She propped up the pillows behind her and began to read:

Dear Frances,

It was good to hear from you. I know we have never met, but I am your aunt Mary, your mother's sister. I was the first of nine children and born in Italy. Your mother was the second child, and she, together with six more children, was born in Rio de Janeiro, Brazil, South America, but three died. Eventually we came to the United States and settled in New York, where sometime later my mother had her last child, Ralph. Growing up in New York was hard. Our parents never seemed to have enough money to feed and take care of so many children. We all had to work and do our share around our "flat" and when possible get outside jobs to help support the family. Your mother was never really close to me or her other brothers and sisters. She thought she was too good to live with us and was always dreaming of becoming famous as an actress. After my parents arranged for her to marry, we seldom saw or heard from her again. We did hear that she had two children, but were never sure what happened to her or her children. Do you see her? Do you know where she lives?

A Matter of Survival

Shortly after your mother was married, I, too, was told I was to be married to a man named Mike, and he is still my husband today. He has a business as a shoe maker. We settled in upstate New York and have lived here ever since we were first married.

I also have two children and would like you to meet them someday. I have a daughter who is just about your age, and I think you two could become good friends. Please write back to me, and we can arrange for you to visit us. We do not travel to the city so it would be better if you came here. It will be necessary for you to go into the city and take a bus to our town. The bus ride will take you about an hour or so. If you would like to visit us, please let me know, and I will give you further traveling instructions. I look forward to meeting you. Write soon.

Aunt Mary

After reading the letter, Frances was more than curious about her mother. What would ever make her mother act so bizarre and be so mean to her? After all, from what the letter said, Frances was the only one she had. Sometimes Frances felt sorry for the strange and unloved life that her mother must have had, but not sorry enough to want to see her again. She was deathly afraid of her.

Frances felt totally exhausted from her day. After reading the letter, she didn't have the inclination or the energy to think about her family. She decided when she got around to it, she may write back to her aunt and perhaps someday even visit her knowing it would take at least two or more hours of travel. Right now all she wanted was to sleep. *Mornings come fast,* she thought, and with that, she closed her eyes, happy to have found Kay, and fell into a deep sleep.

Months passed. Frances was still waiting to hear from her father, but no return letter was received.

Mrs. O'Neill became more and more dependent on Frances's help. She wondered to herself what she would ever do without her. Frances had learned to cook quite well and loved it, and she also took great pleasure in taking care of Mrs. O'Neill's home. She busied herself with her duties, offering to do more and more for Mrs. O'Neill. The children grew to love

Frances very much. The little boy was now in second grade, and Frances helped him every afternoon with his homework. The two little girls were in kindergarten and seemed to enjoy attending the same school as Timmy. Each day Frances would walk them to school and retrieve them at the end of the school day. The children looked forward to Frances meeting them. They learned very quickly that Frances would often hide something sweet in her pocket as a much-anticipated treat. Frances was looking forward to spending the summer months with them, as the school year was ending soon.

Mrs. O'Neill had told Frances they would be spending vacation time out on Long Island as a family. Mrs. O'Neill and the children would stay over the course of several weeks, and Dr. O'Neill would spend two weeks at the beginning of the summer with them. Thereafter, he would visit the vacation rental home as often as possible. Frances was told she would be sharing a room with the children. This would allow Mrs. O'Neill the freedom she wanted and needed.

Frances looked forward to this arrangement with great anticipation, as this would be a fantastic way to spend the summer. She had never been anywhere farther than Queens. Her weekly meetings with Kay would have to be put on hold for much of the summer, but Frances did suggest to her that perhaps she could come to visit her on her day off. Frances summoned all her courage to ask if Kay could also visit the vacation home while they were staying there. Mrs. O'Neill consented, saying that Kay could even stay over for a night or two, so long as it didn't interfere with her duties, making it very clear she must never leave the children unattended. Frances, of course, accepted these terms.

It was now the last week of school, and as she walked to pick up the children, she thought again about her father. It was funny that he never wrote her back, as Kay and her aunt had. It had been months since she'd sent the letter to him, but then again, he had really never showed her any affection. She decided to put the whole thing out of her mind.

As the children exited the school, one could sense the excitement they all felt as they ran from the doors. It was strange, but Frances was generally the only one to come for the children. It was even more unusual for the children to have a chaperone to and from the school, but Frances and the children seemed to appreciate their daily walks together. As customary, they greeted her with hugs and laughter, excited to tell her what went on in school that day and wait with eagerness for the hidden treat in her pocket.

"Frances, Frances, what did you bring us today?" they inquired.

Frances laughed and pulled out a little wax bag that contained three large chocolate chip cookies. She had baked this special treat earlier that day. Frances was cooking and baking quite a bit these days, and Mrs. O'Neill would compliment her on her culinary abilities. Frances had to admit that she not only loved taking care of the O'Neill's home, but she enjoyed the cooking, particularly the evening meal. Mrs. O'Neill's mother would tease her, saying that her cooking accomplishments were surpassing Mrs. O'Neill's rather quickly. Still, after all this time, Frances remained very shy and quiet. When someone such as Mrs. O'Neill or her mother complimented her, she would get very embarrassed, usually turning a crimson red. They would laugh, saying that someday she would learn to accept a compliment as a compliment and it was nothing to be ashamed of. Still, even with their encouragement, Frances never seemed to talk with anyone else outside the O'Neill family except, of course, Kay.

Along the way home, Frances noticed everything seemed to be in full bloom now. The trees were spreading out their branches, almost as if they were demonstrating how proud they were of their magnificent leaves. An assortment of many flowers was also in bloom, as if they too were showing off their bright colors. It was just four blocks to the house, and Frances never got tired of the display of nature, nor would she ever take it for granted. It was a lovely area to live and work. Frances was now very contented.

As they reached the front door, the children ran in, anxious to greet their mother, who was in the kitchen relishing the last of her quiet tea time. Frances started to speak first to Mrs. O'Neill, saying the children were getting so wound up with the anticipation of school coming to an end in just three more days. She was laughing and teasing them at the same time. All of a sudden, Frances realized that Mrs. O'Neill was looking at her rather seriously.

"Frances, a letter came for you in today's mail. I put it on the dresser in your room."

Mrs. O'Neill saw the color drain from Frances's face, and Frances's heart started to pound faster than it had in a long time. *Could it be from my father?*

Mrs. O'Neill, sensing Frances's anticipation, said to her, "Frances, why don't you go into your room now, and take all the time you need. Don't worry; everything is under control here. I'll get the children a snack."

Frances just nodded. She could hardly walk into the little hallway off the kitchen. She felt like her knees were going to go out from under her. When she entered her room, she saw the envelope on the dresser, and, yes—the return address indicated it was, in fact, from her father.

With trembling fingers she picked up the envelope, retrieved a letter opener from the drawer, and slashed the envelope open. She was almost afraid to take the letter out and did so with much trepidation and apprehension. She couldn't imagine what the contents might be. It read:

My Dearest Daughter Francesca,

It is with a heavy and very saddened heart that I write you. I was shocked and surprised to receive your letter, but don't mistake me; I was at the same time very glad to hear from you. You have no idea how many times over the years the guilt I have felt for not living up to my part as a father to you and to your brother. I have thought of you both so many, many times. With the receipt of your letter, I feel as if all the past years have now come to a crashing end. There have been so many times I wanted to contact you just to let you know that I am still alive, although I'm not in the best of health. As I said before, I have often thought of you, but I was never able to gather the nerve to meet or get in touch with you. It took all my courage just to finally answer you now. Up until receiving your letter, I assumed you would not want anything to do with me. For this reason alone, I was very happy to hear from you. I want you to know that very often I have reflected back to when you were a little girl. I had such terrible built-up resentment because I felt I was pushed into a marriage that I didn't want, and shortly after being married, I felt I was then burdened with a daughter who I only saw as a deeper trap and another mouth to feed. You no doubt remember that your mother and I did not get along well. She appeared to be somewhat strange from the very beginning. I desperately pleaded with my parents not to go through with this marriage arrangement, but they wouldn't hear of it. You probably don't understand all of this, but maybe someday we can talk about this further.

I want you to know that I would like very much to see you, and although it has been many years since we saw each other last, I do hope you will be able

A Matter of Survival

to forgive me for being such a poor father. It is probably hard for you to believe, but I know that I always loved you no matter what I demonstrated in the past. When I was a young man, it was considered a weakness for an Italian to show love to a daughter. I am not trying to make excuses for my behavior, but would like to ask your forgiveness so that maybe we could try to build a relationship together in the future.

You have many years ahead of you, Francesca, and hope you will allow me to be a part of them. I was surprised to hear that you were living and working for a family in Queens. I had assumed after leaving the home, you would still be living with your mother. How long did you live with her?

I would like very much for you to come to visit me. Please do try. Maybe we can start over—they say it is never too late. I am living just one block from where we lived before. I now have a wonderful woman who takes care of me, and I am grateful, because she has literally saved my life. I would also like you to meet her as well.

In case you do decide to visit me, I am attaching a separate sheet to this letter with directions of how you would travel from Flushing to the Belmont section of the Bronx. When you reach the Bronx, it will be necessary for you to change buses. Don't let this frighten you. The area looks very busy, but just follow these directions, and I am sure you will be fine.

Please do write back to me and let me know when you may like to come for a visit. I look forward to hearing from you.

You are probably curious to know about your brother. He is fine and is living in Italy. We have written to each other over the years, although not often. Looking forward to hearing from you again.

Your Father

Frances sat on the bed in a somewhat stunned trance. She was quite taken back with how "soft" he sounded, not at all like the man she remembered or even had envisioned him. *"Francesca?" What is that all about?* She had never been called "Francesca" before. She decided right then and there she would make every effort to see him before leaving on the summer vacation. Maybe he could answer her questions regarding her brother and even her mother.

She separated the letter from its attachment and took it out to the kitchen. She wanted to show the direction sheet to Mrs. O'Neill.

"Mrs. O'Neill," Frances asked, "would you please be good enough to look over these directions and let me know if you think I would be able to make the trip by myself?" Mrs. O'Neill sat quietly and read the directions. As usual, she did not want to ask Frances too many questions as to why she wanted to travel so far away to an area she knew nothing about.

"Frances, the directions seem to be very clear, but your destination is a bit far away from here, and I think it will take you well over an hour and a half. We have only been to the Bronx a few times and that was when we took the children to the zoo, and I can tell you one thing, it is not like here in Queens. The area where you need to change buses is a very busy one and looks somewhat rundown, but I suppose you could make the trip, if you feel you really need to do it. Remember one thing, Frances, if you should get lost or confused, you can always ask a policeman, or if one is not around, ask a woman, and I'm sure you'll be fine."

Frances just shook her head, a little more than apprehensive about the pending journey, but she decided yes, she did want to see her father, and if this was the only way, she would have to do it. The two women sat in silence until Mrs. O'Neill broke it, saying, "Frances, I decided a long time ago to respect your privacy and that is why I have never asked you about your background or your family and I won't now, but please remember I am here for you if you want to talk to me."

Frances thanked her for her kind words, but she couldn't bear to tell anyone about her past. She tried desperately not to think about her past life with her mother. It made her shiver with fear, and she would try to push the horrific memories deeper and deeper into her mind… and then there was the home. She didn't even want to think about the loneliness she'd felt while living in the home, much less talk to anyone about it.

Frances was content with her life now and decided she really loved the O'Neill's. They'd provided the only sense of security she'd ever felt, and she was sure she was going to stay with them for a long, long time. She could not remember ever having loved someone before, except maybe her baby brother, who she desperately hoped someday she would see again.

A Matter of Survival

Mrs. O'Neill got up from her chair. She was visibly upset for her young employee. Frances also stood up, intending to take the directions back into her room, when suddenly Mrs. O'Neill put her arms around her and just held her tight. Frances could not ever remember any adult, except maybe the nuns in her desperate times, doing this to her before, and the comfort of Mrs. O'Neill's arms was astonishing to her.

Thirteen

THE MEETING

That night, after completing all her duties and helping the children get ready for bed, Frances was anxious to retreat to her room. She quickly took a bath, and before sitting on the bed, she grabbed a box of stationery. First she wrote a quick note to Kay, saying that she would not be able to meet her on the following Monday. She told Kay, although it might be hard for her to believe, she was planning to visit her father. Frances knew she had never spoken of her father to Kay before, so she was sure this was going to come as quite a surprise to her.

Frances leaned back on the bed for a moment and remembered how occasionally Kay would question her about her family, but she had always been reluctant to discuss it, and the subject would be dropped. Frances knew Kay would never understand, because she came from a large and wonderful hardworking family. She then folded the note, placed it in an envelope, and addressed and sealed it.

Then she took out another piece of paper from the box and wrote a note back to her father. She told him she was happy to have heard from him and was planning to visit the following Monday. She said his directions were fine and she understood them. She estimated she would get to his apartment somewhere between eleven o'clock and noon, as she wasn't sure how long the trip would take. She ended the note saying she was looking forward to their meeting and was anxious to see him.

She mailed the notes the following morning.

As the next several days passed, Frances looked more and more forward to visiting her father. She was unsure of what results the meeting would bring, but still the same, she anxiously anticipated their meeting.

Monday finally came, and Frances decided on a pretty yellow dress that again Mrs. O'Neill had given her. She also wore white high-heeled pumps and a pretty little matching clutch handbag. The dress looked quite nice on her slender body. Clothes looked good on her, especially; the combination of yellow against her dark hair looked striking. She had prepared her pocketbook the night before, being sure to enclose the directions and the necessary money to make the trip. She considered that it might be nice to bring something sweet with her for the visit and made a mental note to stop by the bakery before boarding her first bus.

Once she was dressed, she left via the front door, passing Mrs. O'Neill in the kitchen. Mrs. O'Neill scanned her young employee with a look of approval and simply wished her a pleasant day and a safe trip. Frances headed toward the direction of the local bus stop, and as she walked the now-familiar three blocks, she was delighted that it was such a nice morning with no forecast of rain. She was pleased to see people waiting on line, indicating the bus had not arrived at her stop yet and she did not miss it. Frances quickly entered the bakery near the bus stop and purchased two different kinds of cake. It was very seldom that she let herself spend this amount of money at one time, but, then again, this was an unusual occasion.

Just as she finished making her purchase, the bus pulled up to the stop, and she quickly made her exit from the shop and boarded the bus. Once she deposited her coin, she thought, *Maybe it's my imagination, but the driver did seem to glance at me with a look of approval.* She could easily sense he liked the way she looked. She also noticed he didn't immediately pull away from the curb as usual. He hesitated because he was following her with his eyes in the rearview mirror. She quickly took a seat without looking around and could feel herself blushing bright red. The driver chuckled to himself and continued on his normal route.

After a brief time, she glanced at the directions provided by her father and realized she would be getting off the bus at the next stop. It would be necessary to transfer to another bus. She pulled the overhead wire indicating her stop and exited through the rear door. Frances then walked two long blocks to the next bus stop. She waited about fifteen minutes, and the bus finally came. Once on the bus she took a seat near a window and now was able to view the scenery presented before her. She enjoyed the ride as the bus passed though neighborhood after neighborhood, sometimes appearing as if it was going through the country while other areas appeared to be very busy and city-like. This bus ride took much longer than she anticipated, and finally after an hour, she came to an area where everyone was to leave the bus, as it was the last stop.

She again referred to her notes and started to walk down the busy block, which contained many rundown apartment buildings and old-looking stores, hoping to see a sign that would indicate where she was to get her next bus. By this time she was getting tired of the trip and had to tell herself more than once that she was fine and would reach her destination soon. Finally the last bus she needed to board came, and again she got on it, asking the driver to please be sure to let her know when the bus would be nearing her stop at 182nd Street.

Right now she might as well have been in a foreign country for all she knew. She was definitely in unfamiliar territory. It must have been a half hour later when the driver indicated to her this was the stop she was looking for. Frances exited the bus with a combined feeling of anticipated excitement and, at the same time, a little fear of what she may find ahead. The note indicated she was to pass over the main road at the intersection and walk straight for two blocks where she would find the expected address. As she walked the two short blocks, the streets seemed overcrowded with people everywhere. She saw many women carrying large bags of groceries, obviously in preparation for their family's evening meal, many of whom had their children following along, as they too were required to carry some of the smaller bundles containing the family's necessities. There were children everywhere, and if they were not helping their mothers, they were playing on the sidewalk, and sometimes it was even difficult to pass them. As she walked along the streets, she passed a variety of shops where the wares spilled outside the storefronts. It appeared to Frances that everyone in the Bronx seemed to be very busy and preoccupied, not like everyday life in Queens at all.

A Matter of Survival

Finally she reached the apartment building she was seeking and noted there was a drugstore built right into the corner of it. She also noted there was a clock in the window, which read twelve fifteen. The trip had taken her more than two hours, much longer than she had estimated.

Once she entered the rather old building, she glanced at the mailboxes on the ground floor and noted her last name on one of the boxes, which also read "2B." She thought how ironic it was that this was the first time she had ever seen her name on anything other than her own personal belongings. *Well*, she said to herself, *here goes nothing*. Frances climbed the two sets of stairs and finally stood in front of a door that read 2B. She hesitated for a moment, not sure what to expect, not even sure if she would recognize her own father. She took a deep breath and pressed the doorbell. After just a few seconds, an attractive older woman, who was very nicely dressed, answered the door. The woman had a dark complexion with neatly groomed black hair that just showed a little touch of gray at the temples. She wore simple makeup and just the tiniest bit of rose lipstick that showed off her beautiful skin. She had a pretty face and an even prettier smile as she greeted Frances.

"You must be Frances. I'm Jenny, and I have been so looking forward to meeting you," she said. "Your father is expecting you; just follow me."

As Frances walked into the entry of the apartment, she could smell something delicious cooking on the stove, and even above the cooking, she could also smell the cleanliness of the apartment. The woman showed Frances into the living room, and the man who was sitting in a big easy chair immediately rose to his feet. No one had to introduce him to her. She recognized him immediately, even though his appearance was now much older, and for some strange unexplained reason, he seemed to be somewhat softer to her. She had thought about him many times as a hardened and, to some extent, a mean man. It was obvious to her that he was not well, appearing to be rather frail and thin, but then again she really didn't have anything to compare him with. Even with his illness, he still was a good-looking man.

At first they both silently just stood there, looking at each other. Finally, he was the first to move as he took her hand in his. His eyes started to tear up at the sight of her, and he could hardly speak. When he did speak, his voice was quivering, and the words sounded dreadfully shaky, almost like a crystal glass hitting the floor.

"Francesca, it has been too long and I know it is my fault, but all the same I was very happy you decided to write me, and now at last you are here." With that Frances also started to feel tears stinging her eyes. She could hardly get the words out, but then proceeded to speak to him.

"There is so much that I don't understand. If you say you wanted to see me, why did you never look for me, never try to contact me?"

Her father put his hand out to indicate they should both sit down on the sofa. Once they did, he again took her hand and started to speak.

"Francesca, when I left, you were just a small child. You have no idea how much I hated my life with your mother from the very beginning. Our parents weren't concerned about our happiness—they didn't have that themselves. Life was hard for them. They were trying to make a living here in America, and having so many children made their life even harder. Sometimes I think they resented their own children, and they didn't care what happened to them.

"When I protested this marriage arrangement to my parents, they said their decision was made. They said we didn't have to like each other, because in time we would grow to do so. They were just glad we were leaving our families. My parents were very poor people and the responsibility of so many children was just too much for them to handle. This was the easiest way they could get rid of their 'hardships,' by just marrying them off. When I first met your mother, she looked very pretty to me, and appeared to be very quiet. We didn't know each other and had met only a few times before our wedding day. I think she may not have wanted to get married as well. Once we were married, she resented that she had to take care of me and our home. She was always saying she was meant to be a star like the ones she saw in the movies. What nonsense this was! After a while, I couldn't stand even listening to her gibberish. I don't expect you to understand this, but I grew to quickly hate her and my life as well. In the Italian families, for whatever the reason, only boy children seemed acceptable. So on top of everything else in my life, my wife's first child turned out to be a girl—you, Francesca.

"It has been in the more recent years, after I had become very ill, that I began to think more and more about you and your brother too. As the years went by, I felt ashamed that I was not there for you. You both had to

A Matter of Survival

suffer so much because of the anger and resentment your mother and I had for each other. Francesca, please I know I cannot change the past, but I am asking your forgiveness now, and hopefully we can build a future together."

Frances just sat on the sofa and listened to her father pour his heart out. She'd never realized he had had such an unhappy life while married to her mother. She thought, *I guess he couldn't imagine what my life became like because of him.* She decided right then and there not to discuss her past with him. Perhaps he was right, asking her to start their lives all over together. It didn't make any sense to continue to hold resentment toward him any longer. Family was family.

When Frances finally spoke to her father, she simply said that she was glad to have found him and agreed to look forward to the future and said she would visit him as often as possible. He then for the first time placed his arms around her and kissed her so sweetly on her forehead, saying he really did love his little girl, and with that, Frances decided all the past was forgiven.

After taking her eyes off her father, Frances looked around the room and noted what a pretty room she was sitting in and how odd it was for it to be inside such an old and rather rundown building. But what was really odd was how quickly she forgave her father for all the misfortunes she had endured.

He seemed pleased to have his daughter with him now after so many years of them not knowing each other.

"Francesca," he inquired, "I am just curious as to why you are not living with your mother. I assumed that after leaving the home, you would go to live with her."

Frances shook her head. She didn't want to tell this stranger any more than she had to. She just replied, "It didn't work out too well." She also told him she was happy living and working for the O'Neill's, and as far as she could tell, she would be content to be working for them forever.

Her father smiled softly and said, "That's fine, but someday you may want to have a family and a home of your own."

Up until this point, she never gave much thought about having her own family.

Frances asked her father why he was calling her "Francesca." He smiled, explaining that Francesca was her Italian name, but he supposed the Sisters at the home had decided to Americanize it by calling her Frances. They both laughed at her name change, since Frances had no idea what it meant to be an "Italian."

Frances and her father talked for more than an hour. She learned that a few years ago he almost died because he had been very sick. Because of his illness, it had been necessary for the doctors to remove one of his kidneys, which also caused many other health problems. He said he felt lucky to still be alive. He told her that Jenny was the woman he'd wanted her to meet and that she was wonderful to him. The more he spoke about Jenny, Frances realized they were living together without the benefit of marriage. She had never known of anyone who lived together without being married. The Catholic Church outlawed such arrangements. Still, she made no comment about this to him. As their conversation started to wind down, Frances finally got up the nerve to ask about her brother.

"Please tell me where he is, Father. I would really like to write to him."

"He is living with relatives in Italy and is happy to be there. I do keep in touch with him," her father said. "He recently finished college and now is an engineer. I don't think you can write him, because as he was raised in Italy, he doesn't speak English." Frances thought it just didn't seem fair that she had a brother and didn't know him. Frances's father didn't seem like he wanted to discuss the subject anymore, and with that he called Jenny into the room.

Jenny was very pleasant to Frances, saying she was sure she must be hungry after her long trip from Queens. She said she had prepared something for the three of them. One thing Frances did discover was that Jenny was a wonderful cook and prepared a very enjoyable lunch of homemade soup, which she served with tasty Italian bread and a variety of cheeses and cold meats. She had also prepared espresso for the three of them. They sat over lunch for almost two hours. Frances and Jenny cleaned up the kitchen together with her father sitting at the table, joining them in idle talk.

When the dishes were all put away, Frances realized it was starting to get rather late; it was approaching four thirty. She decided it would be best to start heading back to her place in Queens. Frances's father thanked her again for coming and asked her to visit again. He seemed to genuinely appreciate their visit together and said he would look forward to many more whenever she was able to come. Frances had already told them she would be spending most of the summer months on Long Island, but she did promise to write and also promised she would visit him and Jenny when she returned.

Jenny gave her a polite kiss on the cheek and said she also enjoyed meeting her and would look forward to their next visit. Her father then proceeded to walk her to the door and then decided instead to walk her down the stairs so that he could watch her walk to the bus stop. Once they reached the street, he put his arms around her and thanked her again for forgiving him and coming to see him today. Frances smiled, returned his hug, and walked back to the bus stop.

It took her even longer to get back to the O'Neill's as her bus connections were not what she had hoped for. She didn't get home until almost seven thirty.

There was no doubt that she was exhausted. She went right to her room after greeting Dr. and Mrs. O'Neill. Mrs. O'Neill was a little curious about her adventure and asked how the trip went.

Frances simply replied, "You were right; it was a rather long trip, but it was worth it. Right now I am so tired, I just want to take a bath and go to bed."

The O'Neill's smiled at her and simply said good night.

Fourteen

SUMMER FUN

*I*t was a delightful experience for them all, especially Frances, to live at the beach. The atmosphere at the beach house was very casual and needless to say very relaxing for everyone. Even Kay managed to come out twice during their stay. Mrs. O'Neill liked having Frances's friend visit them, and she was pleased to see that Kay enjoyed the beach and playing with the children as much as Frances.

One time while the girls were at the beach, Frances stopped to observe her friend. Kay was turning into a striking young woman, and more than once she would see the young men looking at her in an admiring way. Then, out of nowhere, Kay asked Frances if she realized that so many of the young men were looking at her. They both laughed at this, because Frances was sure they were looking at Kay, and Kay was sure they were looking at Frances. They didn't even realize it, but they both were quickly turning into very attractive young women. Frances was still very shy. She confided to Kay she was sure if any of them spoke to her, she would probably die right on the spot. Again, they both laughed.

The rest of summer was filled with wonderful days at the beach. Their dinners were always easy and delightfully filled with delicious seafood. Sometimes the O'Neill's would go out to dinner together, and Frances would babysit the children at the beach house. They would stay up later

A Matter of Survival

than usual as Frances would cajole them into playing board games together, and there was the laughter, always laughter.

Unfortunately, the summer came and went so quickly, but the memories of these happy times would forever linger in all their minds.

Fifteen

Now That's an Attractive Young Man

Three years had passed, and Frances was now nineteen. Mrs. O'Neill still loved having Frances in her home. It wasn't long after Mrs. O'Neill had first hired Frances that she came to realize she was an invaluable employee, and she didn't hesitate to financially reward her, giving her young employee several nice salary increases.

But to her, Frances seemed more like a niece rather than an employee. The children were becoming older and growing like weeds, and with that came the realization she probably would not need Frances's help much longer; even still, she couldn't imagine her life without her young employee. How empty her home would seem without Frances.

Frances was so much a part of their family that they included her in the many family celebrations. There were even times, when all the chores were completed, when Mrs. O'Neill and Frances would look through the latest fashion magazines together, as Mrs. O'Neill subscribed to many of them. It was obvious both women loved clothes and viewing the latest styles. Occasionally Mrs. O'Neill would invite Frances to travel into the city with her so she could help in selecting something for a special fund-raiser or other charitable event. She learned that she could depend on Frances for suggestions, and she discovered Frances had a keen eye for what was truly smart-looking.

A Matter of Survival

Frances loved the trips into the city with Mrs. O'Neill. They not only would go to the best shops and department stores, but their outing always included a delightful place to lunch. Frances would be in awe of the lovely ladies in the restaurants and admired how elegantly they were dressed. On one such occasion, Mrs. O'Neill told Frances her husband wanted her to pick out a fur coat for his Christmas present to her, and she wanted Frances to help pick it out.

This was one of the most exciting trips of all. After lunch they visited a well-known furrier, and after trying on many coats, Mrs. O'Neill finally selected a full-length Blackglama mink coat. Even she had to admit it was a little more than she had wanted to spend, but just the same, she loved it and decided to buy it. Frances loved it on her. While looking approvingly at herself in the mirror, Mrs. O'Neill noticed Frances also seemed to be admiring the gorgeous assortment of furs.

"Frances, I have an idea," Mrs. O'Neill said excitedly. "Why don't you buy yourself a coat?"

Frances gasped at the suggestion saying. "Oh no, I can't afford such a luxury."

"Well, you don't have to buy one like this, but let's look and see what we can find."

Of course, the salesperson was delighted with the prospect of selling two coats and was now mentally adding up her commission. Frances spotted a lovely dark-brown sheared beaver three-quarter walking coat, which she thought was just perfect. Both the saleswoman and Mrs. O'Neill encouraged her to try the coat on, and Frances had to admit, even to herself, that it did look great on her.

"You know, Frances, you should treat yourself now while you're young and before you have too many of life's obligations," Mrs. O'Neill said encouragingly. "Besides, you know you will have your Christmas bonus to look forward to."

Frances smiling decided to buy the coat, and as it turned out, it was one of the happiest days she could ever remember.

As they traveled back home to Flushing, Frances was still smiling and said, "I still can't believe this is really happening to me. I'm so grateful to you, Mrs. O'Neill, for encouraging me to purchase the coat. I know I will always love it and be proud to wear it."

Mrs. O' Neill, grinning at her young employee, replied, "I'm glad your decision has made you so happy and I know you will never regret it."

The two women continued traveling home in silence glowing with the knowledge that their coats would be sent to them in just a few days.

The holidays came and went, and as it turned out, it was a long and cold winter. Frances was happy for the opportunity to proudly wear her beautiful coat, even if it was only to church every Sunday.

Before they knew it, winter finally faded into spring, and spring quickly turned into summer, and plans were made to spend time at the beach again. Frances loved her "adopted" family and was still happy as ever to be living and working for them. She also loved taking long walks with the children on the beach and, of course, they were always anxious to find an assortment of seashells. Each year, new shells adorned their room.

Frances eventually learned to confide in Mrs. O'Neill. She told her about her many trips to the Bronx to visit her father. At first Mrs. O'Neill was surprised that Frances had any family at all, particularly a father. She knew she had lived at St. Joseph's and always had assumed she was an orphan. Even though she was very curious to learn of Frances's background, she never asked pointed questions. She knew Frances was a very private person, and if there was anything she wanted to tell her, she was sure Frances would confide in her, and sometimes she did. Still, Frances never seemed to talk with anyone else.

During the rest of the year, Frances and Kay met frequently. Occasionally they would go into the city and just walk around, admiring all the beautiful ladies shopping at the beautiful stores. Sometimes they would share a new movie together and have a bite to eat before catching the subway train back to Flushing. When they arrived at Flushing, they would continue on their separate ways, catching the appropriate bus that would take them home.

A Matter of Survival

One Monday Frances and Kay met in Flushing and, as usual, did a little shopping and had a light lunch.

During their conversation, Kay said, "I have to leave earlier than usual since I promised to help my mother with a family gathering. I know it means we will have to part earlier than usual, but I will look forward to next week."

Frances replied, "It's okay. I certainly understand. We'll meet next week under the clock."

After lunch they said their good-byes giving each other a warm embrace.

Frances decided not to stay in Flushing to window shop as she often did and instead chose to head home. She didn't feel like being alone today. She hoped she would find Mrs. O'Neill at home. Usually on Mondays Mrs. O'Neill's mother would visit the family. Frances felt it would be nice to sit and have a cup of tea with the ladies.

For some reason, as she waited for the arrival of the bus, she felt a little depressed and was trying to suppress the horrors of her past. She was thinking of her father. Although she was glad that she had made amends with him, she couldn't help but wonder why, if he was supposed to love her so much, why hadn't he visited her at the home? Why, even when she was old enough to leave the home, did he not look for her, and even more importantly, why did she have to write to him first? She wished he had tried to find her. *I guess these are answers I will never get,* she thought. *And then there is my mother—oh no, I'm not going there, I'm not even going to think of her.*

The very memory of her mother would make her shake with fear. Up until now she'd put those horrible recollections away, way in the back of her mind, and she didn't want them to come to the surface, ever!

While she was deep in thought, the bus arrived, and she realized there were people waiting for her to move. She mumbled a soft apology to the person in back of her and entered the bus. She took her seat and looked up at the person who had received her apology and realized this person was a very handsome young man. As he turned to find a seat, he decided to sit near Frances. He spoke first. "Apology accepted. You seemed so deep in your thoughts that I decided to just wait for you to move on, but the people in back of me weren't so kind. They were obviously in a hurry."

"I'm sorry. I guess I lost track of where I was for a few minutes. I didn't mean to hold up all those people."

Frances smiled and was surprised at herself for being so friendly to this stranger. He asked if he may sit next to her, and she smiled affirmatively. After a few minutes, he said, "My name is Charles, but everyone just calls me Charlie. So what's your name?"

"It's Frances, but everyone just calls me Fran."

They both laughed at her mimicking him. For whatever reason, she'd just made that up. She was surprised at herself for talking so frankly, and maybe even flirting, with this attractive young man. This was so unlike the shy Frances she always had been. He inquired as to how far she was going on the bus, and she told him. She was going to get off about halfway before his stop, so he decided to make the most of their meeting.

Frances found him very charming. Even though she did not know this young man, she was very attracted to his natural wit, not to mention his very good looks. She told him vaguely about her job working for the O'Neill family, and he told her he was working at the airport and was on his way home. He lived with his family, and when he talked about them, it was in such a good and loving way. Charlie told her there were seven children in his family, and he was the third oldest. There were also two dogs, two cats, and maybe a bird in its cage, that is, if his sister didn't open the door and let it out again. They laughed at this. Charlie described his mother as the one who "ruled the roost" with her brood of kids. Still, she did so with a stern but loving hand. He laughed when he spoke about her, saying he had the best mom that anyone could ever want. He obviously loved her dearly.

"I'll tell you one thing about her, and that's if she says no, the answer is no, and she never goes back on her decision no matter what. There have been many times I've tried to change her mind, but like I said, no is always no." They both laughed.

Before they knew it, Frances had to get off the bus. She told him she would have to leave now and say good-bye, but she also said she'd enjoyed meeting him and their conversation. She was sorry her stop came so soon. With that she pulled the overhead wire, got up, and started to exit the bus.

A Matter of Survival

As she was getting off, he called to her to wait, and for some unexplained reason, he decided to get off the bus with her. He even seemed surprised at himself for his actions.

Frances stood there on the sidewalk with a puzzled look on her face. When they both looked at each other, they laughed at his spontaneous decision. He spoke first.

"Frances, I would like to invite you to have a soda or coffee with me. Is there a place near here? I just didn't want to end our conversation. Please, please, say yes."

Frances, again surprising herself more so, said, "Yes." Then, what was even more amazing, she added, "You know what, Charlie? I'm glad you decided to get off the bus with me."

Again they laughed. Frances thought how nice it was to be with someone who could make you laugh so much in such a short time. She mentioned that there was a soda shop down the next block and just around the corner. Perhaps they could go there.

Charlie was beaming. He was so very happy to have met this sweet and very pretty girl. He was trying hard to be on his very best behavior, using the best manners he could remember, which his mother had drilled into him. While he didn't come from a rich family, it was a happy one where good manners were always stressed. His mother would always say, "Someday you will meet a nice girl, and you will have to know how to treat her."

As they walked, he was secretly hoping he would have enough money in his pocket to pay for whatever she ordered. If not, he would have to figure a way to charm the shopkeeper into trusting him to come back the next day. He would say anything that would spare him the embarrassment of not being able to pay the bill. He thought, *Where did I ever get the nerve to ask her to stop with me when I'm not even sure if I have enough money?*

When they reached the shop, the proprietor indicated they could sit at any one of the booths along the wall. He let Frances in first and then sat down across from her. The owner came over and asked if they wanted to see a menu. Charlie held his breath and was relieved when Frances said she would only like a cup of tea. He decided to have a Coke. Now he could relax, knowing this chance meeting wasn't going to break the bank.

They sat in the booth talking for almost two hours. She told him about growing up in a "convent." Right then and there, she decided she was never going to tell anyone again that she was raised in an orphanage.

She told Charlie more about her job with the O'Neill's and how she loved taking care of the children. He seemed very interested in everything she had to say. He thought, *This is a very genuine and lovely girl and she is the prettiest girl I have ever seen.*

Frances surprised herself. She knew she was shy, but yet sitting with this young man over a cup of tea, she felt very comfortable and very much at ease. She liked him and liked him even more so because he made her laugh so much. There seemed to be a glow about him. He was one of the friendliest people she had ever met.

She learned Charlie was working at the airport (now known as LaGuardia Airport) loading freight and cargo onto clipper ships for Pan American Airways. Frances thought how marvelous it was to be able to work at the airport and to have such an important job. Of course, it really wasn't an important job, but to Frances it seemed very glamorous.

Charlie told her all about his family, and he did so with such feelings of love as he spoke. He had two older brothers, and he was very close to them. Then there was a younger sister, another brother, another sister, and finally a little brother who was only four years old. Frances could hardly keep up with the description of all his siblings, but they did sound delightful. She loved hearing about all of them. His description of family life was not one of wealth, but rather one that held a closeness that very few families had.

Charlie stopped and looked at the clock above the counter where elaborate sundaes and sodas were being prepared for the shop's more affluent customers. It was now almost five fifteen, and he suggested to Frances they had better start heading home. He knew his mother would be concerned about his whereabouts since he usually got home about three thirty, but today was different. He didn't want to leave this girl. She laughed at everything and seemed so interested in whatever he was saying. She also participated in the conversation—but not too much, just enough.

They got up, and Charlie paid the bill at the register, remembering to return to the booth to leave a tip on the table. He knew the tip was small, but still he was glad he remembered it.

A Matter of Survival

Frances thanked him for the tea and said she really enjoyed the afternoon. She assumed he would continue his trip home, catching another bus where he had originally gotten off. They walked to the bus stop, and then Charlie asked if he could walk her home, feeling this would give him a few more minutes with her. She thanked him again, now looking forward to the walk back to the O'Neill's. As they walked the three blocks, Frances felt very proud of the neighborhood, almost as if she was personally responsible for it being so well kept. This was her life now, and she was very proud to have him walk her home. As they crossed the street, Frances showed him the big white house where Dr. O'Neill had his shingle hanging proudly on the front lawn.

Frances looked directly at him, saying, "I guess this is it, Charlie. I live here so I will have to say good-bye now. Thank you for a wonderful afternoon."

Charlie was not going to let this girl leave him without making some future arrangements for them to see each other again. He asked her to go out with him the following Friday night, that is, of course, after her work was done for the O'Neill's. Charlie added maybe they could go to a movie in Flushing, and Frances said she would like that. Still, her chores and responsibilities with the children would have to be finished before she could leave. She said she would also like to ask Mrs. O'Neill for permission.

Charlie smiled. He had a good feeling inside knowing that Frances also wanted to see him again. He offered his hand and thanked her for a good time, and when she took it, he was sure that a jolt of electricity went right through his hand.

"If all goes well, I will pick you up at seven thirty this Friday night. Okay?"

"Okay," she replied. "I'll see you at seven thirty."

Frances turned and entered the front door, closing it softly behind her. She leaned against the door, remembering all that had transpired that afternoon. Then she walked into the kitchen, anxious to confide in Mrs. O'Neill about the day's events.

$\mathcal{C}$harlie watched her go into the house and close the door. He stood there for several seconds, almost hoping to get a glimpse of her one more time, but, of course, he didn't. So instead he turned and headed back down the three blocks to the bus stop to continue his journey home.

He had just about reached the corner when he saw his bus coming toward him. There were a few people also waiting to board the bus, and he followed the other passengers. As he deposited his fare, he noted the bus was very crowded and it appeared he would have to stand all the way home, but right now that didn't seem to bother him at all. He walked to the rear of the bus, holding onto the overhead handles, and when he reached the back, he realized he was walking along with a silly smirk on his face. He was a happy man tonight!

Finally his stop was approaching. He pulled the wire and exited the bus. He had a five-block walk from the bus stop to his home. Glancing at the shop on the corner, he read the clock inside and realized it was now six thirty. Surely his mother would be wondering where he had been all this time. He had hoped she wouldn't be angry with him for being so late, but if she was, it would be worth it.

He finally reached the front door and went inside. His mother was in the kitchen, finalizing the evening meal, and once she saw Charlie, she put her hand on her hip, asking, "Where were you for so long? I've been waiting for you to come home. I needed you to go to the store for me. It's a good thing your brother, George, came home earlier than expected and went to the store for me instead."

Charlie just went up to his mother and gave her a big squeeze, almost lifting her off the ground. They both laughed.

"So where were you? Did you have to work late?" his mother inquired.

"No, Mom, I wasn't working, but I met this terrific girl today, and we stopped for a soda, at least I did. She had tea."

His mother looked at him thinking, *Oh no, not Charlie too.* It was obvious to her that her young son Charlie was now also "smitten."

Her oldest son, George, had been going out with a neighborhood girl for about a year now, and she knew things were getting serious. She anticipated that young George would be leaving home sometime during the next year. And then there was her son Joe, who had been seeing another neighborhood girl for years now. They'd known each other since grade school, though, and she never felt it was quite as serious.

"Are you going to see this girl again?" she asked her son.

"As a matter of fact, we have a date this Friday night, and Mom, I can't wait to see her."

⸻

When Frances entered the kitchen, Mrs. O'Neill was sitting at the table with a cup of tea. She was enjoying a last-minute bit of solitude before getting the little ones ready for bed. Dr. O'Neill wasn't home; he was making his usual hospital rounds tonight. So Mrs. O'Neill sat alone in the kitchen relishing her last few minutes of down time while the children played upstairs. Then she looked up at Frances and saw a glow about her and a smile on her face that couldn't be hidden.

"Well, Frances, what have you been up to today? You look fantastic. Did you and Kay have a nice day?"

Frances proceeded to tell Mrs. O'Neill all about the day's events and how Charlie had invited her to stop for a soda and how they sat and talked for two hours. It wasn't until she took a deep breath did she realize that Mrs. O'Neill was smiling at her as she was talking nonstop.

"Mrs. O'Neill, he asked me out for this Friday night to see a movie, and you will have a chance to meet him. He's picking me up at seven thirty."

Mrs. O'Neill was happy for her young employee and could not ever remember seeing her so elated.

Friday night came quickly. Mrs. O'Neill suggested they should eat dinner a little earlier than usual. She almost seemed just as excited for Frances's date as Frances was. She was more than anxious to meet this young man, and she wanted to give Frances extra time to get ready for her evening out. Frances had already planned what she was going to wear and had fixed her hair earlier in the afternoon. She could hardly contain her excitement at the prospect of seeing Charlie again and was anxiously looking forward to their evening out together.

At exactly seven thirty, the doorbell rang. Frances went to the door and invited Charlie in to meet Mrs. O'Neill. He took one look at Frances in the pretty red-and-white dress she was wearing and again thought, *She's the prettiest girl I've ever seen.* He was still deep in his thoughts, admiring this young woman, when Frances interrupted.

"Charlie," Frances said, "I would like you to meet my employer, Mrs. O'Neill."

For a second or two, Charlie was almost at a loss for words as his eyes were totally fixed on Frances. He quickly responded that it was a delight to meet her and said Frances had spoken so well of her, her husband, and the children.

Mrs. O'Neill smiled, saying, "We feel the same way about Frances. She is more like a member of the family than our employee. I hope you have a nice evening."

Charlie bent over and offered his hand to Mrs. O'Neill, and as they shook hands, he said it was an absolute pleasure to meet her. Frances had the funniest feeling. This was the first time she had introduced Charlie to anyone, and she was very proud of the way he conducted himself.

With that, they left the house and walked the three blocks to the bus stop, exchanging small talk. Once they got on the bus, Charlie told her it might be nice to see the movie playing at the local theatre in Flushing. She nodded with her approval. It turned out to be a comedy and one they both liked. When the movie was over, he suggested they take the bus back and perhaps it might be nice to stop at the soda shop again.

The bus came right away, and once they were seated, they started to recollect scenes from the movie. They laughed together as they recalled the many funny antics. The bus ride seemed to go by faster than usual, and in less than twenty minutes, they arrived at their stop. Once they exited the bus, they walked together toward the soda shop. It was a lovely evening with a light, cool breeze. As they walked, they could feel the crisp leaves under their feet as the first signs of autumn were now showing themselves.

The owner of the soda shop was again working at the counter and recognized the young couple right away. After greeting them with a warm welcome, he indicated they should take the empty booth near the wall. The shop was filled with many more people than it had been last Monday. Obviously, Friday was a big date night for many young couples.

A Matter of Survival

Charlie, having just gotten paid that day, asked Frances if she would like something to eat. She declined and said she would be happy just to have a soda, so he ordered two sodas. They sat and talked as if they had known each other for years. Both felt very comfortable in the presence of the other. When they started to compare notes, they realized they were the same age, only Charlie was born three months before her. They also admitted to each other that in the past they hadn't dated very much, if at all, but now they were enjoying each other's company. Of course, much of the conversation revolved around Charlie's beloved family. Frances didn't have too much to say about her family, except that her father lived in the Bronx, and also she had relatives who lived somewhere in upstate New York.

They sat silently for a few minutes, and then Charlie blurted out, "Look, Frances, I have an idea. If you could ask Mrs. O'Neill for a Sunday off, I would like to take you home to meet my family. I know you will like them as much as I do."

"Yes, Charlie, I would like that very much. I will ask her tomorrow. Maybe we could plan to do it the week after next."

Charlie was so happy. He wanted very much to share his home life with Frances. Charlie knew that Frances didn't have the best childhood, and for this reason, he wanted her to see what a real family was like. He was anxious to hear Mrs. O'Neill's response.

As they prepared to leave the soda shop, he asked Frances if he would be able to see her again, and they agreed on the following Friday. It had been a delightful evening. One of the things Frances liked about Charlie was that no matter who he came in contact with, he always made the other person feel good about meeting him. Everywhere he went, people would smile and laugh at his sense of humor and his charismatic personality. No matter where they went, people seemed to gravitate toward him and his laughter. He seemed to be one of those people you just wanted to be around.

As they walked toward the O'Neill's, Frances thanked him for such a wonderful evening. She didn't mention it to Charlie, but this was her first date, and it had been a very delightful evening for her. Frances had never thought about dating much before, but decided if she had, she would want it to be just like this evening.

Charlie smiled, said it was he who enjoyed the evening, and just like that, one block from the O'Neill's home, he turned her toward him and kissed her ever so softly. Frances found herself kissing him back, and there they stood in the darkness with only the shadows of the streetlamp giving off the slightest bit of light, with their arms clutched around each other.

Suddenly, Frances became embarrassed, and she was glad he wasn't able to see her in the darkness as she was turning bright red. *I guess I will always be shy,* she thought. They continued their walk, and when they reached the house, Charlie said, "Fran, I hate to let you go. It was wonderful to be with you tonight, and I will be counting the days until next week."

"Thank you again," she said. "I will also look forward to our seeing each other next Friday."

As they reached the door, he kissed her on her forehead, and she went inside.

Dr. and Mrs. O'Neill were still up and sitting in their living room. As Frances went by, she smiled and headed toward the kitchen. Mrs. O'Neill got up and followed her.

"Frances, did you have a good time? Your young man certainly is a charmer."

"Mrs. O'Neill, I had a fantastic time, and I know I haven't known him for very long, but I think he's terrific."

Mrs. O'Neill, laughing at her, said, "Oh boy, I think we have love in bloom. I'm happy for you that you have met such a nice young man, Frances."

Frances continued, "Mrs. O'Neill, he wants me to meet his family a week from Sunday. Do you think it will be all right for me to have the day off?"

Mrs. O'Neill smiled and said, of course, she could have the day off, and as a matter of fact, it might even be nice for her and her husband to go out together with the children.

Frances went into her room, changed into her nightgown, washed her face, and brushed her teeth. She was eager to get into bed to cuddle under the covers, to recall what a marvelous evening she had had. She closed her eyes with her last thoughts about this new man in her life. She couldn't wait to tell Kay.

A Matter of Survival

The following Monday, Frances met Kay as usual in Flushing, and they greeted each other warmly. Their agenda always consisted of first and foremost window shopping, and as they started to do so, Frances told Kay she needed to talk with her. At first, Kay was concerned that there might be something wrong, thinking it was about her mother, but then Frances told her the whole story of what had transpired the week before when Kay had to leave earlier than usual. She told her all about the chance meeting she had had with this nice and very good-looking man. Kay laughed and was delighted to see Frances so happy.

"Okay" she said, "ask him if he has a friend for me."

They both laughed as they continued on their day together. Frances truly loved Kay. If ever she could have had a sister, she would've wanted her to be just like Kay, her best friend.

As planned, the next Friday, Charlie took Frances out again, only this time he suggested they go bowling. Frances had never bowled before, or even been in a bowling alley, so this was a whole new experience for her. They had a good time and laughed at how poorly they both did. Charlie wasn't much of a bowler either.

Afterward they stopped again at the soda shop and, as usual, they enjoyed each other's company. He was delighted that Mrs. O'Neill had given Frances the following Sunday off so he could introduce her to his family. He had already warned his brothers to "be nice."

"I will pick you up early, about ten o'clock, and we can go to Mass together. My mother sets out Sunday dinner after the last Mass, so we usually eat around one thirty," Charlie told her.

Frances started to speak very softly. "Charlie, I hate to tell you, but I'm very nervous about meeting your family. The only family I have ever really known has been the O'Neill's. Don't get me wrong, they have been wonderful to me, but I am still only an employee. I don't know what real family life is like, not to mention all your brothers and sisters."

He laughed at her, saying, "They're all going to love you."

Sixteen

MEETING HIS FAMILY

Before Frances knew it, Sunday was here. She had already planned the clothes she would wear to meet Charlie's family, taking extra care that everything would look perfect. She had recently treated herself to a pretty little gray suit and had also bought a gray-and-white print blouse to go with it. Frances decided to wear black shoes and carry a matching bag. She also decided that her little white veiled hat would look perfect with the new outfit. Even though she was nervous with the anticipation of meeting Charlie's family, she was still very excited at the same time.

Charlie was right on time. He wanted to be sure of that. Frances opened the door to greet him, and before she could say hello, he took one look at her and whistled at how terrific she looked. Frances laughed at him while blushing at the same time. He teased her about it, which made her blush even more. They both laughed.

They walked the three blocks to the bus stop, only this time they headed toward Bayside. The bus came, and since it was Sunday, it was less crowded than usual. They took their seats, and Frances watched the scenery passing through the bus windows. Everything seemed much quieter today. It was still early, and very few people, if any, were heading to work.

Charlie told Frances they would be getting off the bus shortly, and after he said this, her stomach felt like it was doing flip-flops. She took a deep breath and said to herself, *I can do this today.* Once they got off the

A Matter of Survival

bus and crossed the street, Frances noticed there was a bakery on the corner and asked Charlie to stop, saying she wanted to bring something to his mother. She made her purchase of some delicious-looking butter cookies. There was also a flower shop near the bakery, and again she asked him to stop so that she could purchase a small bouquet for his mother. With that, Charlie bought a rose corsage for Frances and then pinned it onto her jacket. Frances was delighted. No one had ever given her flowers of any sort before. Today was really special.

They walked five long blocks to the church to attend Mass. As it happened, Charlie's house was very near the church. He told Frances many of the family's activities took place around the church's schedule of events. He loved living close to the church and particularly loved hearing the church bells announcing when Mass was going to begin. It was easy to see that he had exceptional values for such a young man, a quality that she greatly admired in him. She observed him during the Mass and again noticed qualities that were admirable.

Once Mass was over, they crossed the street to Charlie's house where his mother was standing in the doorway. Tucked in just behind her with his head peeking out was the cutest little blond boy. She assumed the youngster didn't know what to make of this new lady who was visiting his home.

Charlie greeted his mother with, "Hi, gorgeous. How's my best girl?"

His mom and Frances both laughed at his carrying-on. Once the door was opened, he threw his arms around his mother, planting a kiss on her right cheek. His mom laughed again.

"Mom," Charlie said, "this is the girl I told you about. Frances, this is my mother, and behind her is my little brother, Tommy."

Frances extended her hand to his mom. She appeared to be a very pleasant woman, and Frances thought in her younger years, she must have been very pretty. She had long gray hair, which she pulled back into an elaborate bun, tucking it against the back of her head. Frances noticed she wore no makeup and was simply dressed in a dark-blue dress with an apron to cover herself while cooking.

"It is so nice to meet you, Frances. Charlie has mentioned you several times, and it is a pleasure to have you at our home."

Once inside Charlie introduced her to his two sisters and another younger brother. With that, his older brother, George, entered the room, and they were also introduced. Frances made a special note to try to remember which name belonged to whom. His mom retreated to the kitchen, saying she had to check on the dinner; little Tommy followed her close behind.

Dinner was almost ready when Charlie's other brother, Joe, came into the house. Charlie introduced Frances to him. At first he was very quiet and kept staring at her, making Frances feel uncomfortable. The silence was finally broken when Joe started to speak first.

"You know, young lady, Charlie tells me you're an Italian girl. We don't have Italians in this neighborhood. I do hope you eat something else besides spaghetti."

Charlie was furious with his brother. *It's so much like him to pass a snide remark to my girlfriend,* he thought.

Frances was quite shocked at this remark and said, "You know, Joe, I wasn't raised in an Italian family if that really makes a difference to you." She turned to Charlie. "Charlie," Frances said, "I think I will see if your mother needs help with the dinner."

As soon as she went into the kitchen, his mom smiled at her, saying, "Don't pay any mind to Joe. He's always saying something stupid. I think he was just trying to embarrass his brother. Of all my children, he is the one with the sharpest tongue. No matter how many times we ask him to behave, he always does what he wants, so most of the time we just ignore him. My three older boys, of whom Charles was the last one, are very competitive with each other, but most of the time they really do get along. Believe me when I say the first one up and out in the morning is the best dressed."

Frances helped Charlie's mother bring the food into the dining room. The table was not elaborate but nicely set. Charlie's father walked in the front door after apparently attending the last Mass. Charlie made the introductions, calling him "Pop." Once everyone was seated, Pop proceeded to say grace. Frances had never seen this done anywhere except the convent.

Charlie's mother spoke first. "Frances, I understand you work for a doctor's family in Flushing. How do you like doing this work?"

A Matter of Survival

Frances told her about the children, the summers on Long Island, and how good the O'Neill's were to her. His mom seemed genuinely interested in whatever Frances said, and after a while she found herself to be very drawn to this loving and caring woman. It was obvious that all her children and her husband adored her.

George said after dinner he had plans to visit his girlfriend, adding it was a pleasure to meet Frances and he hoped they would meet again soon. Charlie's sisters were very warm and quite nice to her. On the other hand, Joe insisted on cracking many Italian jokes, laughing all the time. This was really making Charlie angry. *I'll deal with him later,* he thought. At this point Frances was enjoying everyone's company, except maybe Joe, but she accepted him as the showoff in the family and decided to ignore him completely.

Then young Joe interjected, "You know what, Frances? Our family comes from a long line of royalty. As the story goes, there was an Austrian duke going back to the days of my great-grandfather for whom Beethoven wrote a symphony. We were repeatedly told by our great-uncle to 'remember to conduct yourself like dukes and duchesses, because you come from royalty.' So remember when you are speaking to us, you are speaking to royalty."

He made a deep bow as he finished his little speech. With that, they all laughed at Joe, including Frances. The family certainly didn't look like royalty and, yes, this story had been passed down through the years, but it really didn't matter to anyone now. It had simply become the family joke.

The dinner Charlie's mother prepared was delicious, and the rest of the conversation at the dinner table was very pleasant. There was a fair amount of teasing along with lots of laughter. Then it seemed like all of them started to poke fun at Joe.

"See what I have to put up with, Frances?"

They all laughed again. Once the dishes were cleared, Charlie suggested to Frances they go for a walk around the neighborhood, and Frances agreed, putting her suit jacket back on. With that, they proceeded out the door.

As soon as they got to the street, Charlie asked if she was offended by his brother's comments, and Frances said no, because she wasn't even sure what it meant to be Italian. He said Joe had a "big mouth" sometimes and was not the most tactful one in the family, but you could always depend upon him when he was needed. Charlie told Frances that the neighborhood where he lived was mostly made up of German, Irish, and Polish, and maybe a small mixture of other nationalities that he didn't know too much about. This was his life, his neighborhood, his family. Frances looked up at him and said, "I liked them all."

Seventeen

COURTING

Mrs. O'Neill decided to give Frances every other Sunday off. She felt that since Frances now had a beau, she would probably appreciate the extra time for herself. Frances was very happy to spend these days with Charlie.

From then on, they dated most Friday and Saturday nights, and when Frances had the day off, they would go out together on Sunday. Before they knew it, a year had passed, and Frances found herself falling more and more in love with this marvelous man. There was so much laughter and love between them. Occasionally, they would even go into the city and just walk around or take in a movie. While they didn't have a lot of money to spend, Charlie made every date seem very special.

One Sunday, after careful planning, Frances decided to take Charlie to meet her father, and they made the long journey to the Bronx. Of course, her father and Jenny loved Charlie. Everyone loved him! Charlie thought it rather strange that Frances only recently had gotten to know her father, but decided not to push the subject with her. Her father seemed so mellow and kind. Frances found it hard to believe how terrible her father must have been years ago and thought perhaps he was one of the reasons why her mother wasn't quite mentally right. *Could the severity of his attitude towards Dolores have caused her to become so unstable?*

They decided in a few Sundays, they would plan to make the trip to visit Frances's Aunt Mary and her family in upstate New York. It would take them about two and a half hours each way to make this outing, but Charlie believed Frances should get to know her family.

Once they arrived at their destination, they received a welcoming reception. Frances's two cousins were happy to meet them. Her oldest uncle, Tony, and her youngest uncle, Ralph, were also there. Ralph was only a year older than Frances, and she loved him for his warmth and sense of wit. Frances also liked and respected her uncle, Tony, who was not only the oldest but seemed to be the wisest. He was especially nice to her.

Charlie was curious about Frances's mother since neither Frances nor her relatives ever spoke of her. He was not sure whether her mother was even still alive.

Then there were the many Sundays when Charlie took her to his home, and she would join the family for Sunday dinner. This was Frances's favorite Sunday destination. She grew to enjoy Charlie's family more and more each time she visited them. She genuinely adored his mother. Frances felt she was the kindest woman she had ever met. His mother always was doing something for everyone in her family, never asking anything for herself. Sometimes she and Charlie's mother would sit in the modest kitchen, sipping tea and talking about the kids and what it was like to raise such a large family. In particular Frances loved Charlie's little brother. He was an extremely adorable child with bright blue eyes and blond hair. She would often bring him a little toy or something special. It wasn't at all unusual for Frances to bring him a cake or a pie she'd baked. The young child looked forward to her visits, even asking his brother when Frances would be coming to see him! He wasn't as shy as he was when she had first met him. Frances thought, *If I ever have a child, I would like him to look like little Tommy.*

Then there was Joe, still always teasing her about being Italian, but Frances realized it was just his way of making fun. Of all of the children, it was obvious he was not Frances's favorite.

One bitterly cold Sunday afternoon in January 1938, they were all gathered around the dinner table at Charlie's home. As usual, his mom had prepared a delicious dinner, and today she had even managed to make a delicious homemade soup to accompany it. The soup was a welcome addition to the Sunday meal since it made you forget how very cold it really was outside. They were laughing and enjoying dinner and each other's company when George announced to everyone that he had news. He said he had already discussed this news with Mom and Pop, and now he wanted to tell the rest of the family. The news was that Anne and he were going to be married sometime in the next few months, probably in April. The girls were excited that there was going to be a wedding in the family. Then Joe chimed in, saying to his brother, "Well, I'm happy for you, and I wish you the best of luck."

But then he added, "Don't be surprised if Katherine and I decide to tie the knot early next year. We need to save a little more, but it seems inevitable as we are starting to make plans."

How exciting this was for all of them, except Mom, who somehow seemed a little saddened by the news. Sensing that something was not quite right with her mother, Charlie's older sister inquired, "Mom, what do you think of all this?"

His mom hesitated and, taking a breath since she was almost on the verge of tears, said, "I just want my boys to be happy. I knew we would be faced with this someday, and now the time is here. Time passes so quickly. It seems as if it was just yesterday when you were all little. So now I guess we will have to just look forward to having two more daughters."

They laughed at her sentimentality.

That night when Charlie took Frances home, he seemed to be rather quiet, which was very unlike him. They boarded the bus and sat down. Still, he had very little to say. Frances asked him if everything was all right, hoping she hadn't done or said something to offend him or his family. But he just shook his head and said no.

Once they departed from the bus, Charlie suggested they go to the soda shop. It was Sunday night so the owner would close the shop earlier than usual, but still they had an hour to linger. After ordering two sodas, Frances asked, "Charlie, is anything wrong? You seem so serious tonight."

With that, he spoke to her softly. "Frances, we have been going out now for over a year. Listening to my brothers today made me realize that I would like for us to get married more than anything else. I know between the two of us we have nothing. I've only managed to save a very small amount from my salary each week. At twenty-one years old, I know we are both young, but still, I would like it if we too could make plans for the future. If you don't want to plan for marriage, I'll accept it, but I hope not."

Frances sat there in the booth in stunned silence. All the way home, she was wondering what was wrong, and now she discovered nothing could be more right!

She smiled. "Charlie, I would absolutely love to marry you. I don't think we need all that much. I'm sure we could make a go of it if we spend what little money we have wisely."

It was now the beginning of March 1938. They decided they would get married in August.

Charlie rolled his eyes and said, "I hate to tell Mom the news. I don't want her to be upset, but I hope she'll understand."

Frances was so happy; the thought of being married to Charlie was a dream come true. She couldn't wait to share the news with Mrs. O'Neill.

Charlie walked Frances to the O'Neill's front door. They gave each other a long lingering kiss, and both agreed they had made a terrific decision today. Even though the outside temperature had dropped considerably and it had grown bitterly cold, neither one of them even seemed to notice. They made plans to see each other the following Friday.

Frances wished him a good trip home, and with a quick kiss, she told him again how much in love she was with him. Charlie, smiling, made his way back to the bus stop. He didn't even notice the light snow that was beginning to fall. *Wow,* he thought, *I'm the happiest man alive.*

The next morning Frances told Mrs. O'Neill her news.

"Frances, I knew you would be leaving us someday, and I'm pleased that you will be leaving under such fantastic circumstances. This is happy news, and I can't wait to tell Dr. O'Neill and, of course, my mother, who I know will be just ecstatic. I'm sure you know, Frances, Mother has also grown quite fond of you, just like the rest of us."

Frances could hardly contain herself until Friday came. She busied herself doing her usual chores and was grateful the O'Neill children were so well behaved. They rarely gave her a hard time, probably because they were as fond of Frances as she was of them. She so desperately wanted to be with Charlie all the time; to wait a week without seeing each other seemed like an eternity.

A Matter of Survival

When Friday finally came, Frances got ready, choosing an especially pretty skirt and blouse. She even decided to pull her hair up high on her head, and she was pleased with the results. She decided her outfit would look particularly nice with her beloved fur coat. Finally, at seven o'clock Charlie was at the front door. They were going to take in a local movie and stop at the soda shop later.

The movie was a romantic one, and Frances cried at the end of it. Charlie teased her, saying, "It was only a movie; you shouldn't take it so seriously."

Yes, he was laughing at her. It certainly wasn't a movie to his liking, but he knew she would like it.

When the movie was over, they headed to their usual bus stop, stopping by the soda shop for a little bit of extra time together. The owner now acknowledged them both by name. They took a seat at one of the booths against the wall. Charlie ordered soda, and Frances had tea.

Once their drinks arrived at the table, Frances started to speak first, telling Charlie how excited she was about planning for the wedding. She promised to make him the best wife possible. She said she was going to guarantee his happiness always as she was planning to spoil him to no end. Charlie sat quietly, just kind of smiling at her, and she said, "What, what is it? You're laughing at me, aren't you?"

Charlie responded softly, "No, Frances, I'm not laughing at you, I just love you so much. By the way, I have a little surprise for you." Frances looked puzzled and couldn't imagine what he meant. With that he pulled a little blue velvet box from his pocket and placed it in her hand.

"Open it," he said.

Frances's hands were trembling, and upon opening the box, she saw the cutest ring she had ever seen. It was an engagement ring with one tiny gleaming stone right in the center.

"Charlie, I just love it. Thank you."

He made it clear to her that while he didn't have much money, he still wanted his fiancée to have an engagement ring. Charlie had bought it from a reputable jeweler on Main Street who had recommended the setting. It also had a matching wedding band. Frances thought it was perfect. He took her hand and placed the ring on her finger. She just kept staring at it as if it was the biggest and the best, because to her, it was.

Eighteen

The Wedding

Frances and Charlie decided to tell his family together. Like George, they wanted to wait to break the news to the family at the Sunday dinner table. Charlie had told his parents just before he left to pick up Frances on Sunday. His mother tried to talk him out of getting married so soon after his brother George, saying that it was supposed to be bad luck for two to leave the family in the same year, but Charlie's mind was made up and there was no dissuading him. He and Frances would be married the following August. Charlie's mom accepted his decision and kissed him fondly.

"Charlie," she said. "We have grown to love Frances. She is a sweet and lovely girl, and we would more than welcome her to become a member of this family. We love you both, and you certainly have our blessing."

When everyone was finally gathered around the table, Charlie broke the news. His sisters and brothers were happy for them, even Joe, who teased Frances once again, saying, "I guess my Italian jokes didn't deter you one bit. Good for you, kid." With that he leaned over, kissed her on the cheek, and said, "Welcome to the family, sis."

It was an exciting afternoon. George had brought his fiancée to dinner as well, and it was fun to share the wedding plans with each other. They were both going to be married in the nearby church. Anne's family seemed to have the means to give Anne and George a fine wedding reception at a

A Matter of Survival

well-known restaurant, but Frances and Charlie barely had enough money to get by, not to mention an expensive celebration. No, their reception would be held in the basement of the church. It would do just fine for the two of them. They were so much in love that it didn't matter where their reception would be.

That night on the way home, for the first time Charlie asked Frances about her mother, saying that he wasn't sure if she even was dead or alive, because she never spoke of her. Frances was quite taken back, but told Charlie when they reached the soda shop, she would tell him her reasons.

It was so cold that night that they decided to order hot chocolates. They sat in their usual booth along the wall, drinking the hot substance. Charlie saw that his future wife appeared quite shaken. Finally, she gathered the courage to talk about her past. She related the whole story to him. He sat there in shock, horrified at the story that was being told to him. It made him love her even more, and he vowed to himself he would always protect her.

"Frances, I am so sorry that your mother was so awful to you. You say she is mentally ill. I don't know anything about mental illness, but if you want, before we get married, we can go together to visit her, and perhaps maybe you could have some kind of relationship with her."

Frances said she wasn't sure if this was a good idea, but she would think about it.

Spring came early that year, and the cold, hard winter was behind them. They were making many decisions these days. First, they made arrangements for the church as well as its basement party room. Frances had selected her gown from a sample shop and was paying it off a little each month. She was grateful that Mrs. O'Neill had given her several pay raises during the past several years, which had enabled her to save a good portion of her salary. Even though her savings were small, the money would help out with their plans. They hired a caterer who would supply the food at their reception, and they also decided where they were going to live. There was an apartment house just one block from the bus stop and four blocks to Charlie's home. Frances loved the idea, as it would be an easy walk for her to visit with her mother-in-law. Charlie even managed to buy a used car from one of his neighbors. It was several years old, but they both thought it would be terrific to own their own car. Things were looking up for them.

One of the first trips they took was to visit Frances's aunt Mary in upstate New York. Frances wrote to Aunt Mary, telling her the news of their engagement but asking her to keep it to herself. She said she wanted to be sure to tell her cousin Christina also in person, as well as hopefully her favorite uncle, Uncle Ralph, and perhaps Uncle Tony.

They arrived the following Sunday at Aunt Mary and Uncle Mike's home where they were greeted warmly. It was so much better to make the trip in a car; it took half the time. Frances was pleased to find that her cousin Christina and her uncle Ralph were also waiting for them. Frances and Christina had been writing to each other often over the past several months. They had much in common; they were just about the same age, and Uncle Ralph was only one year older than Frances. Everyone seemed to love Ralph; he had a great personality and always made you like being with him. Frances couldn't wait to tell her relatives the good news. Finally, when everyone was seated in the parlor, Frances and Charles made the announcement of their impending marriage. Frances asked Christina to be her maid of honor, which made Christina feel very important. She was delighted to be asked. Uncle Mike got out a bottle of champagne that he had been holding forever and decided this would be the occasion to break it open. They all toasted to Frances and Charlie's happiness.

It was turning out to be a delightful day, and then Aunt Mary asked Frances if she was going to invite her mother to the wedding. Frances replied that she didn't think her mother would even want to be there.

"Frances, we all know your mother is not quite right, but for this happy occasion, why don't you two try to make up? Go visit her, as I recently have. She really seems much better. You and Charlie should decide to do whatever you think best. We will abide by your decision, no matter what it may be."

"It's funny you asked us, Aunt Mary, because just a few days ago, we were discussing the very same thing. I guess we will try to contact her and see how it goes."

The subject was dropped by all, and they continued with their visit. Christina was excited to be the maid of honor. Frances had had a tough

A Matter of Survival

time deciding who to choose, Christina or Kay, but she decided on Christina because she was family. She hoped Kay wouldn't be too hurt and in time would come to understand her reasoning. On the other hand, the selection for Charlie's best man was an easy one. It would be his older brother, George.

On a Sunday a month before the wedding, Charlie persuaded Frances that they should visit her mother. Frances didn't want to give her mother any advance notice of their arrival, so she didn't write a note.

The apartment was easy enough to find; she recognized the area immediately. Frances, trembling at Charlie's side, ascended the staircase to the second floor. Frances considered turning around and forgetting about this whole thing, but Charlie offered her words of encouragement and held her hand all the time. When they reached the door, it was he who rang the bell. A few seconds later, the door opened just a little with her mother peeking through. Once she realized it was her daughter, she swung the door open and threw her arms around the girl she hadn't seen in several years.

"Oh Frances, I'm so glad you came to see me; I have missed you so. Please, please, do come in, and bring your gentlemen friend in with you."

When they entered the small apartment, Frances was stunned to see it was as neat as a pin. There weren't many fancy furnishings, but still it looked very well cared for.

"Do sit down," her mother requested, beckoning Frances to sit near her, but Frances instead stayed with Charlie on the couch. Her mother seemed nicer than she ever remembered her being, but she didn't want to take any chances.

Frances started the conversation.

"Mother, I came to see you because I wanted you to meet my future husband, Charlie. We are getting married next month, and we would like you to be at the wedding, if you would like."

Her mother jumped to her feet. "If I would like? Of course I would be happy to be there. This is wonderful news, Frances. You must fill me in on all the details on how you met, how long you have been dating, where Charlie comes from, and what he does for a living."

Before Frances had a chance to answer her mother's questions, she interrupted herself, asking, "Why don't we continue this conversation over some nice cold lemonade?"

This was certainly welcome with the heat in the apartment. It was almost unbearable, and except for a tiny fan in the room, it seemed like the air just hung there without moving. Frances's mother listened carefully to all the details. She was most pleased to learn that her niece, Christina, was going to be her daughter's maid of honor.

"Please, please, Frances, let me ask you just one thing. Can you please get married from here? After all, this was your former home at one time. You can use my room to get into your gown, and Christina can get dressed here also."

She sounded so sincere; actually, she sounded so normal. So with Charlie's encouragement, she accepted her mother's offer and said she would bring her and Christina's gowns to her apartment the day before the wedding, which pleased her mother to no end. Frances also said it would be nice if she could come back after the wedding to change into her honeymoon suit, and then she and Charlie could leave from her apartment. It was all settled, and they decided to say good-bye now. Frances's mother hugged her daughter as she left and thanked her for the visit and especially for inviting her to the wedding. She said she would start to look for a dress for herself that very next day.

They left the apartment and walked to the car. Charlie was pleased the meeting had gone so well, but Frances's past experience told her otherwise. She was thinking all the time, *Don't trust her.* Still, she was glad to have made amends with this lady and realized she hardly knew her at all.

Charlie was happy now. He and Frances had made their plans final. The one thing that did bother Frances was Melody; they had lost contact with each other a long time ago, and she had no idea where to reach her. She desperately wanted to share this happy time with her. Once Frances left the home, Melody never did return to St. Joseph's again or even give the Sisters an updated address. It seemed when Melody left, she left all memories behind. Still, Frances hoped she was happy and wished they might see each other again someday.

As the wedding day approached, Frances was spending more and more time with Charlie's mother, asking her for all sorts of advice. She would bring her over to their new apartment for suggestions. "Mom," as Frances had come to think of her, was always such a positive person. She gave some great suggestions to Frances, which she accepted and implemented right away. They would go shopping with all the kids, and it never ceased to amaze Frances how she was able to keep track of so many offspring, especially in the department stores, but she hadn't lost one of them yet.

As promised, the day before the wedding Charlie drove Frances to her mother's apartment, bringing Frances's and Christina's gowns with them. Her mother seemed to be glad to see them and actually looked very nice. She invited them into the apartment to show Frances her dress. It was perfect, Frances thought, a light-blue lace that would set off her gray hair exquisitely. Frances thanked her mother again and said she and Christina would be there the first thing the next morning.

As soon as they left her mother's apartment, Charlie said he wanted to speak to his "soon-to-be wife." Frances was both curious and surprised. She thought everything had been taken care of in preparation for the wedding. Charlie turned toward her in the car and said, "Frances, there is just one more thing," and with that, he handed her a prettily wrapped small box.

Frances couldn't imagine what it might be and replied, "Now what did you do?" Upon opening it, she was overjoyed to see a beautiful gold cross.

"Oh Charlie, I absolutely love it, and I will wear it tomorrow with my wedding gown. Thank you so much!"

With that she gave him a kiss, telling him she loved him so. Charlie remembered all too well the story of the cross she once had and wanted to give her this one as its replacement.

Even though Frances did not sleep well, morning came quickly. Christina had slept with Frances at the O'Neill's the night before. In the morning she and Frances gathered their prepared toiletries, Frances's suitcase, and her honeymoon outfit and brought them out to Christina's car. They were trying to be very quiet because it was only 6:00 a.m., but this didn't deter Mrs. O'Neill. She had prepared coffee and pastries for the girls and didn't want them to leave without having something to eat.

She beckoned the girls into the kitchen. Frances could see the excitement in Mrs. O'Neill's mannerisms. She was truly very happy for Frances, and she loved Charlie, but then again, who didn't? They sat together for the next half hour discussing all the arrangements that had been made for the big day. Frances was more than happy. After the reception they were going to return to her mother's apartment to change their clothes and then head upstate for their honeymoon. Frances was so innocent, and it showed when she asked Mrs. O'Neill what was going to happen to her on her wedding night. This took Mrs. O'Neill by complete surprise.

"Frances, haven't you discussed this with your doctor?"

Frances replied, "Actually, no—we just went for the required blood test."

Mrs. O'Neill smiled and said, "Just do what comes naturally. You'll see. Just love each other."

Frances wondered if Charlie knew what to do, but she didn't want to think of that right now. She was just looking forward to living with her perfect husband, her soul mate.

The coffee and pastries were delicious, and both girls loved starting out their morning this way. Frances hugged her employer and said she didn't think "thank you" was enough for all she and the doctor had done for her. They were wonderful people, and she loved them both dearly.

"See you at the church," Frances exclaimed, and the girls left the house and climbed into Christina's small car.

When they arrived at Frances's mother's apartment, it was still early, only a little after seven o'clock. The streets were quiet, typical for a Saturday morning. Frances wanted to break the silence by shouting, *Wake up, everyone. Today is my wedding day,* but, of course, she didn't dare. It had been arranged that Uncle Ralph would drive Frances, her mother, and Christina to the church, and after the wedding reception, Ralph would take Christina back to get her car. This was so like her uncle. He was such a help to anyone who needed him. She would meet her father and Jenny at the church. Her father was going to give the bride away. Frances thought, *How silly is this? He gave me away years ago. Oh well, let's bury all those bad memories; now I can look forward to a wonderful life with the man I adore, soon to be my husband.*

While Frances and Christina were changing into their gowns, Frances felt guarded; she had a strange sensation that something was wrong with her mother, but she couldn't put her finger on it. She decided to just leave her alone and not ask if anything was wrong. Frances busied herself with getting ready and helping Christina with her gown. The girls finally finished with their makeup, hair, and dressing. They made sure Frances had something old—Charlie's mother's handkerchief, which she had worn on her wedding day; something borrowed were Kay's pearl earrings, and then there was the traditional blue garter, which her sister-in-law Anne had given her to wear under her wedding gown.

Both girls stood in front of the mirror, admiring their joint efforts, when Frances's mother entered the room. She stared at them both and then walked directly over to Christina. Turning her back to Frances, she said, "Christina, you look beautiful."

Frances thought, *Nothing has changed; I just want to get out of here and go to Charlie. She almost had us all fooled, but she has that "sick" look today, and I can't deal with it now. I just have to stay away from her.* It was now eight forty-five, and Uncle Ralph was due to arrive any minute.

When she heard his voice she uttered, "Thank goodness." Uncle Ralph arrived as promised, announcing he was ready to take them to the church. When he saw Frances, he said, "Frances, you look stunning and make a beautiful bride. Charlie is a very lucky man."

Frances glanced at her mother. She knew that look; she was furious, listening to her brother complimenting her daughter. Frances whispered to her uncle to be sure to put Christina and herself in the backseat and her mother in the front. *I will not let her ruin my wedding day, no matter what. Once we're at the reception, other family members will keep her occupied, and I'll be sure to avoid her at every moment possible.*

The flowers for Frances and Christina were waiting for them in the back of the church. Frances's gown looked stunning on her. It was made entirely of an exquisite lace design with a square neckline and a stand-up collar. At exactly nine thirty, the organ music started, and then Christina, followed by Frances with her father next to her side, walked down the aisle, and she smiled as she saw her beloved Charlie. Once they reached the altar, Frances's father raised her veil and kissed her softly on the cheek. He then took her hand and placed it in Charles's hand, and together they stood in front of the priest to make their lifetime commitment before God. It turned out to be a lovely ceremony.

The reception that followed was one of very little formality, but one of good fun and lots of merriment. The food was sufficient with plenty of sandwiches, salads, beer, and, of course, the wedding cake. The music was provided by three local men who played a variety of instruments, making it very often sound as if they had ten musicians.

As promised to herself, she stayed far away from her mother. She danced with her father, father-in-law, and brothers-in-law and finally got to dance with her beloved husband. She laughed and whispered to Charlie that she needed to talk with him before they went back to change at her mother's apartment. Finally, it was time to cut the cake. She and Charlie smiled as they fed it to one another. Then the wait staff proceeded to distribute the cake to all their guests. Before the wedding reception was over, Frances went to her mother-in-law and thanked her for everything. She told her Charlie was everything good and kind because of her. The two women embraced, and Charlie's mother was happy her son had found such a lovely girl to marry. It was obvious, even though she wouldn't admit it, of the three girls her eldest sons had chosen, it was Frances who was her favorite.

The wedding reception flew by very quickly; it didn't seem possible that they were there for four hours. It looked like everyone was having a great time celebrating the new marriage. Everyone, that is, except her mother. Frances glanced over her way a few times, noticing she had that strange look about her. Most people wouldn't think anything of it, but with Frances's past experiences, she wasn't so sure. Frances decided to put these thoughts out of her mind. She didn't want anything to spoil her day. The music was now stopping, and the guests were starting to gather their things. Many came over to say good-bye to Frances and Charlie and wish them well, often depositing an envelope in Frances's hand.

Once the room was clear of the majority of guests, Uncle Ralph told Frances he was going to bring her mother and Christina back to her mother's apartment. He wished her a good and safe honeymoon trip. He said he would be sure to see them when they returned. The newlyweds gathered up any remaining wedding gifts. They were going to be deposited at Charlie's parents' house for safekeeping until their return from the honeymoon. At last everything was over and done, and most of the gifts were already at his mom's.

Frances and Charlie got into their car, and as they started toward Frances's mother's apartment, they noticed Charlie's mother watching them from her doorway. She waved good-bye and at the same time blew a kiss to

A Matter of Survival

them. Charlie thought, *How did I get so lucky to have such a great mother, and a now a great bride?* He was a contented man.

Once they were on their way, Frances spoke first. "Charlie, I can't put my finger on it, but I think my mother is looking for trouble. I can sense it."

Charlie answered saying, "Fran, you're just being nervous—don't let it get to you. Just as soon as possible, we will get dressed and leave. Remember, honey, you are not alone anymore. I'm here to protect you."

With that Frances put her head on his shoulder and snuggled close to him, feeling secure because of his positive attitude.

Once they arrived at the apartment, they climbed the stairs and knocked on the door. Dolores was still wearing the lovely blue gown.

Frances spoke first. "Mother, we are just going inside the bedroom to change our clothes and will be right back. Thank you again for letting us use your home for this."

Frances hurriedly put on a little white-and-black suit she'd recently purchased. Charlie said he had a surprise for her about where they would be spending their wedding night, and she should just look pretty. He too quickly changed, and they gathered their belongings together with suitcase in hand.

Frances stepped out of the room first, and then she saw the horrifying sight of her mother coming at her with a kitchen knife. Frances screamed and Charlie came rushing out of the room coming to his wife's aid. Her mother was rambling incoherently, something to the effect that her life was terrible and it was all because of Frances. He quickly wrestled the knife away from her pushing Dolores into one of the living room chairs and shouted, "Don't you move!"

Frances was in shock holding her hand to her mouth as she watched this terrifying scene.

Charlie breathlessly yelled to Frances, "Take whatever you can carry and go out to the car. I'll follow you shortly."

Frances was afraid for him, but he just said, "Go!"

Within a few minutes Charlie was downstairs, tossing some of the remaining items into the back of the car. He then slipped into the driver's seat, visibly shaken.

"Frances, you were right to warn me about her. What a crazy woman she is. Let's just get out of here and get on with our honeymoon."

Frances was terribly upset and quite shaken that this could happen to her, even on her wedding day. The scene brought a flood of horrible buried memories to the surface. Frances then took a deep breath suppressing tears and at that point made up her mind: once and for all, she never wanted to see her mother again, and this time there would be no going back on her word!

Nineteen

MARRIED LIFE

Charlie had planned their wedding night, giving it much consideration. He wanted it to be extra special, and although their budget was tight, he wanted it to be something they would always remember. He had reserved a room at one of the new hotels near the airport and even remembered to buy a bottle of inexpensive champagne for them to share—something he debated since neither of them were drinkers, but tonight would be different. If anything, he thought, it might give him the needed courage to pursue the wedding-night ritual, since he was just as inexperienced and as innocent as his bride. If it weren't for his brother George filling him in on the details of consummating the marriage, he would have been at a total loss.

When they arrived at the hotel, Frances was more than pleased to find that Charlie had gone to so much trouble and expense. She knew Charlie didn't have a lot of money, but she loved him even more for his thoughtfulness. The desk clerk surmised it was their wedding night and graciously gave them an extra-special room for the night at no additional charge.

Frances wasn't exactly sure what was going to take place but figured surely her husband would know this. Once in the room, she changed in the bathroom, putting on a gorgeous nightgown and robe that Mrs. O'Neill had given her as a wedding gift. Frances felt elegant and very special in her new nightwear. She'd never had anything so exquisite before.

Charlie gave her a pleased and approving smile, and with that Frances blushed with nervous anticipation. He then went into the bathroom and donned the new pajamas, robe, and slippers his mother had given him just a few days before the wedding. He never even gave a thought to wearing something brand new on his wedding night. Just before leaving the bathroom, he glanced in the mirror and thought how lucky he was to have a mother who was perfect, and now he had taken the perfect wife. He hoped he could please Frances tonight, but he was also very nervous. *Oh well, I'll just hope for the best,* he said to himself.

Charlie tried and tried to open the champagne bottle. He kept trying to turn the top, but he couldn't seem to master it. They both laughed and decided not to drink it anyway since neither of them were drinkers. There was a small radio in the room, and Charlie turned it on, scanning the stations until he was able to find some very soft, nice music. He lowered the lights in the room and took Frances in his arms, telling her she was beautiful and how happy he was tonight that she had agreed to marry him. They both agreed their future looked wonderful as long as they always had each other. He kissed her softly and walked her to the bed. For a long time, they just lay next to each other, kissing and giving each other soft caresses. Then Charlie reached over and turned off the last light in the room. Only a soft glow of light coming from the bathroom shone into the room. His hands gently covered her body, and despite their inexperience, they somewhat awkwardly consummated their marriage.

They slept until eight o'clock the next morning and dressed leisurely. They wore comfortable clothes for the trip as they were planning to have a four day honeymoon at a resort in the Poconos. Charlie estimated the trip would take them no longer than three to four hours. He'd had the car checked at a local service station before the wedding. All seemed good, except he was warned he needed new tires. Charlie didn't have money for new tires, so instead he just purchased a tire repair kit together with a hand-held air pump. They had a quick breakfast of coffee and donuts and decided they would get a light lunch once they got on the road.

When they approached their car, which had been parked on the street, they were both taken back. Apparently, his brothers thought it would be funny to decorate the car with a "Just Married" sign and tie old shoes

A Matter of Survival

and tin cans on the back bumper. They decided to drive a short distance with all the nonsense tied to the back of the car, and after about an hour of driving, Charlie's heart sank at the sound of a flat tire. There was no mistaking the sound; it couldn't be drowned out, even with the sounds of the rattling tin cans. He managed to pull the car over to the side of the road, and with Frances reading the directions from the repair kit, he repaired the flat and proceeded on the trip, but not before removing the "Just Married" extras.

A half hour later, the same sound began, and again they got out and fixed the tire, patching it with the glue provided and then using the hand pump to pump it up again. The anticipated trip of what was supposed to be three to four hours was now taking them more than twice as long since they had a total of ten flat tires on the way to the resort. By the time they got there, they were both exhausted but laughing hysterically at their old car.

As soon as they got to their room, they both freshened up and went back down to the resort's restaurant for a bite to eat. They were very hungry, as they never did have a chance to stop for something to eat on the road. They were too busy repairing tires. They were both grateful that they weren't planning to leave the resort until it was time to go home, and they decided not to worry about the car until then. They each ordered a sandwich, coffee, and a piece of chocolate cake. At least now they were full and contented.

Charlie suggested they walk on the outside grounds since it was a delightfully warm evening. After a little while, they stopped and sat on one of the benches. There was very little conversation between them. They just sat there holding hands. The bench overlooked a pond, and there was a family of ducks swimming in it. Frances said to Charlie she hoped they would have a family of their own someday, just like the ducks. Charlie said their kids would look rather odd if they looked like those ducks. They both laughed.

They were quite tired and decided to retire to their room and get an early start tomorrow. The hotel had a nice pool and other facilities they planned to enjoy as much as possible. They retired to their room, made love, and fell into a deep sleep, cuddled in each other's arms.

Morning came, and both felt well rested. They showered and got dressed for breakfast. The morning meal was included in their room rate, so they wanted to be sure not to miss the promised big breakfast. They were both famished and took full advantage. Frances even managed to smuggle some extra fruit and rolls in a napkin so they would have something for later in the day.

The next days passed very quickly. They'd savored every minute of each day, and now it was time to return home. Before they left Charlie checked the tires, but all he could see were the ten patches he had placed on the defective tires. *Here goes nothing,* he thought. He and Frances climbed into the car. They didn't say anything to each other, but they both kept their fingers crossed, hoping for the best. They had been driving for only about an hour and a half when the awful, familiar sound began. They gave each other a pained look, and Charlie pulled the car over to the side of the road. Frances didn't have to read the repair directions anymore; they both knew them by heart. They finally made it back to Bayside, this time with just seven flat tires. So all in all, while traveling on their honeymoon, they had a total of seventeen flat tires. Charlie and Frances decided no matter what else they had to buy, the first thing would be new tires.

Instead of going directly to their apartment, they decided to stop by his parents' home and, of course, Mom was delighted they did so. She heated some leftover homemade turkey soup, prepared turkey sandwiches, and added a treat of some homemade cookies. It was delicious and, as usual, Mom took pleasure in watching them enjoy her cooking. They told her the incredible story of the seventeen flat tires and how much longer the trip took, but they also told her how very much they liked the resort. They never mentioned the incident with Frances's mother. This was going to be a dropped subject from now on.

Before they left to go to their own apartment, Mom put together a package for them consisting of bread, milk, eggs, and coffee. She didn't want them to have to have to stop anywhere tonight. They welcomed her thoughtfulness and told her how much they appreciated all she did for them. With that they thanked her for dinner and left, kissing her good night and saying their good-byes to Pop and the younger brothers and sisters.

A Matter of Survival

It was a quick ride home, just four blocks from Charlie's mother's house, and now it was time to start married life.

They entered their small four-room apartment, and when Frances glanced around, she thought it was just perfect. They had been able to buy a small kitchen set, a three-piece living room set, two matching end tables, and a coffee table. They also placed an area rug in the center of the room. Through someone Charlie worked with at the airport, they had purchased, for a very reasonable price, a used bedroom set that was in exceptionally good condition. Before the wedding Frances had painstakingly examined all the pieces of furniture, moving them into several different locations until she was pleased with the final outcome. She had also managed to buy some sheer curtains, which certainly dressed up the old windows. She was now quite proud of her new home.

The fourth room was bare, except for the many boxes and cartons still to be emptied. They had received many wedding gifts, which were now housed in this small room, and she was more than anxious to go through them. Frances wanted to take her time and promised herself she would leisurely empty them one by one.

The next morning they slept later than they usually did. Because Charlie had to return to work the following day, they both wanted to devote the day to staying in bed, making love, and cuddling in each other's arms for as long as they wanted. It was almost ten thirty when at last Frances decided to get up. She took a pretty housecoat from the closet and tied her hair up with a matching ribbon. She kissed her husband on the head and told him she was going to prepare him breakfast with the provisions his mom had provided. Both Charlie and Frances never did get dressed that day. They decided to just lounge around for one last day before their new responsibilities set in.

Charlie rose quite early the following morning at five thirty. He was due into work at seven and didn't want to be late on his first day back. Frances lingered in bed a few extra minutes, listening to the shower running in the bathroom. She smiled to herself and decided she had better get up and make her husband breakfast and pack him something for lunch as well. There were still eggs, juice, bread, and coffee left, which she prepared for him. She also found some canned meat in the pantry and thought this would do just fine to make him a sandwich for his lunch. She didn't want him to skip lunch.

Charlie came into the kitchen wearing his airline uniform, and Frances loved how clean and handsome he looked. He sat down at their little table to eat the breakfast Frances had prepared. He gulped his coffee down, and she quickly poured him another cup. He drank the second one almost on the run. Then he took her in his arms and gave her a lingering kiss goodbye, telling her he loved her and was looking forward to their evening together, and with that he was out the door, ready to start work. Frances watched from the living room window as he drove away thinking she had never been this happy before.

She poured herself coffee and just sat there in her little kitchen, trying to remember all the wedding gifts they had received. *Oh well,* she thought. *I better get started on cleaning up the kitchen and get to work in the spare roo*m. Once the kitchen was cleaned and dishes put away, Frances went into the bedroom and found a housedress to put on, then washed her face and brushed her teeth. She quickly ran a comb through her hair. If anything, she felt neater and cleaner. Frances decided that she would work in the spare room for a portion of the morning and then she'd leave the apartment later in the day to buy something for dinner. She thought it may even be nice to stop in the afternoon to visit with her mother-in-law.

She entered the spare room and saw so many boxes she hardly knew where to start. *I guess I'll start in one direction and make my way around the room, emptying them as I go,* she decided. As she sat on the floor, she enjoyed the fun of going through the gifts. Originally they had rushed through the gifts together, but now she would take her time to appreciate each one separately. No rush today. There were the pretty dishes given to them by his brother George and his wife, a toaster given to them by Charlie's other brother, Joe, a pretty pair of candlesticks and a matching bowl from Kay and her mother. The gifts seemed to go on forever. Frances would accumulate a number of them, bring them into the kitchen, wash them carefully, and place them somewhere around the apartment. Frances didn't realize how quickly the time was passing because she was so busy. When she glanced at the clock and saw it was nearly noon, she decided she'd better put the rest off until tomorrow. She took a quick shower,

A Matter of Survival

dressed, and gave a quick look around the kitchen, trying to decide what to prepare for dinner. She was certain she would make up her mind later when she was at the grocery store. For now she wanted to visit with her mother-in-law, who she now called "Mom."

Frances walked the four blocks to Charlie's boyhood home, and although it was a hot and humid day, she didn't seem to feel the heat or let it bother her. All she could think about was how happy she was and wasn't it great to have a home of her own with a husband who she loved so very much. *Life doesn't get any better than this*, she thought. Within just a few minutes, she reached her destination and waited outside the door until little Tommy came and gave her a big smile. It was obvious to Frances that this little guy was her favorite of all Charlie's brothers and sisters. Little Tommy called to his mother, and it was she who let Frances in. As usual she gave her a warm greeting and invited Frances into the kitchen for a cool glass of iced tea. Charlie's mother was glad Frances felt she wanted to spend some time with her. Again she said to herself that her son had made a perfect selection when he found Frances.

The two women sat and talked about the wedding, the honeymoon trip, and all the flat tires they'd had on the trip. They laughed together. It was wonderful the closeness they felt to each other. Then Frances went on to tell Mom about the marvelous wedding gifts they received and invited her to visit the apartment to see them. Mom smiled, saying it wouldn't be easy to visit with all the kids, but that she would try to get there as soon as possible. Frances then asked Mom what it was like to raise so many children. The children seemed to be Mom's whole life, and it never seemed to bother her that there always was so much work with having such a large family. Frances confided to her mother-in-law that she and Charlie wanted to start a family as soon as possible and hoped to have at least four children if they could afford it. His mother was pleased, knowing they were so much in love and happy together. She told Frances, "Love always seems to find a way."

Frances decided to conclude the visit, knowing she still had to stop to buy something for dinner. She said her good-byes and proceeded to the grocer. She also purchased a few additional items they needed, but knew carrying the groceries might pose a problem.

She finally made it home and walked the two flights of stairs to their apartment. Once inside she hurriedly put her purchases away and started to prepare the dinner. It wasn't before long before Charlie arrived home. He looked hot and tired, and she sent him to shower and then sit in their living room to relax before dinner. She was so proud of her husband. She knew he was a hard worker when she married him, but to realize he was doing this for them made her love him even more.

After dinner, they both went into the spare room and unwrapped many of the remaining wedding gifts. It did his heart good to see how happy Frances was. The two sat on the floor, opening boxes, and finally when the last box was emptied, Charlie said, "You know what, hon? This is going to make a great room for a baby."

They both laughed at the prospect of them becoming parents. She related her day to him and how she had visited his mother, saying she only hoped she could do as great a job as his mother when it came to raising a family. He assured her that he didn't have a doubt in his mind that she would make a fantastic mother, and besides, if she needed advice, his mother was just four short blocks away.

Charlie then looked seriously at Frances and told her someone at work had a side job caddying at the local golf club, and they were looking for additional caddies. He figured this would be a good way to make some extra money, and besides the salary, the tips were quite good. The only drawback would be that it would cut down on their time together as he would be working at the golf club on his days off. Frances hated to see him take on additional work, but she knew if they were planning to start a family, the extra money would come in handy. Charlie decided he would give it a trial run.

They picked up the extra paper and empty boxes together, and Charlie bundled them up for the trash. All the while they seemed to work in silence thinking of the prospect of Charlie taking on extra work. Frances knew she would miss having him around on his days off, but it probably would be worth it. When they finished working, they shut off the lights and went into the bedroom. They made love and fell asleep in each other's arms.

The weeks turned into months. The caddying job worked out better than expected. Charlie would rise extra early on his day off and drive to the golf course, getting there by six o'clock. He found that if he started early

A Matter of Survival

in the morning, he could be home by noon, and he and Frances still would have the day to spend together. She knew she'd married a good man. Not only did he give her all the money from his airport job, but now he would caddy on the golf course and then give Frances his day's pay, plus any tips he made. She learned to budget the household finances well and put as much money into a savings account as possible. The account was starting to build very nicely. Some Sundays they would visit his mother and have Sunday dinner with the family, and other Sundays they might make the trip to the Bronx to visit Frances's father, and occasionally they would make the trip upstate to visit her aunt Mary and her cousins. If they were lucky, Frances's Uncle Ralph would also be there as well. They were both very fond of him, more than anyone else in her family. It was hard to believe that he was her mother's brother.

Twenty

The Next Phase

A year passed, and after many months of trying, Frances was still was not pregnant. Without saying anything to her husband, she was beginning to be concerned that something might be wrong, and hesitantly, almost fearfully, she made an appointment with the doctor.

When the day arrived for her appointment, she said nothing to Charlie, but as soon as he left for work, she got dressed and made her way to the local bus stop to travel to Flushing. She had also made arrangements to meet with her friend, Kay, after she finished at the doctor's office. Kay was now seeing someone rather steadily, and Frances felt he was a marvelous young man. She hoped Kay would be as happy as she. Frances decided that if the doctor did find something wrong, the only person she wanted to share her problem with was her good friend.

Frances entered the doctor's office, noting that there were two people ahead of her. She tried to busy herself, glancing through the worn magazines in the waiting room, but she couldn't seem to concentrate on any of the articles in them. As she sat there, she thought, *Charlie would probably be upset with me for making this appointment by myself,* but still she didn't want to worry him. Right now she felt very nervous, and the longer she sat there, the longer she imagined herself never being able to produce children. Her negative thoughts were becoming louder and louder in her head, and she felt panic starting to stir inside her. She decided to get up and get out of there as fast as she could.

A Matter of Survival

Just as she was going to stand up, Frances heard her name being called by the doctor's nurse. The nurse called out her name again. Frances stood up, certain her knees were banging together so loudly that everyone could hear them, but everyone just kept looking at their magazines. Frances cautiously walked to the doctor's office. This was the same doctor she'd visited just prior to her wedding, and although her previous visit had been short and uneventful, she liked this kind man and was glad she had chosen him to be their family doctor.

When she entered his office, he smiled and indicated for her to sit down. She sat straight in the chair facing him.

"How are you, Frances? What brings you here today?" he asked her.

With that Frances blurted out almost hysterically, "I can't have children."

The doctor could hardly contain himself. Chuckling, he said to her, "And what makes you think that?"

Frances replied quickly, defending her panic. "We have been trying for a year now, and I still have not become pregnant."

"Only a year?" he questioned.

"Yes," Frances replied, "and every month I still get my period."

"Frances, tell you what," the doctor replied. "I'll give you a schedule to review, and I'm sure within the next few months you'll be back here telling me you may be pregnant. Frances, today I'll give you a checkup, but I think you should go home and relax and don't worry about it."

After giving Frances a general physical, he told her as far as he could determine, she was in perfect health.

"As I told you before, go home and forget about making babies and just love your husband. I'm sure everything is fine with the both of you. Get dressed, and we will talk in my office."

Frances dressed quickly and entered his office. She sat in front of his desk and watched him write notes in her chart. She was anxious to hear anything else that might help her. The doctor, now looking over his eyeglasses at her, and said, "If you find you are still not pregnant a year from now, come back into my office and we will talk again. In the meantime, I want to assure you that you are just fine, and you should stop assuming the worst."

Now Frances started to blush at her foolishness. She thanked him and left the office.

After checking the clock on the nurse's desk, she realized she had only a half hour to meet Kay. She was eager to tell Kay that there wasn't anything wrong with her. Frances left the doctor's office feeling a sense of relief. She was looking forward to someday having a little one of her own. She now was sure she was going to tell Charlie about her unwarranted fears and today's visit to the doctor. He would probably tease and laugh at her, but just the same, she was glad she'd gone to see him.

Frances looked to see if a bus was coming, but no luck. She decided not to wait for a bus, but to rather walk the eight blocks to meet Kay. Even though she realized she might be a few minutes late by walking, it was such a gorgeous day that it would be invigorating. She knew Kay would wait for her. They had made an agreement a long time ago that they would always wait if the other was running late. She hurried along, pausing once to glance at a little baby shop en route to her destination. Frances felt a slight tinge of guilt for stopping to look in the window, but she loved the shop's display and how prettily the sweet little items were arranged. Frances thought, *Someday I will be looking at these items for my baby.* She had just two blocks more to walk. As it turned out, Frances was only five minutes late, and Kay wasn't even "under the clock" yet. Frances stood there, catching her breath, and waited for her good friend. After about ten minutes, Kay arrived, also slightly out of breath. The girls greeted each other with a fond kiss, and Kay seemed exceptionally excited.

"Frances, it's such a gorgeous day; let's walk to the park where we can sit and have a few minutes with each other."

The girls proceeded to walk the next two blocks; Frances thought it was amazing how such a transformation could take place in just a two-block area. They were leaving an extremely busy avenue with people walking hurriedly in many different directions to an area that was quiet and peaceful. They found a bench and sat under the shade of a tree that had just sent forth its blooms for admiration.

Kay was carrying a little tote bag saying, "My mother prepared sandwiches for us."

A Matter of Survival

"Up until this point, I didn't even think about eating but I certainly appreciate the thoughtfulness of your mother." Frances replied.

Kay responded saying "There is also a small thermos containing coffee and two cups."

While consuming their lunch Kay said "I have exciting news to tell you. Bobby proposed to me last night, and gave me an enormous engagement ring."

Kay proudly displayed it to Frances. Frances had never seen a diamond that large and jokingly said, "That certainly is a big rock!" and then added "I'm thrilled for you, Kay and wish you all the best."

Kay continued telling Frances they'd decided to get married the following year, probably in October, and although Kay's mother was looking forward to arranging an elaborate wedding, she wanted Frances to share in the planning of the wedding as well. They laughed at the prospect of Kay and her being married ladies. Frances hugged her good friend and was genuinely happy for her.

Kay thanked her and said, "I would just be glad if we would be half as happy as you and Charlie are. I know how much you and Charlie love each other, and I feel the same way about Bobby. Frances, up until now, I thought you got the prize when you married Charlie, but now I got a prize also. It would be fantastic for us to someday be pushing baby carriages together."

Frances's eyes opened wide when she realized she forgot in all the excitement of Kay's news to tell her about her visit to the doctor. When Frances related the story of how nervous she was with the prospect of never having children, and how this had been the reason for her doctor visit, Kay and she laughed together.

"I was so happy when he said I was fine and that he was sure I would become pregnant during the next year."

After their lunch and a visit to the local park, the girls walked toward Main Street where they, as usual, stopped to glance in the stores' windows. Kay needed to buy some things, and Frances stayed with her while she made her purchases. After about two hours, Frances decided she'd better start to head home to prepare dinner. The girls said their good-byes and made arrangements to meet the following week.

Frances boarded her bus and sat down, getting lost in her thoughts. She was happy for her friend and how nice it would be to help her with her wedding plans. Yes, Kay was right in saying Frances had gotten the prize. The only thing that would make her happier was to have a child, a child they both wanted. Charlie was working hard, making good money now, and Frances hoped that eventually they might even have enough money to buy a small house. She had often wished they could buy something closer to Charlie's mother. She stopped often to visit with her. With a mother-in-law like Charlie's mother, Frances never felt deprived about not having a mother. She was lucky to have a woman like this in her life. This was the way she imagined a mother/daughter relationship was supposed to be. Frances admired her so much, especially the way she was able to manage her home and family, and she wanted to be just like her when it came to raising children.

That afternoon Frances stopped at the grocery store and purchased a few items for the evening meal, making sure to buy things Charlie liked. She always wanted to please him in every way possible. She loved to cook and bake and take care of their apartment. Life can't get much better than this, she thought.

That evening she decided to tell her husband about her visit to the doctor and, yes, he did laugh and tease her.

"Well," he said. "We will just have to keep practicing until we get it right."

They both laughed. Then she remembered to tell Charlie about Kay getting engaged. Charlie liked Kay and her family very much and was happy for her.

"Let's get her something nice for her engagement," he told Frances. "After all, she is your best friend and they were so good to us when we got married."

The following month, much to Frances's surprise, her period didn't come at the usual date, and she began to wonder if it was possible that perhaps the doctor had been right and maybe, just maybe, she might be expecting their first child. As the weeks went on, Frances became increasingly sick in the mornings, and if there was any doubt before, now she was certain. She made an appointment with her doctor, who seemed to be genuinely happy for her and told Frances according to his calculations, she

A Matter of Survival

would have her baby sometime around mid-March. He gave her a prescription for vitamins and told his nurse to put Frances on a monthly schedule to visit him. He assured her that since she was in such good health, her baby would be very healthy as well.

When Frances left his office, she was beaming. She couldn't wait to share her news, not only with her husband and in-laws, but Kay and Mrs. O'Neill as well. Then she decided not to tell her friends just yet. She wanted to wait a month or two before saying anything as she just couldn't believe it herself. Now her life was complete.

For their next get-together, Kay had arranged for them to meet at Kay's house. Today there seemed to be much more of a commotion at her home since so many of her brothers and sisters were home that day. Kay's mother invited the girls to sit with her in the kitchen while she started to prepare dinner. She gave them tea and some cookies she had prepared earlier in the day. They talked about the upcoming wedding and the arrangements that had been made so far. Kay's mother had chosen to have an elaborate reception at one of the hotels in the city. They had also made arrangements to reserve the local church, deciding on a wedding date the following May. Frances knew this date would be perfect for her since her baby was due in March. Frances couldn't hold back her news any longer and suddenly decided to tell her friend and her mother the happy news.

Kay was surprised that she didn't guess her good friend was expecting. "I guess I was so wrapped up in my own wedding plans that I didn't notice you may have gained some weight."

Kay was sincerely happy for Frances and hugged and kissed her. Kay's mother congratulated Frances and wished her the best, saying now there was something else to look forward to besides the wedding. Frances decided right then and there that she would ask Kay to be the godmother to her baby.

The following week, Frances stopped by to visit Mrs. O'Neill, who greeted her, as usual, very fondly.

"What a nice surprise this is, Frances," she said.

Mrs. O'Neill prepared a pot of tea and set out some fancy cookies, and the two sat very comfortably at the familiar kitchen table. Frances always felt at home with Mrs. O'Neill, who was delighted to learn the good news.

She was very encouraging to Frances, saying she would make a wonderful mother with all the experience she had gained while living with them.

Finally, after a month or so, they decided to have Sunday dinner with Mom and Pop and the rest of the family. When they got to Charlie's parents' house, Charlie's brother George was there with his new wife, Anne. Of course, Brother Joe showed up with his girl. They were all there for Sunday dinner as well. It was great that everyone was together that day. Frances and Charlie wanted to share their news and let his parents know they were expecting their first grandchild the following March. The future parents were so excited that they could hardly contain themselves.

Once everyone was seated at the table, Charlie declared he wanted to share some good news with the family. He proudly told everyone he and Frances were expecting their first child in March. With that Anne screamed, "I can't believe it. We are also expecting our first child in March."

Everyone laughed at the coincidence of two babies being born into the family at almost the same time. The family was certainly growing with two grandchildren now on the way. What a happy occasion this day turned out to be. The men reached over to each other, shaking hands and offering hearty congratulations to one another. Then, of course, Joe piped up, offering his congratulations also, but he could not resist letting the moment pass without saying, "Frances, I bet you are going to have a dark little Italian baby, and its first words will probably be 'feed me spaghetti.'"

He laughed at himself while his brother looked at him like he wanted to punch him out right then and there. He probably would have if it weren't for Pop telling Joe, "Button it up and stop teasing Frances."

"Let's see what you'll produce when the time comes," his mother interjected.

Joe, as usual, would not let the subject drop; instead he reminded everyone again he came from royalty, and the way he said it, it sounded like he was the only one in the family who was supposedly a direct descendant of the Austrian duke. Again everyone laughed at him, except maybe Frances. She no more felt like an Italian than anyone else in the room. Frances hated the fact that there was so much prejudice against Italians. For some reason, which she didn't understand, the Italian people were looked down upon. She believed maybe it was because the Italian people were among the last group of immigrants who migrated to the United States, and most were labor who did not speak English. Still, she never felt like an Italian and couldn't understand why Joe had to tease her so much about her heritage. Secretly, she began to worry about what her child would look like. Would it be a dark Italian baby, or would it be light like the Irish/German heritage from her husband? After all Joe's teasing, she was sure she would have the dark Italian baby Joe predicted, but the baby was theirs and she would love it no matter what.

After dinner the women got up to help clear the table, but Mom said the expectant mothers should go inside, put their feet up, and just relax. She and her girls would do the dishes and clean up the kitchen. Frances and Anne welcomed the attention they were getting, not only from their husbands, but also from their mother-in-law. Mom was so sweet and considerate. The women were grateful to their mother-in-law for her kindness to them. They assumed she could sympathize with them since she too had had so many children. She knew what it was like to want to just relax, and so they did. After an hour or so, Mom came in from the kitchen and presented them with a tray of tea and small cakes, telling them she thought they would enjoy the treat, and they certainly did.

Twenty-One

A BIG SURPRISE

During the two girls' pregnancies, they would often visit Charlie's mother and father, not only on Sunday afternoons, but during the week as well. Mom would shower lots of attention on the girls, pampering and doting on them at every visit. Many times she would either prepare lunch or tea with splendid snacks for them. Needless to say the women relished all the attention they were receiving and were anxious to present their mother-in-law with beautiful grandchildren. It was fun to discuss babies with her, and they asked her many questions about taking care of a little one. They thought her experience was invaluable.

The only time that Frances didn't like visiting Charlie's mother was when she found that Joe was home. He never let the opportunity pass without making a wisecrack about Frances having a dark little Italian baby and pointing out that Anne would be the one to have the beautiful baby with Irish/German heritage. Even Anne felt sorry for Frances and kept telling her to ignore him, but sometimes it wasn't easy.

The holidays came and went, and Frances and Anne were growing considerably bigger every week. They were both now beginning to waddle and commiserated over the pregnancy ills that each one experienced. They were happy to share their complaints with Mom, seeking to find out what her pregnancies had been like; Mom would tell them how much they would love the babies once they came and their present discomfort would become a distant memory.

The family had gotten together for another Sunday dinner in February. As was his habit when they arrived, Charlie hugged and squeezed his mother, but this time his father chastised him, saying to leave her be.

Charlie looked at his father, saying, "What's with you, Pop, are you jealous because I'm showing Mom affection?"

Pop chose not to answer his son but instead just shrugged his shoulders. Charlie dismissed his father's attitude, attributing it to old-age grumpiness.

Everyone then gathered around the dining room table. All the usual people were present, including Joe and his girl. Charlie complained about how difficult it was working at the airport during this particularly cold winter. Joe said they should all look forward to the warm weather next June would bring. Charlie, being somewhat puzzled, asked his brother why he was talking about June now when it was still so cold and icy outside.

Joe smiled and replied because he and his girl had gotten engaged for Valentine's Day, and they planned to get married in June. The winter months were long and cold, and today was no exception, but still, this announcement did give the family something else besides the babies to look forward to. Right now June seemed to be an eternity away. Frances glanced over at Charlie's mother and saw the sadness in her eyes. She knew Mom's heart broke a little as each one left the family, but she never voiced her opinion about this to them. She and Pop gave their blessing to their second eldest boy, and Charlie's mother said she and Pop hoped they would be as happy as their other two sons who'd recently taken wives.

Frances had what she thought would be her last appointment before the birth of her baby the first week in March. She had a question for the doctor. She was embarrassed, but she decided she would swallow her pride and just ask him outright. After his examination, she got dressed and sat across from his desk, waiting to ask him her question.

"It appears as if the baby will be born right on schedule, and I want to see you every week until its birth," he said.

Frances nodded her head in agreement and steadied her nerves. "Doctor, I have just one question to ask you, and I'm not sure what you will think of me."

"What is it, Frances?" he asked her curiously.

Frances took a deep breath and blurted out, "Doctor, please tell me, how is the baby getting out of me?"

The doctor smiled at her and said, "Now I know why I've always referred to you as 'my little baby girl.' Frances, the way you conceived this child is the same way your baby will come out. Don't worry, I'll be right there with you, and I promise I will take good care of you."

It had never occurred to him until today that Frances didn't have a clue about the birthing process, but he should have realized it when she had told him she was raised in a convent with the nuns. He went on and explained to her what she should expect. She left his office thinking to herself the birthing process was going to be horrible, but then again, she wasn't the first woman to give birth, so she would just have to trust her doctor. She liked him and was glad he was going to help her deliver the baby.

Early on in her pregnancy, Frances had converted the spare room into an adorable nursery. First, she had Charlie paint the room a very pale, soft yellow, which was her favorite color, and the woodwork a glossy white. They purchased a white crib with a matching dresser and also found a good mattress on sale in one of the local shops in Flushing. Frances then hung sheer crisscross dotted swiss curtains on the windows. She added a fluffy white area rug and a few inexpensive pictures, which made the room complete. She couldn't get over the transformation of the bleak and stark room into what was now a sweet little nursery, ready to welcome the arrival of the new baby. She was proud of how the room turned out. Frances loved decorating her home, and it showed.

With the baby being so close to being born, it was difficult for Frances to take the bus to meet Kay. Since Charlie was now working the afternoon shift at the airport, he suggested he drop her off at Kay's before driving to the airport and pick her up later that evening. Kay's mother had invited Frances to stay for dinner, thinking the girls would have time together to not only plan for the upcoming wedding, but also plan for the new baby. Frances was happy she had decided early on to ask Kay to be the godmother to her baby. Charlie stopped in to say hello to Kay and her mother. They were always pleased to see him. Kay's mother insisted on preparing something for Charlie to eat; she wanted him to have some dinner before he went to work. Charlie sat at the kitchen table while Kay's mother seemingly magically produced a delicious meal of chicken accompanied by a rich and hardy Italian sauce. She had given him a side dish of spaghetti and some crusty Italian bread as well. He gulped the meal down as quickly as he could, knowing he was limited for time and didn't want to be late. Kay's mother watched him with pleasure as he savored every forkful of her dinner. He thanked her, telling her she was the best Italian cook he knew. He kissed his wife and left, saying he would be back for her sometime later that evening.

After Charlie left for work, the girls spent the rest of the afternoon together going through wedding books and talking about the impending marriage. During this time alone, Frances and Kay also discussed the responsibility of Kay being godmother to her baby, a responsibility Kay was genuinely pleased to perform which meant she promised to always supervise the religious education of the child especially if the parents should die and there were no other relatives to oversee the teachings of the Catholic faith.

Later that evening Kay's mother prepared a delicious meal, not only for them, but for Kay's two sisters and three brothers as well. They all sat down together at the large dining room table. Frances thought, *How fantastic it is to be invited to be a part of this family.* Since the family was in the bakery business, they had plans to create the most memorable wedding cake possible. The way they all talked, it was obvious the cake was going to be a work of art, a cake like no other. Kay announced that Frances and Charlie wanted her to be the godmother to their baby. Kay's brothers chimed in, saying now they would also plan on making the most beautiful christening cake as well. It would be their gift for the new baby. Frances was delighted with the excitement they all shared.

After the dishes were done, the girls sat around the table with Kay's mother, talking more about the wedding and the baby. Since they were planning to hold Kay's wedding at a magnificent hotel in the city, it seemed as if no expense was to be spared for the event. Frances had never gone to such an elaborate affair and was looking forward to this very luxurious wedding. Frances was glad that by the time Kay was to be married, she would be a normal size again. She wanted to wear something special.

It was now approaching nine o'clock. Frances had expected Charlie an hour ago. She assumed that maybe he got stuck at work, which was not at all unusual. Kay, her mother, and her sisters were still sitting around the dining room table when finally Charlie arrived. When he came in, he looked a little pale. He said to Frances, "You'll never guess who had a baby."

Frances replied, "Oh no, Anne had her baby first. She wasn't due until after me."

Charlie quickly responded, "No, my mother had a baby!"

Frances was embarrassed in front of Kay's family. "Charlie, that's a terrible thing to say."

He repeated it again. "I'm telling you, my mother just had a baby. I stopped there after work tonight, and I am not kidding; my mother had a baby today."

Frances was mortified that her husband would make such a joke in front of Kay and her family. She knew full well that she had just seen her mother-in-law a few days before, and Mom had waited on her and Anne in the usual way.

Embarrassed, Frances got up from the table, saying they had better go home as it was getting late. As she put on her coat, she thanked Kay and her mother and hurriedly left their house.

As they got into the car, Frances said to Charlie, "Wait, I don't want to go home just yet. I want to go to see your mother. I really don't believe you, but I still want to go to see Mom."

Charlie, almost in disbelief himself, repeated his words again to his wife. "I couldn't believe it either, but my mother did have a baby girl today."

They drove to Charlie's parents' house, and when Frances entered the house, she discovered Mom was not downstairs as usual. She immediately went upstairs, and sure enough, she was in the bed, holding the most beautiful baby she had ever seen.

"Oh Mom," Frances said sadly to her mother-in-law. "Why didn't you tell us? I can't believe you waited on us, catering to our every need and listening to our pregnancy aches and pains, and here all the while you were also expecting a child and never said anything."

"Frances," Mom said, "I was embarrassed to be expecting a baby at forty-five. At first I thought I was going through the 'change.' I never believed I was going to have a baby at the same time my two daughters-in-law were expecting, and, not only that, my other son will be getting married in just a few months. I didn't know how to tell anyone that I was also expecting a baby. So I figured it was best not to say anything to either you or Anne."

"I can't believe you hid it so well." Frances laughed. "Come to think of it, you were always wearing an apron over your dress, and when you were sitting, you seemed to be holding the newspaper in front of you all the time. Now it makes sense, and I can understand why Pop was acting so strangely when Charlie would hug and squeeze you. Mom, I have to tell you, she is the most beautiful baby I have ever seen, and I hope my baby is just like her. I am very happy for you, and now my baby will have a playmate as well."

Mom smiled and said she was glad the news was finally out and she didn't have to hide it anymore.

"Yes, she is really beautiful. She reminds me of Tommy when he was born. It's hard to believe I have eight children, although two are married and one is about to be married."

Frances held her hand. "You know what, I just realized this baby will be an aunt to my baby and Anne's."

Frances tidied her mother-in-law's pillow and tucked in her sheets and brushed her hair. She then changed the new baby's diaper so Mom could rest. When she was finished, she placed the neat little bundle back in her mother's arms.

"Let me get you tea or something light to eat if you want. It's about time I wait on you for a change."

Mom said she would welcome a cup of tea if Frances would join her. Frances went promptly downstairs to the kitchen to prepare it. She arranged a tray with a pot and two cups.

As she was waiting for the water to boil, she heard her brother-in-law, Joe, chastising his father, saying that he should have known better and what was wrong with him for getting his mother pregnant at this late stage. He was trying to be funny, but actually he sounded quite cruel. Frances, overhearing his comments, just shook her head and said to herself, *That certainly sounds like my brother-in-law.* Then she heard him talking to

Charlie, again repeating that he was going to have a dark little Italian baby, and it wasn't going to be like any of the other babies in the family. Charlie had started to retaliate, almost sounding angry with his brother, when Frances decided to call to him to help her carry the tray upstairs, using her size as an excuse.

She asked Charlie to take it to the top of the stairs and was glad when she heard Joe leaving the house. She thanked her husband and suggested he sit with his father, who probably needed consolation after Joe's biting words. When she brought the tray into the front bedroom, she witnessed Mom smiling at her newborn and showing the joy of just giving birth. She then poured the tea and watched her mother-in-law sip it slowly, welcoming the favorable brew. Frances sat next to the bed sipping a cup also. Frances started to speak.

"Mom, I think it's wonderful that you have this little one. We'll be able to push the carriages together. Won't that be fun? I can watch you take care of your baby, and you can teach me all I need to know about mine. It's too bad I didn't know you were expecting, because I would have felt more at ease asking you questions about giving birth."

Then she related the story of her last doctor's visit. The two women laughed as they sipped their tea. Mom told her she would have been too embarrassed herself to explain it to her anyway, so it was probably for the better that she spoke to her doctor.

Frances just smiled and said, "I think it's best that we not stay too much longer so you can get some much-needed rest."

Frances took the baby and carefully placed her in the cradle next to Mom and Pop's bed. With that she kissed her mother-in-law on the forehead, saying, "Congratulations."

She took the tray back down to the kitchen, washed the few dishes, and suggested to Charlie they go home. It had been quite a day; yes, quite a day!

The next day Frances got up early, prepared breakfast for Charlie, and watched him go off to work. She quickly showered and got dressed. She needed to get an early start, as she wanted to visit her mother-in-law. Frances was sure she might need her assistance with things around the house, or even with the new baby. Much to her surprise, when she arrived, she found her mother-in-law in the kitchen with the baby in a little bassinet sleeping soundly while she worked.

"Mom, why did you get out of bed so quickly? I was sure you would need at least a couple of days to recuperate after delivering a baby."

Mom said she was fine and would take a rest later in the day. It seemed to Frances that her mother-in-law never doted upon herself. She claimed it was better to get out of bed and just move around rather than stay still thinking of your aches and pains. Frances learned to develop this philosophy as well. Mom was right. If one was to stay in bed, it would be easy to dwell on the discomfort, so it was better to get up and do some light work around the house. Sure enough, the discomfort would go away.

Nevertheless Frances stayed and helped her prepare dinner for the rest of the family and tried to straighten up downstairs. All of the other children were in school, so this was a perfect opportunity for Frances to help out. One thing was for sure, the nuns had taught her to work quickly and thoroughly.

Frances helped Charlie's mother with as much as she possibly could, but she had gained so much weight and had become so much larger than her normal size, it was difficult for her to do as much as she really wanted to. She reminisced back to all the recent times when she'd visited, and now to find out that her mother-in-law had just about been ready to deliver her own baby. She had still been taking care of her own family, not to mention also taking care of her daughters-in-law when they came to visit. What a strong woman she was; both mentally and physically.

Now that Frances's due date was quickly approaching, Kay would visit Frances at her apartment. Kay would often tease Frances about how neat and organized she was. She would jokingly tell Frances once she was married, she would need her help in organizing her new home and in putting things were they belonged. Kay said she didn't have a clue.

Frances assured Kay she would be more than willing to do so, but, of course, it would mean she would be bringing the baby along with her. They would just have to work more quickly and pace themselves around the baby's schedule. Kay chuckled, calling her friend "Superwoman." Sometimes Frances couldn't tell whether Kay was more excited about the baby or her own wedding.

Twenty-Two

A New Family

A week after Charlie's mother had her baby, Frances was lying in bed one night, unable to sleep, when suddenly she felt a strange, sharp pain inside her. She looked at her husband sleeping peacefully beside her and decided not to disturb him, but rather got up and went into the bathroom. Another pain came, only this time it was more intense, and she remembered the doctor telling her this would happen. Ironically, she wasn't frightened, but rather felt excitement building inside her at the prospect that a new life was going to be born sometime in the very near future. Her doctor had prepared her well. At this point she felt she had no choice but to wake her sleeping husband.

"Charlie, I think you better get up. You are going to become a father soon."

He awoke, and it was he who looked frightened at the prospect of his child being born.

Frances decided to take a quick shower and get dressed. Her suitcase for the hospital had been packed several weeks ago. Charlie rose out of bed quickly and got himself dressed, anxious to help his wife with anything she needed. Within just a few minutes, Frances stepped out of the bathroom, fully dressed. Charlie had already gotten their coats, gloves, and scarves out of the hall closet and placed them on the living room chair. As it had just snowed two days before, it was still very cold and icy outside.

Charlie wanted to be sure they would be warm on their journey to the hospital.

The car was freezing cold when they got into it, but Charlie brought a small blanket with him so Frances could put it on her lap until the car warmed up. There was very little traffic on the road at three o'clock in the morning, and he tried to drive as carefully as possible without letting his nerves get the best of him. After about twenty-five minutes, they finally reached the hospital and fortunately were able to park right near it. Taking the suitcase, Charlie escorted Frances inside, noting the sign that read "Admitting." Charlie sat his wife down in a nearby chair while he gave the admitting clerk all the necessary information. The clerk called the doctor and told Charlie to wait for a nurse, who would be with them shortly.

The pains now came steadily to Frances, and within a few minutes, a nurse came with a wheelchair to take her to the upper-floor delivery room. Charlie, who was now very nervous, followed the women, and the nurse indicated he should go into the fathers' waiting room. He kissed his wife, telling her he would be right outside.

After what seemed like an eternity—or more accurately, eighteen hours of labor—the doctor finally came out to tell Charlie he was now the proud father of a beautiful baby girl. His wife was fine and sleeping peacefully. Charlie, greatly relieved, was anxious to see his wife and the new baby. After a while they brought him to her room. She was still very groggy from the delivery. She barely spoke to her husband, but did ask if he had seen his little baby girl. At this point he said he had not, but told her he was going to as soon as he left her room. Frances fell back asleep.

Charlie found the nursery easily enough. He was anxious to see his daughter. He was convinced he would recognize her, as she would no doubt be the darkest little Italian baby in the room, but he couldn't find a baby with that description. Just then a nurse in the room held up his daughter for him to view. He couldn't believe it! The nurse was holding the fairest and cutest little blond-headed baby. She was perfect. Wow, he couldn't wait to show her off to his brother, Joe.

Frances remained in the hospital for five days. Not because she was ill, but in 1940 women who had a normal childbirth stayed for four to five days. On the fifth day, Charlie was impatiently waiting to take both his wife and new baby daughter home. He wanted all of them to get on with their life as a family as soon as possible. They decided to name their baby Patricia since she was born just a few days after St. Patrick's Day.

Charlie had arranged to take a week's vacation to coincide with the birth of his child. He loved watching his wife taking care of the new baby, but he didn't want to handle the infant. She seemed so little, and he was fearful he would make a mistake, perhaps even drop her. After two days Frances insisted he sit in a comfortable chair and hold the little life in his arms. After that, he never seemed to want to put his daughter down.

Even though it was quite cold outside, they decided to bundle up the new baby to visit Charlie's mother. Because it was a Sunday, he was secretly hoping his brother, Joe, would be there. He couldn't wait to show off his precious daughter. They hadn't seen his mother since she'd had her baby.

Even though the car ride was a short one, Frances wore her beloved beaver coat. Now more than ever she appreciated the warmth of it; she could keep the little infant cuddled next to it and be sure she wouldn't be affected by the cold.

Sure enough as soon as they got inside the door, Joe hurried over to see the new baby, and for once he didn't have anything to say. He just stood there with his mouth open in disbelief. Frances and Charlie were very proud to show off their daughter to him. Mom was happy they came to visit and insisted they stay for dinner. Mom's baby was asleep in a bassinet, and she persuaded Frances to put the new infant in with her baby. Because the infants were so tiny, there was plenty of room for them both. It was adorable to look at the two babies sleeping together. If they didn't know any better, they even looked like twins.

Frances said to Mom, "Let's hope they will always be close as they grow. They will be perfect playmates."

Charlie couldn't have been happier. He loved his wife and his daughter and was very proud to be a family man.

Frances had made arrangements for Baby Patricia's christening celebration at one of the local restaurants. Kay was delighted with the new baby. Looking at the little one, she told Frances she wanted to have a baby just like hers and said she couldn't wait to be married so that she could get started on her own babies. Charlie had asked his brother George to be the baby's godfather, and George was pleased his brother had asked him. Since George and Anne had had a baby boy ten days after Frances and Charlie had their baby, there were three new infants in the family, all born within a month of each other.

Kay bought the baby the sweetest christening outfit with tiny flowers and delicate lace trim on it. The day of the christening went very well. Even her father and Jenny came, making the trip from the Bronx.

Two months after the christening, Kay had the most elaborate wedding imaginable. It was done with incredible sophistication and in very good taste. Kay, of course, made a stunning bride. Her mother saw to it that every detail was taken care of and made certain nothing would be overlooked. It was the most exquisite affair Frances had ever attended, not that she had attended many affairs at all. Kay's wedding was held in one of the most superior hotels in the city. It was nothing like Frances's wedding, which had been held in the church hall.

The days passed into weeks and then months. Charlie was working many extra hours at the airport, trying to work as much overtime as possible, and he still continued to work as a caddy on his days off. They decided to set themselves a goal. If they wanted to buy a house somewhere near his mother, it would mean making sacrifices now, and later they could enjoy the fruits of their labor. Frances loved being home with her daughter and taking care of their apartment. Since she particularly liked cooking, she was able to prepare economical and very tasty meals.

Charlie couldn't wait until he got home from work, just to have some special time to play with his daughter before her bedtime. He was proud that her first word was "Da Da," and no one could convince him that most babies' first words were the same. They loved watching their little one grow and perform all the things that babies learn to do, and before they knew it, it was the baby's first birthday.

It was now March 1941 and Charlie's mother and Frances decided it would be fun to celebrate their children's first birthdays together. The little girls seemed to be right on schedule together. They both walked and started talking within days of each other. It was fun watching them. While they didn't actually play with each other yet, they would play near each other, keeping a watchful eye on the other. Frequent visits to Charlie's mother proved to be a strong indication the little ones were becoming terrific playmates. Whenever the girls saw one another, their excitement could hardly be contained which made everyone laugh just to watch them.

Almost nine months passed, and Frances and Charlie were planning to look for a house the following year hopefully in the spring. Before they knew it winter was upon them and the weather was now turning very cold. Charlie's caddying job was put off for the winter season, and he loved having the extra time to spend with his wife and daughter. It was now the beginning of December and the holidays were quickly approaching. It was an exciting time for them as they prepared for Patricia's second Christmas. As they discussed plans for the upcoming holiday, delightful Christmas music was playing on the radio. Even though little Patricia was not even two years old, Charlie was so enthusiastic that he wanted to buy her everything and anything he saw in the stores. Frances would laugh hysterically at him.

While they were enjoying their happy thoughts and plans, a news bulletin interrupted the pleasant music with the unbelievable announcement that the Japanese had attacked Pearl Harbor and the realization hit them that their country may be thrown into war. They were stunned. They glued themselves to the radio and the next day their fears were soon founded when President Franklin D. Roosevelt in a speech to the nation stated, "Yesterday, December 7, 1941—a date which will live in Infamy—the United States of America was suddenly and deliberately attacked by naval and air forces by the Empire of Japan." He then asked Congress for a declaration of war against Japan.

Needless to say the merriment of the holidays quickly ceased and for the most part it was a very quiet Christmas. Patriotism was first and foremost on everyone's mind.

*

After a very cold and icy winter, the season finally passed. New York in the spring was a delightful place to be, and to observe everything coming back to life again was a special treat. Each year Frances was in awe of the change of season and happy her daughter's birthday was on the first day of spring.

Frances would enjoy watching her young daughter as she stood up in her crib, looking out the window. She seemed to take particular delight in seeing the flowers and leaves bloom on the trees. The child would giggle and get excited watching the birds land on the branches that appeared outside the window. Frances couldn't have been happier. Her baby was growing quickly and doing more and more each day.

Time flew by. Watching their daughter, who now was two and a half years old, grow up was amazing. Charlie would delight in teaching her all sorts of new things. One they liked the most was when he would ask her, "How much do you love Daddy?"

He taught Patricia to reply by saying, "I love you more than tongue can tell," but she insisted on learning it in her own way and would repeat it as, "I love you more than 'tonkin' tell."

It made them both laugh, and invariably she would repeat it again and again. She learned very quickly the more she said this to him, the more her father would relish it and lavish avid affection on her. They were so proud that their child had platinum blond hair and deep-blue eyes. Charlie would ask everyone and anyone, "Isn't she the cutest kid you ever saw?"

There was no doubt about it; his little girl was the apple of his eye. They were particularly pleased to show her off to Charlie's brother, Joe. He never did say anything negative about Italians to them again after Frances gave birth, and his poor sense of humor seemed to vanish. It looked as if Charlie had the last laugh on his brother.

Charlie did think it was strange that Joe, the one who had always bragged about the wonderful child he would produce, had been married for almost two years now, and still there was no sign of children. Obviously, Charlie had more sense than his brother, because he never mentioned or questioned him about this.

Frances and Charlie continued their plans, saving as much money as they possibly could, and it seemed as if their dream of owning their own home was becoming a close reality. The ways things were progressing, perhaps in just a few more months they would have enough for a down payment on their very own home.

Twenty-Three

Life Changes

It was late, about midnight, one hot summer night in July, 1942, and Charlie's mother was exhausted. Sometimes between taking care of the house and her children, it all seemed to be too much for her. She had finally gotten the last of her older children to bed earlier and thought, *Thank goodness they are all asleep.* She and her husband were still awake, lying in bed and trying to catch an occasional warm breeze from the open window. They had the radio on and were listening to the day's news.

Except for the low volume on the radio, the night was quiet. Suddenly, however, in the distance they could hear someone leaning on a car horn. At first they decided to ignore it, but the sound got louder and louder until it seemed to stop right in front of their house. The sound of the horn was incessant, and now everyone who was asleep in the house was fully awake.

"Joe, you better find out what is going on outside. Whoever it is they seem to be persistent to get someone's attention," Charlie's mother said.

With that her husband grabbed his trousers and slippers, put them on, and went downstairs to look out the front door. He observed a car that had stopped directly in front of the house. The car was horribly mangled and appeared to still have someone behind the wheel. At first Pop didn't recognize the car, or the driver, until he got closer to it. He couldn't believe his eyes, because it was his own son, Charlie, who had obviously been in a terrible

A Matter of Survival

accident. The first thing Charlie mumbled to his father was that he didn't want to go home and upset Frances.

Pop had difficulty opening the door on the driver's side, but after several tugs, he managed to pry it open. Pulling Charlie from the car proved to be no easy task. He saw his children watching from the front doorway. Calling to his teenage son, Sandy, he told him to come outside and help him to get his brother out of the car.

The two of them could hardly carry Charlie into the house. They couldn't close the car door so they had no choice but to leave it open. They managed to get him into the house and set him down on the living room couch. At that point Mom came into the room and gasped at the sight of her son. She quickly grabbed a kitchen towel, dousing it with cold water, and tried to wipe her son's face.

"Oh my gosh," she exclaimed. "He's covered with blood. I think we had better get him to a hospital. I can't imagine what happened. Charlie, please can you speak to me?"

Charlie lay on the couch; at first, he seemed too weak to speak to his parents. After a few minutes, he finally managed to tell them some of the details of what had happened. He started to speak, but his breathing was terribly labored and he seemed to be gasping for air as he spoke. He said while he was stopped for a red light, another car that was speeding slammed into his. The impact was so severe it caused him to lose control of his car; it flipped over three times. The car stopped only because it hit a traffic light on the corner, and the force was so strong that it knocked the light down onto the street. When the car finally stopped, he discovered he wasn't able to get out of it. The young man who hit him gave him his name and address, but he also told him his father was a well-known politician and Charlie shouldn't cause trouble. Charlie said it seemed like the young man appeared to have been drinking. He was sure of this because he smelled of liquor, yet he remembered his words were very clear. The only other thing he could recall was that the young driver had threatened him, saying his father would see to it that he wouldn't be charged with anything, and repeated again that Charlie shouldn't cause any trouble. Taking a deep and labored breath, Charlie further spoke, saying, "I don't know how I was able to drive here, but somehow I did. Even though it was late, there were a couple of people who saw the accident and tried to help me, but I just wanted to get here to you. All I could think of was that I didn't want Frances to see me like this. I didn't want someone from a hospital ringing our bell and telling her I was hurt. She's probably wondering now why I haven't come home yet. Even when I work overtime, I'm home long before this."

Mom and Pop both tried to persuade him that he needed to go to the hospital and get checked by a doctor. Charlie, however, was very insistent and absolutely refused to listen to them, saying he was sure he was fine, and he just needed to rest. He said he knew he hadn't broken anything, and the only thing that bothered him was that his head hurt where he'd gotten cut. He just wanted to rest on the couch.

Mom got his head to stop bleeding and placed a bandage over the deep cut. Other than the cut on his forehead, he didn't appear to have any other serious injuries. His mother thought it was a miracle he was alive. They were able to get his shirt off, loosen his belt, and remove his shoes, trying to make him as comfortable as possible. Mom had sent one of the girls upstairs to get a light blanket and a bed pillow, hoping that if he just slept he would feel better. Still, she wished her son would have let them take him to the hospital.

At last Charlie finally fell asleep on the couch. Mom and Pop decided Pop should go to Frances to tell her what happened and Mom should stay by Charlie's side. They decided it would also be a good idea if he took their oldest girl with him, knowing Frances would want to see Charlie right away and she would need someone to stay with the baby.

It was close to two in the morning when Pop hesitantly approached the apartment door. It was obvious Frances was waiting up for Charlie, because she immediately answered after Pop rang the bell. She gasped when she saw her father-in-law, knowing full well something dreadful had happened.

The first thing he said to her was, "Charlie is all right."

He proceeded to tell her about the accident and why he had driven to them rather than going to her. Needless to say, she wanted to go to her husband immediately and was grateful that Charlie's sister was there to watch the baby, who was sleeping soundly. Frances dressed quickly, and she and Pop hurriedly walked the four blocks to his house, only this time the familiar few blocks seemed to take forever. Neither one of them spoke, but she was sure her heart was pounding so loudly that they both could hear it.

Once they reached the front door, Frances pulled at it, wanting to enter the house as quickly as she could. She saw her mother-in-law sitting next to Charlie with her hand over her mouth. Frances looked at her husband's normally handsome face, which had now become distorted due to the swelling the injuries had caused. He looked awful and quite disfigured. He hardly resembled her husband at all. She felt her heart breaking for him.

Frances tried to call to Charlie to let him know she was there, but there was no response. Again, they discussed the possibility of getting him to a doctor, but Charlie's mother repeated his absolute refusal to seek medical attention. They decided to let Charlie rest on the couch. Then they would see how he was in the morning. Frances and Charlie's mother decided they would take turns sitting at his side. Frances told Mom to go to bed and she would stay with him first. She cuddled up on the living room chair across from him, watching for any signs of distress.

When the morning came, Charlie woke and said he just wanted to go home and get into his own bed. As they were leaving the house, Frances saw the car parked across the street and was amazed that he got out of it alive. She couldn't believe he had been able to drive it to his parents' house in the condition it was in, but somehow he had.

With the help of Charlie's father, they walked the four blocks back to the apartment and got Charlie into bed as quickly as possible. Frances helped him undress, and before she knew it, he was fast asleep again. Charlie slept until almost the evening. Frances had prepared a light meal for him, which he didn't want. He said he still didn't feel himself, so they both agreed it would be best if he stayed home from work for a day or two until he felt better. Fortunately, there was someone else in the building who worked at the airport, and Frances was able to reach him before he left for work. She asked him to let his supervisor know about the accident and that Charlie would be staying home from work for a few days.

For the next two or three days, Charlie seemed to sleep all the time. After the third day, he said he felt better and would be going to work that afternoon. Frances was afraid for him, but he insisted, saying he was feeling better.

Again, she made him a light meal and prepared his lunch, which was her usual routine on the afternoons when he was working. Frances and Charlie discussed the fact that they would need to buy another car, deciding to look for one the following weekend. Fortunately, Charlie was able to get a ride to work with the neighbor who also worked at the airport, so for the time being they would be okay.

It was almost one o'clock in the morning when Charlie came home, and he seemed quite agitated, which was not like him, but Frances let it go, thinking he still probably was not feeling well. Usually, when he came home, he would kiss his wife hello and look in on his little daughter, but not tonight. Instead he decided to stay up, saying he just wanted to listen to the radio and read the paper. Frances offered to stay up with him, but he snapped at her, saying he wanted to be alone tonight. She decided it probably was best to go to bed because the baby would be waking early, and she, herself, needed to sleep. Leaving her husband in their living room, Frances had an uneasy feeling. He'd acted so belligerent, which was so unlike him, but she shook her feelings off, thinking the accident had probably traumatized him.

When Frances woke in the morning, her husband was still sleeping on the couch. Apparently he had never gone to bed. She tried to wake him, but he wanted to be left alone. She then fed and dressed the baby and got dressed herself, thinking that it would be good to get out and get some fresh air. She would walk to visit her mother-in-law and perhaps do a little shopping afterward.

She spent the day as planned, but even while at Mom's house, she had a terrible feeling inside that she could not shake. While she couldn't put her finger on it, she knew something was wrong. Charlie said he was feeling fine, but somehow, he was different.

Mom prepared a light lunch for Frances, and while they were eating, Mom expressed concern for her son. Frances, not wanting to alarm her mother-in-law, told her he was feeling better and was already back at work. Frances really wanted to tell her the truth, but decided it best not to express her own feelings. Her mother-in-law had enough to contend with taking care of her own family. They had a nice visit, and it was good to see the two little girls side by side. It was not until after one o'clock that

A Matter of Survival

Frances thought it best to go home, even though she didn't want to leave the comfort of Charlie's mother. However, she still had to stop at the store to get something for that night's dinner. She mentally calculated she would be able to stop at the store and still get home shortly after two o'clock.

Surprisingly, Charlie was not home. Frances couldn't imagine where he might be. She prepared dinner anyway, thinking he would be back shortly, but he never came back. She assumed he had gone straight to work.

It was almost midnight when he finally came home. Again, he said he wanted to be left alone and didn't want anything to eat. He didn't want to talk or even see the baby. Frances suggested that perhaps they should start to look for a car since he was off the following day, after he got home from working at the golf course. He agreed and repeated to her that he wanted to be alone. Frances did think it was odd—not just that he was ignoring her, but he hardly looked at the baby. Up until recently, his daughter had been the highlight of his day.

The next day Frances woke up much earlier than Charlie. She showered and dressed and went to check on the baby, who was just waking up. She fed the baby and then dressed her. Once the baby was taken care of, she tidied up the apartment and waited for her husband to wake from his sleep. Normally on his day off, he would get up at dawn and go to work at the golf course. Generally he would be home by noontime.

It soon became obvious he wasn't going to his second job today. She waited for him to get up, which he finally did at about eleven thirty. When he awoke, Frances inquired if he was feeling well and if he wanted her to prepare something for him to eat. Much to her surprise, he again snapped at her, saying he was fine and he didn't want to eat. She didn't dare mention anything about the caddying job, but she did remind him about their plans to look for a car that day. He agreed and got dressed quickly. Once outside, they walked in silence to the bus stop and waited for the bus that would take them into Flushing, where the used car dealers were located. At last they reached the area, where several dealers were more than willing to make a deal to sell a used car. After looking for about two hours, he spotted a car to his liking. Frances tried to tell Charlie that it was too expensive; nonetheless, he wanted that particular car and didn't want to hear any negative comments. By purchasing this car, it would nearly clean out their savings account, which had taken them almost three years to build. They both knew their savings were intended for a down payment on a house. Frances wasn't going to argue with him, though, as she could see his mind was made up.

They drove the car home, again in silence. Frances had the baby on her lap and when they returned to their apartment, he told Frances to take the baby upstairs because he wanted to show the car to his mother and older brother. She asked to go with him, but he insisted he wanted to go by himself. Now she knew something was definitely wrong with her husband. This was so unlike him. Before the accident he had always wanted her and the baby to go everywhere with him, but not today. She exited the car with the baby in her arms, saying she would start dinner and would wait for him in the apartment. He mumbled something back to her and took off down the street. Frances stared after him in disbelief.

Oddly enough Charlie didn't return home for dinner. Frances didn't know what to make of it. It was now seven o'clock. He had left her about three o'clock, and she had hoped he would be home for dinner at five. Frances was frantic with worry. Even though it was late, she decided to put the baby in her carriage and walk to her mother-in-law's. Maybe he was still there, or if not, maybe she would know where he was. When she reached Charlie's parents' home, his mother was surprised to see her. She said Charlie stopped there earlier to show off his new car and then said he was going home.

"Frances, I'm a little worried about him because he was acting strangely," his mother said. "I found it odd that you didn't come with him."

Frances decided to confide in her mother-in-law, telling her that she was also concerned about Charlie's new behavior and didn't know what to make of it. Frances saw that it was getting late, and she had better get home with the baby. She pleaded with his mother, "If he comes back, tell him I'm worried and to please come home."

His mother promised to do so.

Charlie didn't return home until almost midnight, telling Frances he'd caught up with some old friends. They'd decided to go for a ride in his new car, and then they all went to one of their homes. Frances tried to tell him she had been sick with worry, but he didn't want to hear it and didn't seem to care either.

A Matter of Survival

The next day Charlie got up early and went out. Frances didn't have a clue where he was and now instead of worrying, she was angry. Again, he didn't return until eleven o'clock that night. She couldn't imagine where he had been all day and night, and he offered no explanation to her. He simply said he didn't want to talk about it.

First a week passed with the same pattern. Then two weeks passed, and still no answer from Charlie as to where he was going. Finally, she got him to speak with her. She asked him if he was going to work, and he answered affirmatively. Frances then proceeded to ask him if he had gotten paid, because for the last two weeks, he didn't give her his salary, as he had always done in the past. He replied, telling her the airline was having financial difficulty and had asked their employees to be patient, as their salaries would be held up for a few weeks. Once the financial difficulties cleared, they would receive their salary, plus any back pay that was owed to them as well as a bonus. Frances thought this was odd, but she was forced to accept Charlie's explanation since she had no choice.

A month went by, and still Charlie didn't bring home his salary. He was keeping odd hours and never seemed to have a set schedule as he always had in the past. The little bit of money that was left in the bank was quickly being used up. Frances managed to pay the rent, buy a moderate amount of groceries, and pay the utilities, but she was starting to get very concerned. She desperately wanted to trust and believe in her husband, but her instincts were telling her he was not being honest with her. She tried to suppress her innermost thoughts, but inside she feared the man she married and loved so deeply had in fact changed since the accident.

Although she rarely confided in anyone, she decided to speak to her neighbor whose husband also worked at the airport to inquire if they were having the same financial difficulties as well. When she questioned the wife, she was shocked to learn that Charlie was no longer working at the airport, and he hadn't been working there for about a month. Stunned, she thanked the woman for telling her this. Charlie was pretending to be going to work every day. *If he wasn't going to work, where was he going?* She was very uneasy waiting for him to come home.

Finally, he came home about eleven o'clock, the same time he would have come home if he was still working at the airport. As soon as he changed his clothes and got comfortable, she sat down beside him.

"Charlie, what is going on?" she questioned.

She then proceeded to tell him that she was aware he wasn't working at the airport any longer and wanted to know the reason why would he make such a decision without first talking it over with her.

First he looked shocked that he had been found out, and then he said he had a good explanation, but couldn't give her too many details. He started to stammer, telling her an elaborate story of how one evening while working at the airport, two FBI agents had come to talk to him. They wanted his help in watching employees who were suspected of smuggling stolen goods. He said they told him he would now be working for the government in the capacity of an FBI informant, and he would have to work for them for six to eight weeks before getting a salary. Charlie said he was going to make very good money with this new job, so he decided to quit the airline and just follow the suspected employees as the agents outlined. Furthermore, he couldn't give her any additional information right now.

Frances was flabbergasted at this story. It was so convoluted and complicated that for the first time since she'd known him, she was certain he was out-and-out lying to her. Still, she decided to wait another two weeks to see what excuse he would use when still no money would be coming in. She explained to him that they were getting very short on funds and that she had to use their remaining savings just to pay bills and buy groceries. Charlie asked for her patience and promised he would be giving her money shortly.

The next few weeks passed, and every time Frances tried to question Charlie regarding his late hours, or what was worse, his never coming home at all for one or two nights in a row, he was very evasive and put her off, saying he wasn't allowed to discuss government business. Frances was at her wits' end and was quickly running out of money. The rent was now overdue by a week, and there was hardly any food in the apartment. She was now determined that she couldn't shelter her husband any longer. His family was going to find out what was going on in their life.

A Matter of Survival

After a night when Charlie didn't come home again, she got up very early the next morning, showered, dressed, woke the baby, and fed her the last of the breakfast food she had in the cabinet. After cleaning the dishes, she then dressed the baby, making sure she would be warm for the walk to her in-laws' home. The weather was turning much cooler; winter would soon be arriving. There already was quite a chill in the air, and the last thing she needed was for her or the baby to get sick. After putting the baby in the carriage, she tucked a warm blanket on top of her.

When she reached her destination, she discovered her mother-in-law was not at home. Frances felt the tears of frustration building up inside her. She simply did not know where to turn next. She was frantic. The man she had loved and trusted so much was constantly trying to deceive her.

Frances decided to sit on the steps of the stoop and wait for her mother-in-law's return. She sat there and started to pray, *Dear God, please let me get an explanation as to what is going on with my husband. Please, dear God, help me.* Ever since Charlie had had that terrible accident, his whole personality seemed to change. He didn't approach her anymore to make love, nor did he even kiss her when he came home or left the apartment as he used to do. Moreover, he never looked at his child. It seemed he had lost interest in his family and his life with them. Frances could only hope and pray that whatever his problem was, he would come to his senses and get back to his old self. She so dearly loved him and would help him work out whatever his problem was, if only he would talk to her.

Frances waited for a little more than an hour. She was glad the baby was sleeping soundly under the warm blanket, but she herself was getting cold. She was just about to leave when she saw her mother-in-law approaching, pushing her baby carriage, which not only contained her baby, but groceries as well. At first she seemed surprised to see Frances waiting for her so early in the day.

"Is everything okay, Frances?" she asked, sounding concerned.

Frances said she needed to talk to her. Her mother-in-law simply nodded her head, and both women gathered their little girls and the groceries and entered the house.

Once inside they emptied the paper bags of their contents, and Frances helped put the groceries away in the proper cupboards. Charlie's mom put some water in the coffeepot and placed it on the stove so that they could have coffee with homemade biscuits. Fortunately, the little girls remained asleep; right now Frances needed the quiet time to speak to her mother-in-law.

"Mom, I don't know if you have seen Charlie lately, but he's acting very strange, and I don't know how to handle it."

Charlie's mother was obviously surprised by Frances's statement, and said she had been wondering why she hadn't seen him for the last several weeks. Normally, he would stop by several times a week just to check in and to see if she needed anything. She continued that she hadn't seen him for quite some time now, and yes, she was concerned but had been hesitant to ask Frances if something was wrong. Frances blurted out the whole story to her, starting with his buying the expensive car, his late hours, and sometimes not coming home at all. She then related his story about working for the FBI and the fact that he hadn't given her any money for over a month now.

Charlie's mother's disbelief showed on her face. Obviously her son wasn't fine. She said they must insist he see a doctor once and for all; they needed to recount this story to a medical person. Neither woman really knew how to handle the problem of getting Charlie to a doctor, but both agreed they would try together to get him to seek medical attention. She said her son was a good boy. Whatever his problem was, he would come around and be his old self again. Maybe he just needed to rest more.

Frances sat there sipping the hot liquid, which was welcome after the cold wait outside. She did all she could to hold back the tears. Her mother-in-law was the one person in whom she could confide, but still, it was her son they were talking about, and she was clearly being protective.

Mom's young child started to stir and woke up crying, which, of course, woke the other child. Frances thought it best to go home now and promised to let Charlie's mother know if he seemed better, or at least keep her informed of what was going on. Her mother-in-law insisted on giving Frances a few dollars, hoping that Charlie would bring some kind of salary home and prove Frances wrong. She was sure he would do the right thing. After all, this was the son that everyone loved.

A Matter of Survival

Frances bundled up her child and put her back in the carriage. She walked the four blocks to the apartment, deciding to use the few dollars Mom had given her to buy some groceries. She mentally planned what meals she would make and tried to stretch the money as far as possible. She managed quite well, taking into account how many meals she could prepare and still have a little bit left. She was glad that she'd visited Charlie's mother, not only because of the money she gave her, but because it finally felt good to let someone else know the problems she had been encountering.

When she reached the apartment, even though she was exhausted from worry and sleepless nights, she managed somehow to not only carry her young child, but also the few bundles of groceries up to the second floor. Surprisingly, when she got into the apartment, she discovered Charlie was home and was taking a shower. She changed the baby, put her in the playpen, and then put the groceries away. When she finished, she sat down and waited for her husband to come into the living room. He looked quite pleased with himself when he entered the room and handed her a little more than fifty dollars. Frances was shocked and asked how he managed to get the money.

He stated simply, "I finally got paid, and more will be coming soon. This is only the beginning, because I'll be making more money than I have since we got married."

Frances was doubtful that Charlie was telling her the truth, but she decided not to argue with him. At least she could pay the rent and still have a little left over. She thanked him and said she wanted to talk to him. He looked curious but didn't respond to her.

Frances blurted out, "I've noticed that you don't seem to be interested in me or the baby as of late. Can you please tell me, have your feelings for us changed? Charlie, please tell me what is going on."

He only laughed and said it was her imagination. "Of course I love you and the baby. I've just been busy working hard, and right now I have to go out and take care of important business. I don't know when I'll be home again, so don't wait up for me."

Frances still didn't know what to make of this and didn't really believe him anyway.

She kept busy the rest of the day, tidying up the baby's room and painstakingly arranging the little clothes, placing them neatly back in the drawers. When she finished it was sometime around four o'clock, and she decided to make dinner for her and her child. After they both had eaten, she bathed her daughter and put her in an adorable nightclothes outfit. Frances very much enjoyed dressing her little one, so much so that she always looked very special.

Once Patricia had gone to sleep and the kitchen was cleaned up, Frances went into the living room and turned the radio on. It was nice to listen to the soft music coming from it, and it made her forget the problems she was recently experiencing. She decided now would be a good time to go through her own drawers and tidy them up as well. She had nothing better to do that evening and didn't expect her husband to come home. Lately he hadn't been coming home at all.

When she started to straighten out the top drawer, she noticed that her engagement and wedding rings weren't in the place where she was sure she had put them. *Oh,* she thought, *Did I put them in a different place?* But she couldn't remember where else she would have put the rings. The rings meant the world to her. They were special. They were a symbol of the way things used to be, reminding her of how much in love they were. She remembered the joy and happiness she'd felt when Charlie surprised her with the rings, knowing full well that he couldn't afford them but still wanted Frances to have them. They were the perfect gift, and she loved them more than anything else he had given her.

She started to frantically look through all the drawers, even though she knew she would never have put them there. Still she was sure she would find them. Yes, she had been distracted lately, but still she couldn't imagine being so careless with her treasured gift. She silently prayed, *Please dear God, let me find the rings.* She searched everything in the bedroom: first the drawers, then the clothes in the closet, but nothing. Finally, when she couldn't think of any place else to search, she sat on the bed and looked around the room. It was a mess. Clothes were everywhere. She was sure the rings would show up, but still, she had a feeling of uneasiness about her. Frances wasn't one to cry easily, but she now could feel tears of frustration sliding down her face. *What is going on in my life? Could it get any worse?* She sat on the edge of the bed for a very long time, trying to make sense out of the situation, and still could not come up with an answer.

She rose to her feet and started to pick up her clothes one by one. *This is a heck of a way to get organized,* she thought. Still, the work before her had to get done, and she decided to do just a little at a time until she finished the chore at hand. It was well past eleven thirty, and she was exhausted. As she completed her task, she hoped Charlie would be coming home soon, so that she could question him as to whether he had seen her rings, but Charlie didn't come home again that night. As a matter of fact, he didn't come home for the next three nights, and when he finally did show up, he had a story to tell. Of course, he told her how much he loved her and that he was working hard for her and the baby. *Who was he trying to kid, the child he hardly looked at these days?* Something was terribly wrong.

"Charlie," she said, looking at him straight in the eye. "Have you seen my engagement and wedding rings?"

He replied, "Frances, I don't know what you're talking about, but if you can't find the rings now, I'm sure they'll show up. You probably just misplaced them."

Frances couldn't stand this much longer. She sat down at the kitchen table and wrote to her father, telling him she would like to visit the following week and would be bringing Patricia, but that Charlie wouldn't be with her, as he had to work. She also sent off a note to Kay, asking if they could meet later the following week. It seemed that once Charlie had had the accident, she hardly had any time to visit with Kay, or anyone else. Kay seemed very happily married, and she was glad for her.

Very early in the morning the following Tuesday, Frances packed up Patricia and a few items she would need and took the bus, first to Flushing and then another one to the Bronx. Once she arrived in the Bronx, she had to transfer to another bus, which would take her just two blocks from where her father lived. She knew she wouldn't be telling her father what was going on between her and Charlie; she just wanted to feel the comfort and security of family. For this reason she was most anxious to visit her father and Jenny.

When she finally reached her destination, her father and Jenny asked if she was not feeling well. They were concerned as she appeared very tired, looked pale, and run down. Frances made an excuse, saying traveling with the little one to the Bronx was exhausting, and she just needed to rest and catch her breath for a minute.

They were both glad to see her, and as usual Jenny had prepared a very enjoyable lunch. Frances appreciated the lunch even more than they could have possibly realized. She had very little food in the apartment and only a little bit of money left, which she was using for bus fare. At least she knew that she and the baby would be eating well today. Jenny suggested Frances take the leftovers home with her and, of course, Frances didn't object too much. She was very grateful, more grateful than they would ever dream.

While they were eating, they spoke about life in the Bronx, Jenny's family, and her father's poor health. Frances was thankful that he had Jenny to take care of him. Even though Frances didn't know her father when she was a child, and in reality he had abandoned her, still, for some unexplained reason, she had an odd sense of obligation that if he were alone, she would have to take care of him. She was grateful for Jenny's presence.

When they finished the main part of the meal, Jenny served dessert. She went all out as usual, making her homemade cheesecake. This, together with her delicious coffee, was the end to a perfect meal. It was nice to relax with them. They always enjoyed her daughter; Jenny, in particular, would make a big fuss over the little one.

While they were having a second cup of coffee, her father said he wanted to speak to her about something very special. Frances couldn't imagine what the subject might be and was very curious for him to continue.

He started, "As you know, your brother, Peter, has been living in Italy since he was a very young boy. I have been writing to him during the past few years, asking him to come home to the United States. At first he was rather reluctant, saying his life was in Europe, and also he was planning on getting engaged next year so he would rather stay where he is. However, I have been persistent and continued to write several more letters, explaining that because of my poor health, I could not visit him in Italy, but I would like for my son to return to this country to be with me. After all, this is his homeland. In his recent letter to me, he indicated he was having a change of heart and he may be coming back here in a few years, maybe within three or four years. I have written to him telling him that with the war going on, jobs are plentiful for civilians, and once the war is over, it's predicted things will become very prosperous in the United States."

Frances was listening intently to her father. She asked him, "When you write to my brother the next time, please let him know I think of him often and send my love to him. It's just a shame that I don't speak Italian, or I would write to him myself."

Her father willingly agreed to let his son know this. He continued, "You may also be interested in knowing that he was delighted to hear the news from me that you had Patricia."

It was a very pleasant afternoon, and she loved the conversation with the both of them, particularly when her father told her about her brother. She was glad she had chosen to leave the apartment and visit them; even though it was a quite a distance to travel, she felt the trip was worth it. She not only felt better, but she was certain she looked better than when she'd arrived. Now, as she glanced at the clock, it was almost three thirty, and Frances knew she had better start to head home. It was going to be a long trip back—even if she made good connections, it would still take her about two hours to reach Bayside.

Jenny must have sensed something was wrong, because not only did she give Frances the leftovers from lunch, but she also included the rest of the cheesecake, a loaf of bread, and a box of macaroni as well as a few other items from her cupboard. She never said a word about the extra items. She just packaged everything up for Frances in a heavy-duty knitted shopping bag. At the last minute, Jenny also placed some cookies and additional treats in the bag for the youngster. When Jenny got through making up the package, they all laughed at her efforts. Both her father and Jenny decided to walk with her to the bus stop to help her carry everything. Once they reached the bus stop, her father decided he would take the bus with her too, just to make sure she was able to transfer easily to the next bus. Jenny chimed in, saying that she also wanted to go with them. So all three, together with Frances's little one, took the bus to where she was going to transfer. Actually, Frances was very grateful to have their company, as well as their help. They assisted her in getting on the next bus, knowing that this would be the longest part of her journey. She kissed them both and sincerely thanked them for the wonderful afternoon.

Frances almost fell asleep on the second bus. Her child was cuddled next to her and was soundly sleeping against her breast. Frances had the bag under her feet and felt secure knowing that after this bus, she would just need to take one more, and after a short walk, she would be home. *In a little while, we'll soon be home. I wonder if Charlie will be there. I love him so much. I wish I knew what was going on. I can't understand why he is acting so different...and of course, there is still the matter of the rings, and my not being able to find them. I can't imagine what happened to them. Oh, I don't want to think about all this now; I just want to look out the window and watch the neighborhoods pass by.*

Twenty-Four

The End Is Near

Frances was glad when she finally reached the apartment. Little Patricia had woken up just as they were approaching their stop, which made it easier to carry the bag and hold on to her child's hand. When they got to their apartment door, Frances rang the bell, hoping Charlie would be home to let them in, but there was no answer. She then struggled with her handbag, searching for the key.

Once inside it was obvious to her that Charlie had not been there, as it seemed everything was just as she'd left it. She set the little one down on the rug in the living room and placed two toys next to her. She went into the kitchen and put away the items that Jenny had given to her. Frances was grateful to have the leftovers and even more so for the few extra items Jenny had placed in the bag.

Then she went into the living room and picked up Patricia from the floor. She brought her into the kitchen and gave her a small portion of the leftovers for her dinner. Frances herself was not hungry, or at least didn't have an appetite. She was lonely and depressed, wondering where her husband was. The only thing that made her happy these days was her daughter. She liked taking care of her and took great pride in keeping her looking pretty. After her daughter was fed, she prepared the bathtub for her. This was always a special time as Patricia delighted in splashing and playing in the water. Usually Frances enjoyed this part of the evening as well, but not tonight. She was distressed and didn't know where to turn next. She hadn't seen anyone in the last two weeks, because it was difficult to answer questions about her husband. Today, however, was different; she was pleased she'd decided to force herself to visit her father. As it turned out, it was probably the best thing she could have done. Even though the trip was a long one, it was good to see other people, and surprisingly neither her father nor Jenny asked too many questions.

She took the young child out of the tub. As always she loved the smell of her when she was freshly washed. Frances dried her off, put on her pajamas, and then combed her hair. She took the child into her room, hugged her ever so tightly, and kissed her cheek, telling her how much mommy loved her. She then placed her in the crib, putting her favorite toy teddy bear next to her. She looked so adorable as she snuggled up to the toy that Frances almost started to cry. She thought, *How we are going to manage if Charlie doesn't come home?*

Once her daughter was in her bed, Frances cleaned up the bathroom and then took a shower herself. When she was finished getting into her nightgown and robe, she decided to make tea and perhaps she would prepare a piece of toast with the bread that Jenny was so good to provide. She would then force herself to try to relax and maybe listen to the radio for a short while before going to bed. Frances retrieved the bread from the refrigerator and then was shocked to discover the absence of the toaster, which had always sat on the end of the kitchen cupboard.

"Now where did that go?" Frances said out loud to herself.

Up until this point, she'd probably been so preoccupied that she didn't even notice the missing toaster. Frances just shook her head. She thought Charlie had not been to the apartment while she was in the Bronx, but apparently he had, and it was now very obvious he'd helped himself to their toaster. She couldn't believe it. *What is going on with him?*

Frances felt a touch of panic within her. Her husband was no longer the man she knew or married. How could she resolve this situation, if he wasn't coming home when she was at home? She also wondered where, or better still, if her husband was really working. If not, how had he been occupying his time? It all proved too much for Frances. She was exhausted and decided she might as well just go to bed.

A Matter of Survival

"Sleep is a wonderful escape," she said out loud.

But sleep didn't come easily. Frances tossed and turned all night. Unfortunately when she finally did fall asleep, it was about five in the morning.

Frances woke up with a start. She glanced at the clock and realized it was seven thirty, but she didn't feel rested at all. Actually she felt totally worn out, knowing full well it was because of the restless night she'd spent, hoping her husband would come home. Of course, he hadn't come home. The place next to her in the bed was empty, as it usually had been for the last several months. It hurt so much to remember what life used to be like.

"I wish I knew what was going on with him. There was a time when he couldn't keep his hands off of me," she said to herself.

She smiled, thinking back to how happy he used to make her. They'd woken many mornings before their baby and made love. Sometimes even though they'd just made love the night before, he still wanted her the next day. She loved him so much that the hurt erased the smile from her face.

Frances heard her daughter waking up. She dressed quickly, putting on casual slacks with a smart striped blouse. As she looked at herself in the mirror, she was grateful she had lost all the weight from her pregnancy and still had the figure of a young woman.

She went into her child's room, fetching the little one from her crib and bringing her into the kitchen. She carried her little toy bear along with her to the breakfast table. It was always such a delight to watch her. Frances thought, *how quickly the last years have gone by. Patricia will soon be three years old, and it seems as if it was just yesterday that she'd been born.*

She prepared cereal and milk for her daughter and placed a small amount of coffee in the percolator and placed it on the stove. *Well, that's the last of the coffee,* she said to herself. She then took a slice of bread and placed it under the broiler so that she might have toast. Jenny had been kind enough to place a jar of jam in the package, and Frances liked having this with her toast and coffee. As she sat at the kitchen table with her daughter, she played with the little bear, pretending it was walking across the table toward her. She smiled as her daughter laughed with delight. *Thank goodness I have her. She is the only bit of happiness I have now,* she thought. Frances felt a frisson of fear. *How am I going to feed her, and how am I going to take care of us if I don't have a husband?*

Once they'd finished breakfast, she let the child stay in her pajamas and play in the living room. Frances washed and dried the few dishes and placed them in the kitchen cupboard. She then tidied up the kitchen table, placing the little centerpiece of artificial flowers she'd bought last year in the middle of it. She decided to dust and sweep the carpet in the living room, and then she made her bed.

Once the apartment was taken care of, she took her little girl into the bathroom and got her washed and dressed. She loved combing Patricia's hair and placing it different styles. Today she would have two long braids with ribbons tied on the ends to match her outfit. By the time she'd accomplished everything she wanted, it was almost ten o'clock, and now she was thinking about what to do for the rest of the day. She missed seeing Kay, Mrs. O'Neill, and most of all her mother-in-law, but she didn't want to be asked questions and certainly didn't want to worry Charlie's mother. She had enough to be concerned with just taking care of her family and trying to make ends meet in her own home. *No,* Frances thought, *I can't see her for a while, but maybe someday soon I hope.*

Frances decided to change her clothes and just get out of the apartment. Maybe she would push Patricia in the carriage around the neighborhood. She was just about dressed when she heard a key in the door. She was shocked to see her husband entering the apartment. She started to ask him where he had been, and he simply placed his hand in the air, indicating for her not to ask him anything. He walked right past her into their bedroom, saying he was going to take a shower and change his clothes. Even though he'd indicated he didn't want questions asked, she decided questions did, in fact, needed to be asked.

"Charlie," she questioned, "can you please tell me where you have been? Are you working? Did you take our toaster?"

He stared back at her. He said yes, he was working, but as he told her before, he couldn't tell her anything about his job. And yes, he did take the toaster, saying it needed to be repaired.

"Repaired?" Frances questioned. "I don't remember anything being wrong with it." He then replied that he tried to use it and it had almost caught fire, so he took it to a fix-it shop. Frances just shook her head, not knowing what to believe anymore.

"Charlie, aren't you even going to greet your daughter? She has been asking for her daddy."

He replied that he was too rushed and needed to shower and change his clothes.

"Wait a minute," Frances said rather sternly. "What is going on here? You're gone for days at a time, and you don't even try to give me an explanation. We hardly have any food in the house, and furthermore, it's almost the first of the month and I don't have money to pay the rent."

He then walked over to her, and placing his hand under her chin, he kissed her tenderly, saying that he would be getting paid in a few days and all would be taken care of.

"Don't you worry your pretty head about it," he stated. "Everything is going to be just fine."

His straightforwardness made her feel a little bit better. Maybe, just maybe, he was telling her the truth, but still in the back of her mind, she had those nagging doubts. Then he asked, "Have you seen my mother recently?"

Frances replied she hadn't, knowing she was busy with the children and taking care of her home.

"Maybe it's for the best. She has a hard time taking care of her brood," Charlie said. "I'm sure if she wanted to see you she would come by. I think it's best if you let her be and not bother her anyway."

Funny, Mom never acted like I was bothering her, but maybe Charlie is right. I should let her be.

Then he asked, "What are your plans for today?"

"I really don't have any. Perhaps if it's not too cold outside, I might take a walk by the stores with the carriage."

"Great idea," he replied. "It's not too cold today. It would do you good for you and Patricia to get some air. It's a beautiful October day, and the weather won't be this good soon, so you might as well get out."

Once Charlie showered and dressed, he looked as handsome as ever, and Frances was glad he was home. She then impulsively asked him, "Why don't we all go out together? We could walk to the park and put Patricia on the swings. I visited my father and Jenny yesterday, and Jenny gave me some of the leftovers. I could fix us some lunch before we go out."

"Sorry, I have important work to do today," he replied.

Frances was hurt. At first she thought he was showing her some affection, and then he turned it off as quickly as he'd turned it on.

"Are you coming home tonight?" she inquired.

"Not sure," he said with shrug of his shoulders.

"Oh Charlie, please tell me what is going on with you," Frances pleaded.

"Absolutely nothing but important work," he replied.

Now Frances was almost in tears. She didn't know what to make of him. *What was this important work? Why wasn't he supporting his family?* Frances tried one more time to bring the subject of his family up, saying that before they knew it, it would be Thanksgiving and she was sure his mother would like to have the whole family together.

"I hope whatever it is you're doing will be completed by the time Thanksgiving comes around," she said to him.

He simply replied, "Hope so." Then he kissed her on the head, saying, "Listen, Frances, I have to go now. I will try to be back in a day or two. Don't worry; everything is going to be fine," and with that, he was out the door.

All the while he was here, he never even looked at his daughter. What gives? Frances thought *yes, it was best for me to get out of the apartment.* With that in mind, she fixed a little lunch to take with them. First she put on her nice everyday cloth coat and then put a little jacket and hat on her daughter. She put Patricia, along with her little toy teddy bear and a warm blanket, in the carriage. She planned to spend the rest of the day out, and if it got colder, she would have ample covering for her child.

It was a bright and clear but somewhat crisp autumn day. Most of the trees had started to shed their leaves, and it was pleasant to hear the familiar crunch of the fallen leaves beneath the carriage and under her feet. Little Patricia seemed to be amused being outside watching the activity of the many people as they passed by. Once they got to the park, Frances took out what she had prepared for their lunch and sat on one of the benches, feeling very lonely and saddened. After they finished lunch, Frances put the little girl on a swing and then the sliding pond, which made her laugh and scream with delight. They spent quite a while at the park. Frances felt she didn't want to go home just yet, but decided instead to walk past the stores on the boulevard just to look into the shop windows. It seemed as if she'd walked for hours, but she had to admit it did her good to walk in the cool air. The fresh air was good for her child as well, since she had fallen asleep in the carriage and slept for well over an hour.

Frances realized it soon would be getting dark and she had better head home. As the afternoon started to turn into early evening, the weather also started to change and now it was getting quite windy. Frances tightened the blanket around her daughter and started to head home. As she walked, she remembered there still was a little food left over from what Jenny had given her and almost a full container of milk. She was also sure there was some canned soup in the cupboard, so they would be all right for two or three days. She was glad when she finally reached their apartment building, realizing she was drained from their outing.

She entered the apartment building and pulled the carriage, with Patricia still in it, up to the second floor. As soon as they got inside the apartment, Frances took off her coat, setting it carefully on the living room chair, and then took off the jacket and hat her daughter had been wearing. She let her child play on the living room floor, placing some of her favorite toys there. Frances went into the kitchen to prepare something to eat, which certainly didn't take long to do. She placed mats on the table and the necessary dishes. She realized they both were hungry. She poured milk for Patricia and made a cup of tea for herself. She sat there, sipping the tea and savoring its taste. It was relaxing to just sit for a few minutes. Suddenly little Patricia raised her hand and stroked her mother's face with such a sweet gesture that it almost brought tears to Frances's eyes. She smiled back at the little one and simply said, "I love you too, sweetheart."

She let Patricia leave the table and go back to her toys in the living room while she cleaned up the kitchen. When she was done, she went into the living room to turn on the radio; only this time the radio wasn't there. The radio that normally was on the table next to the couch was missing.

"Now what?" Frances said out loud. "Where has that gone to?"

She felt a sickening sensation come over her. Charlie must have come back while she was out walking Patricia and helped himself to the radio.

No wonder he encouraged me to go out with Patricia. He must have come back to the apartment after we went out.

Frances shook her head and tried to forget about her husband, which, of course, was next to impossible.

"Come, Patricia, let Mommy give you a bath, and then I will read a story before you go to bed," Frances said to her daughter.

With that they both picked up the toys on the floor and placed them in the toy box, all except her beloved teddy bear. Patricia picked up the bear and placed it in her crib. Frances could hear her talking to it, saying that after her bath, Mommy was going to read them a story. Frances smiled and thought how much she loved this little child.

When bath time was over, Frances combed out Patricia's hair, which smelled wonderfully clean. She put the little one's pajamas on her and said, "Okay, now let me clean up the bathroom a bit, and then Mommy will be right inside to read whatever story you want."

The little girl was delighted to go to her room and pick out one of her favorite books. Frances cleaned out the tub and carefully folded the towels on the rack on the back of the door. She noticed her husband's towel also hanging on the back of the door, and she took it with both hands, burying her face into it. She could smell his scent. She missed him so, so very much. She ached for his touch and his caresses and the warmth of his body next to her. Her thoughts were suddenly interrupted by her daughter calling for her to come to read her a story.

"I'll be right there," she answered as she placed Charlie's towel back on the rack. Frances quickly put the shampoo and other bath items away and turned toward her daughter's room.

"Now then, what story did you pick out?" Frances asked.

Little Patricia was smiling; it was her favorite book, one which they read over and over, and she never seemed to tire of it. After the book was finished, she placed Teddy in Patricia's arm, kissed her, and shut off the light.

"I love you, my precious daughter," she said as she closed the door.

"I love you too, Mommy."

Frances smiled. Finally, everything was taken care of for the night, and she could get undressed and get comfortable. *I will surely miss having the*

A Matter of Survival

radio tonight, so maybe I will just read. As she entered the living room, Frances picked up her coat, which she had neatly folded and left on the chair. She took it into the bedroom and opened the closet to hang it in its place, when suddenly she was horrified. Her beloved shirred beaver coat was not hanging where it belonged. Frances now became panic-stricken. She started to slide the items hanging in there one by one: first she looked through the blouses, then she went through the slacks, and then the dresses. No, her fur coat was not there. She even looked on the floor of the closet, but again, her coat was nowhere to be seen. Of course, one couldn't miss a fur coat hanging with the other garments, but she was so distraught she couldn't help herself. She just couldn't believe Charlie would take her precious coat, the coat she loved so much. Frances sat on the edge of the bed with the closet door open, put her hands to her face, and let it all out. Without realizing it, she must have cried for a very long time and finally fell asleep across the bed, never changing her clothes or folding the bedspread down.

Frances woke at about two in the morning and realized she was still in her street clothes. When she looked up and saw the closet door open, she remembered the awful truth. Her coat was gone. Charlie had returned earlier while she was out and no doubt took both their radio and her coat. *How much does he want to hurt me? What the heck is going on? Tomorrow I am going to visit his mother and tell her everything. I'll ask her if she knows anything about his shenanigans. I'm sure she will tell me.* Then Frances got up, went into the bathroom, and looked at herself in the mirror. She looked awful. Her mascara had run down her face, her eyes were red and swollen, and the color of her skin actually looked green to her. She put on her nightgown and thoroughly washed her face, taking extra care to soak her eyes with the cool water contained in the washcloth. She brushed her teeth and then brushed out her hair. At least she felt clean again. The kitchen and living room lights were still on, and as she left the bedroom, she took her robe and wrapped it around her. Frances checked on her daughter, who was sleeping soundly, and she whispered, "I'll find out what is going on. Daddy will come to his senses, and we'll be okay, I'm sure of it."

Frances double-checked the apartment door, and it was, of course, locked. She then turned off the lights and went back into the bedroom. The closet door was still open, a reminder that her coat was gone. She closed the closet door and went into the bathroom, leaving the light on in there. She just didn't want to be in the dark tonight. When Frances looked at the clock in the bedroom, she realized she had been up for about an hour. She lay down in the bed, hoping to get some sleep, but again sleep didn't come too easily. She tossed and turned most of the night, anticipating that daylight would come soon.

She must have dozed off, because the next thing she knew Patricia was at her side, shaking her arm and telling her to get up. Frances smiled at her; it was rare that her daughter would be out of bed before her. She grabbed her in one swoop, placing her in the bed next to her. The child laughed at this surprise gesture and snuggled next to her mother. All of a sudden, little Patricia asked Frances, "Where's Daddy?"

Frances was taken aback by the young child's question. She hesitated and simply decided to say that he was working.

Okay, Frances thought. *We are going to get up and get out of here as quickly as we can and visit Charlie's mother today.* Frances prepared a little breakfast for the two of them. She got the child dressed and then herself. She was more than anxious to visit with her mother-in-law.

It was another crisp, clear, and cool autumn day. Frances could feel the anticipation of winter as they walked toward her mother-in-law's house. It was only ten o'clock in the morning and Frances knew it was very early to be visiting, but she must find out what was going on with her husband.

As soon as she reached the house, she rang the bell. At first there was no answer. Frances rang it again, and finally Charlie's mother answered the door.

"Frances," she said. "How are you feeling? Do you think you should be out so soon?"

Frances didn't know what she was talking about.

"Why, Mom? Do you think I've been ill?" Frances asked.

With that Charlie's mother told Frances to come in and sit down. At first she made a fuss over her grandchild and was delighted to see the two little girls start to play with each other, spreading toys around the room.

Frances started first. "Mom, have you seen Charlie? Has he been here recently?"

A Matter of Survival

Charlie's mother looked surprised. "He had stopped by here three or four weeks ago, telling us you and Patricia had a very contagious illness and we weren't allowed to be near either of you. Then last week he stopped by again and told Pop he needed money for the doctors, and Pop gave him almost five hundred dollars. He said you still were both very sick."

Frances felt weak in the knees and couldn't believe her ears. "Mom, something is terribly, terribly wrong. We haven't been ill. Charlie has hardly been home, and what's more he has been taking things from our apartment. First my wedding rings were missing, then the toaster and the radio, and then last night I discovered my fur coat was gone. He tells me he is working for the FBI, or some other government agency, and he has hardly given me any money for over two months. I don't know what to believe anymore."

Frances was even more shocked when Charlie's mother asked if they had been getting along, because her son was a good boy and would never lie to them and if he did, there must have been a very good reason. Frances discovered her mother-in-law was in a complete state of denial. Charlie was her favorite son, and she loved him no matter what. If he and Frances weren't getting along, it must be because of an issue between them. Maybe Frances wasn't being a good wife. No one in the family had ever acted out in this way. The idea of her son not coming home to his family and being separated from his wife was something she could not possibly fathom. It was obvious that Charlie's mother could not, or did not want to, comprehend what Frances had just told her.

"Mom, you have to believe what I'm telling you is true," Frances pleaded. Still his mother seemed to be in complete denial.

"Frances, I know Charlie wouldn't make up such a story about you and his daughter. Pop gave him all our savings just to help you. I know he wouldn't lie to us." It was obvious to Frances she wasn't going to get anywhere with her mother-in-law, so she decided to leave and just go home. It was all too much for Charlie's mother to comprehend.

Frances walked the four blocks back to her apartment thinking all the while about the conversation she'd just had. She repeated the words to herself, *Pop gave Charlie all their savings, because he told them we had been very ill. Of course, Mom would never believe her son could be so deceitful as to take their savings.*

When she reached the apartment, she decided she did not want to go inside, but rather needed a change of scene. So she took her daughter's carriage upstairs and left it in the apartment. She decided it might be good to take the bus to Flushing and just walk around looking at the shops the way Kay and she used to do. *Oh Kay, I really miss you, but how can I visit with you now that I have so many problems. I can't, just can't, answer anyone's questions right now. I don't have any answers myself.*

Frances gathered a little food together, consisting of some crackers with a small amount of jelly on them, and wrapped them for her trip into Flushing. She would be able to give Patricia something for lunch when she got hungry. Frances didn't want anything for herself. She didn't have much of an appetite these days.

They waited only a few minutes at the bus stop. Once on the bus, Frances decided instead of going to Main Street, she would get off sooner and visit Mrs. O'Neill if she was home. She walked the few blocks to the O'Neill's and was glad she had made the decision to visit Mrs. O'Neill once she saw the familiar house. Frances walked up to the front door and rang the bell. After just a minute or two, Mrs. O'Neill came to the door and seemed delighted to be face to face with Frances and her daughter.

"Oh, I'm so glad to see you both, and to see you looking so well! We were so worried about you. You really gave us quite a scare."

She extended her arms out to Frances and hugged her tightly. Then she reached down to little Patricia and gave her the same welcoming hug. Frances looked at her quizzically. Before she could say anything, Mrs. O'Neill said, "You must stay and have lunch with me. We need to catch up. I haven't seen you for quite some time, and I want to hear all about your recovery."

Frances was stunned. The words sounded familiar, but she shut them out of her mind for right now. Mrs. O'Neill quickly prepared a light lunch of cold cuts and fresh bread and put water on for tea.

"You know, Frances, I miss the days when we would sit in my kitchen and have a cup of tea together. It was always such fun to have you around."

A Matter of Survival

Frances remained very quiet, grateful that Mrs. O'Neill was giving them lunch. Little did Mrs. O'Neill realize it, but this was going to be their main meal today.

Finally, Mrs. O'Neill sat down after pouring tea for them both.

"Frances, tell me, what was the problem with you and Patricia? Did the doctors ever find out exactly what it was? I know Charlie was so worried about you both."

She was going on and on, but Frances only heard her voice vaguely, as if it was coming from far in the distance.

"I know it seemed like a lot of money, but we really did want to help. Dr. O'Neill even offered to refer Charlie to some of his colleagues; however, he told us he already had the best doctors for you, but not enough money to cover their cost."

Frances felt as if she was going to faint.

"You gave Charlie money?" she asked, almost hoping the answer would be negative.

"Of course, we gave him the money. Didn't he tell you? In fact, we gave him seven hundred dollars. We took it from our children's college fund, and Charlie said he would be able to pay it back in just a few months. Frances, you were sick, weren't you?"

Frances couldn't get the words out of her throat to answer her. As hard as she tried not to, she could feel tears starting to roll down her face.

"Mrs. O'Neill, I don't know an easy way to say this, but I have hardly seen Charlie for the last few months, and moreover, we haven't been ill," Frances said, her voice cracking.

Frances could feel her throat closing and her face turning red from embarrassment. Looking at Mrs. O'Neill, it was obvious that she was shocked at what Frances was telling her, but Frances continued, saying, "One thing I will promise you is I will see that you are paid back every penny you gave him."

"I'm sure you will," Mrs. O'Neill said to Frances in a consoling tone. "I am so sorry that you have been having such a difficult time, Frances. Of course, we had no way of knowing you weren't really ill. Charlie always seemed like such a nice young man that we never suspected you were having any kind of trouble."

Frances was ready to burst into tears and instead decided to leave. She told her daughter to finish up her lunch. There wasn't much more to say at this point. Frances didn't want to make any excuses for her husband, because she herself didn't know what was going on with him. She decided not to tell Mrs. O'Neill about her coat.

Frances gathered her things, and Mrs. O'Neill gave her a little package consisting of the leftover lunch so that they would have something to eat later. Frances got up to leave, and Mrs. O'Neill put her arms around her, holding her tightly but not saying a word. Frances thanked her again as she put Patricia's coat on her. Then they just left.

Frances was feeling numb as they walked toward the bus stop. Mrs. O'Neill's words were echoing in her mind: *We gave him seven hundred dollars...*

How could he do that to these wonderful people? They had always been so good to me. I can't stand that he would hurt them so much.

Visibly shaken, somehow she managed to get home. She was exhausted and didn't know where to turn next. She let Patricia play in the living room as she usually did, and Frances just sat down on the living room couch, trying to think of what to do next. *I suppose I should tell someone in the family.* Maybe she could confide in her Uncle Tony, but then again he lived quite a distance away, and it was not easy to get to where he was in upstate New York. *I'll think about this another time,* she thought. *It's all just too much for me to think about right now.*

The next day Frances decided to take the bus into Flushing, just to get out of the house. As she walked along Main Street with her daughter, it was pleasant to look into the various store widows. She was glad she chose to do this today. While she was looking into one of the windows, someone called her name. As Frances turned around, she was surprised to see one of the girls she knew from the convent. They were just about the same age and had grown up together. Frances hadn't seen Connie in quite some time.

"Gee, Connie, it's been a long time since I last saw you. I'm glad that we happened to run into each other," Frances told her.

The woman stared at Frances and remarked what a cute little girl she had. Then she asked, "How is Charlie doing?"

Frances just replied, "Fine."

A Matter of Survival

"You know, Frances, I saw Charlie just last weekend."

"Really?" Frances asked inquisitively.

"Is everything okay with you two?" Connie asked.

"Of course it is."

Connie continued, "Well, I saw Charlie coming out of the movies with his arm around some woman. She looked quite a bit older than him, but yet they seemed to be very cozy with each other. I know he tried to ignore me, but I waved to him anyway."

"Oh no, you must be mistaken," Frances replied.

"Oh no, I'm not. I'm sure it was him. He even went out of his way to avoid talking or introducing her to me."

The woman started again, "If you ask me—"

Frances quickly interrupted and said she saw her bus approaching and didn't want to miss it.

"Good running into you," Frances said and quickly left Connie standing in the street watching Frances and her daughter head for the bus. *I can't believe what she just told me,* Frances thought, but sadly she knew she really had to believe it. *Now I can understand why Charlie never comes home anymore.*

Twenty-Five

THE PLAN

As they boarded the bus, Frances took a seat. Patricia was tired and cuddled up next to her mother. It was evident she would be asleep in a few minutes.

Frances was grateful when her daughter fell asleep, as it gave her time to think of what to do next. *I know what I will do. I will definitely visit my Uncle Tony.* He was older and seemed to be the wisest of all her uncles. Perhaps she could go next week. *He has always been so nice to me, so I will confide in him. I know how much of a disgrace it will bring to the family if I tell them my husband has left me for another woman, but I have to confide in someone.* Frances knew her uncle wouldn't be too hard on her and felt for sure he would help to give her some guidance as to where she should turn next.

When she arrived home, she decided to retrieve the mail before going into her apartment. As she opened the box, she noticed there was a letter from her uncle, Ralph. She hadn't heard from him for some time and was glad to see a letter from him as he was her favorite relative. Since they were so close in age, she felt as if he was more like a brother than an uncle.

Once inside her apartment, she got her daughter settled and sat down in the living room, anxious to read the letter. As she began, she could hardly believe what she was reading. He said he had very sad news to tell her. It seemed that Uncle Tony, while working for the railroad, was high up on a pole when a car lost control, running into the pole and knocking it

A Matter of Survival

down. He was killed instantly. Frances started to shake. Uncle Ralph went on, saying the funeral was going to be upstate in a few days and if Frances wanted to attend, she and Charlie could meet him there. After rereading the letter, the first thing she did was write a note back to Uncle Ralph, telling him it was not possible for her to attend the funeral because Charlie was away on business. She suggested that perhaps when he got back to Queens, they could get together. Uncle Ralph and his wife, Jean, had two youngsters and lived in a small apartment not too far away in Corona.

Frances realized it would now be her uncle Ralph whom she would have to tell about her husband, but she would worry about that later, maybe next week. She wrote further, saying she would like to visit him within the next two weeks after the funeral was over and would write again giving the exact date of her planned visit. Frances sealed the envelope, letting out a deep sigh. She would make sure to remember to mail it tomorrow morning. *How sad it is that Uncle Tony was killed.* She'd liked and admired him a great deal, and now all she could feel was a deep sense of sorrow and depression.

Two weeks passed, and Frances wrote again to Uncle Ralph and Aunt Jean, saying she would be coming to visit them in a few days. The trip to Corona was not a difficult one; it would take her less than an hour. First she would take the bus to Flushing and then the train to its second stop. Once off the train, it was only a short walk to their apartment.

When she and Patricia arrived at their apartment, they were welcomed by both of her relatives and greeted with warm hugs and kisses. Jean had prepared a modest lunch of spaghetti with a very inexpensive sauce she had made with only pork neck bones. Frances knew it must have been hectic for her to assemble this lunch with two children under her feet in their little apartment. Once they sat down to eat lunch, Uncle Ralph asked Frances if Charlie was away again, or was he just still working at the airport. She tried desperately not to show them how distressed she was, but she just couldn't contain herself. Right there at the table, she burst into tears. Uncle Ralph and Aunt Jean were shocked and couldn't imagine what was upsetting her to this extent. Her uncle comforted her and tried to calm her down, giving her some cool water to drink. Once Frances was able to regain her composure, she related all the events of the past months. She told them how Charlie had been taking things from their apartment as well as telling people they were ill and then taking money from them under these false pretenses and lately she'd even received letters from creditors inquiring why they hadn't been paid. She ended by including the conversation she'd had the day she ran into Connie.

Both Ralph and Jean sat there in disbelief. They had thought the world of Charlie and couldn't imagine what had gotten into him. Frances was relieved to find out Charlie had not asked her uncle for money, but then again, he knew they had nothing so she assumed this was why he didn't even bother.

Uncle Ralph at first sat there quietly, and then he spoke softly and calmly to Frances. He said that she must make future plans for her and Patricia, and when making these plans she should be sure not to include her husband. Uncle Ralph said it was obvious he was a lost cause. Now they must concentrate on getting Frances and her daughter back to some kind of normalcy. He assured her they would help her. He also suggested it might be best for Frances to try to find some kind of work so that she would be able to support her child and herself. Frances would then need someone to watch Patricia while she looked for work. He was fantastic and gave Frances all of his support.

The mood had now become very somber and depressing. Listening to this entire conversation, Jean didn't know what to say and then blurted out, "Why don't we all have another helping of bones?" Even though Frances and Ralph may have been having this serious conversation, they both had to stop and laugh hysterically at Jean.

Frances stayed with them until late afternoon, and although they didn't have much for themselves, Jean made a small package of food and a small amount of coffee for Frances to take back to her apartment.

Frances bundled up her little daughter since the weather was now getting colder. She knew it wouldn't be much longer before winter would be upon them. She hugged her uncle and his wife while thanking them over and over again for listening to her and for their advice. She left saying she would keep in touch as much as possible, and Jean asked Frances to come back to them the following week.

A Matter of Survival

Once Frances and her daughter were on the train heading back toward Flushing, Frances had a chance to think about Uncle Ralph's suggestion, which was for her to look for work. His advice was good and very sensible. She would have to make arrangements for someone to watch her young child, but who? At least Uncle Ralph's advice made her calm down and start to plan for her future. Frances started to think about what kind of work she could do. She knew she was a good worker and had received an excellent education at St. Joseph's. The war had been going on now for more than two years, and every day she would read in the newspapers that more and more women were working in defense plants. Maybe this would be a good place for her to start. She was so lost in her thoughts that she failed to realize they had reached the last stop and the conductor was telling her they would have to leave the train.

Frances took her daughter by the hand, and slowly they walked up the long staircase to the street. Fortunately, there was the bus waiting for its passengers, and they got on it. Frances knew they would arrive at their stop in about twenty-five minutes. She was anxious to get home and get settled in their apartment. There was so much to think about in planning for their future, a future that wouldn't include her husband. *How will I pay the rent? How will I care for my daughter? Will I be able to buy food?* It was almost too much to think about tonight. It was totally overwhelming.

She was exhausted as they descended the steps from the bus and started the short walk to their apartment. Little Patricia held her mother's hand. She was very quiet, almost as if she understood that her mommy had problems and it was best just to be silent and stay next to her mother. Finally they reached the apartment and climbed the stairs to the second floor. Before entering the apartment, Frances wondered if Charlie had been there today, and if so, what was missing now?

Much to her relief, everything seemed to be as she left it. She took off her daughter's coat and hat and placed her in the middle of the room with her dolls nearby. Frances took off her own coat and then emptied the bag of food Jean had given her. Frances knew they didn't have much, but still they wanted to share the little they had with her. Their kindness and generosity brought tears to her eyes.

Frances called to Patricia, saying she would have to get ready for her bath and there would be the usual story before she got into bed. When bath time was complete and little Patricia was in her pajamas, she cuddled next to her mother. Frances loved this time with her daughter. She loved her little girl so much; it was breaking her heart because the future was so uncertain, but no matter what, she promised herself to always provide for her child.

Once the little one was asleep in bed, Frances got into the shower. The warm water felt soothing on her aching body. She actually felt more relaxed than she had in a long time as she donned a fresh nightgown. She then prepared a cup of tea for herself, noting that there were only three tea bags left in the box. Once the tea was made, she took the cup to the kitchen table. She reached for a pencil and pad. Frances remembered when she was in the convent and there was a problem that she couldn't solve, she would write it down, and after a while she was writing solutions to the problem. She wrote:

Find a sitter for Patricia.
Find where to look for work.
Figure out how to get to the interview (when one is granted).
Check again to see how much money is left.

She knew full well that the rent would be due soon and there was absolutely no way of getting that much together, but at least she still had a small amount for carfare and a small—very small—amount of food left. The tea did her some good. She decided not to think about all of this anymore tonight, but she promised herself she would go back to the list again the first thing in the morning, It was hard to suppress her thoughts—problems were problems, and she needed to solve them. She lay in bed, asking herself how such a wonderful man could change so much. Whatever had happened to Charlie she wasn't quite sure, but one thing she did know was that ever since he had had that terrible accident, he'd never acted the same. Could the injury to his head have caused his odd behavior? She wasn't a doctor, but she knew he did, in fact, change since that awful night. Remembering back to the night of the accident, Charlie had absolutely refused to seek medical attention. He just wouldn't hear of it, and that was that!

She lay awake, thinking so many scrambled thoughts in her head. Then Frances remembered the woman downstairs, whose husband worked at the airport with Charlie. She may know of someone who could watch her little girl while she tried to find work. Yes, she would talk to her first thing tomorrow. With that thought Frances fell fast asleep.

Frances tossed and turned throughout the night, having the strangest dreams of some monster chasing her, and all the time she was barely in front of it. All at once she awoke and discovered it was seven thirty in the morning. Little Patricia was still sleeping, so Frances got up, put her robe on, and walked into the kitchen. There the pad rested on the table, almost as if to say, *You promised you would get back to me.*

Frances decided to put it off for a little while longer. She was thankful she had the little bit of coffee Jean had given her. As she took the canister from the cupboard, she silently thanked Jean again for her thoughtfulness. She prepared a small amount, placing it carefully in the percolator along with a small amount of water. She placed the pot on the stove and within a few minutes, could smell the coffee perking away on the burner. Once it rested, she poured herself a cup.

Placing the cup in front of her at the table, she thought, *Now back to the list.* Maybe she could get a job waiting tables, but she hated the idea of clearing off dirty plates. She would love to work in the fashion industry, and with some luck maybe she could land a job doing just that. Frances decided to get dressed, and once Patricia was fed and also dressed, she would go downstairs and talk with her neighbor about babysitting.

A little while later, Frances stood outside the door of the apartment on the first floor. She was hesitant to ring the bell but suppressed her fears and decided she must confide in this woman. After just a short time, the woman opened the door and greeted Frances with a welcoming hello and invited her in.

The two woman stood in the entrance foyer with little Patricia at her mother's side. Frances spoke first. "Martha, I was wondering if you knew of anyone who is a responsible person who could babysit my daughter. You see, things have changed, and I now find I must look for work. I can't pay much right now, but as soon as I get a job, I will definitely increase the pay."

Martha didn't seem too surprised at Frances's request and decided not to press the issue with her.

"I would be glad to watch your daughter, Frances," she said. "As a matter of fact, I was thinking of doing something like this anyway, so whenever you are ready, we could start."

Frances was relieved and very grateful. She knew this woman only casually, but she couldn't think of anyone else to ask.

"Maybe I could leave Patricia tomorrow, if that's all right with you," she asked. She said she would let Martha know a time later in the day.

The weather was turning colder. Frances and Patricia walked to the corner candy store so that she could buy a newspaper to read over the want ads. They returned home as quickly as possible, glad to be inside.

Frances let Patricia play with her dolls while she went over the classified ads. There was an ad for a "Girl Friday" in the garment district. Frances thought since she'd always loved fashion, maybe this would be the perfect opportunity to break into the business. The ad said just show up by eleven thirty the next day for an interview. Frances decided to go for the interview, and maybe, just maybe, she would get the job. She took Patricia and flew down the apartment stairs, telling Martha that she would like to leave Patricia with her tomorrow.

Everything was set. She went to her closet and decided what she was going to wear for the interview. Frances was hopeful that maybe she would get the job if she conducted herself properly and showed a keen interest in fashion.

The next day, after dropping off her daughter with Martha, she took the train into Manhattan, walking just a few blocks to the address listed in the ad. She arrived more than a half hour earlier than required and took the elevator to tenth floor. When the elevator doors opened, she entered into an office of chaos and confusion. There was a tough-looking blonde sitting at the front desk. She was chewing and cracking gum so loudly that Frances could hardly understand her. The woman told Frances to have a seat, indicating one of the nearby chairs. There were bolts of rolled fabric everywhere, and the whole place appeared to be totally disorganized to Frances. She noticed there were three other women who were apparently also there for an interview.

After about forty-five minutes, the woman indicated she was to follow her down the hall for her interview. Inside there was a fat, grubby, old

A Matter of Survival

man puffing on a cigar. He looked over his eyeglasses when he greeted her. Actually, Frances didn't like the way he was looking at her. He said he needed help in the office, and part of her duties would be to greet and take care of the buyers who came into his factory showroom. Frances asked just how she would be taking care of the buyers.

The man replied, "I just want you to be extra nice and friendly to them. They like to see a pretty girl when they visit, and I think you will do just fine. Sometimes it might be necessary for you to accompany them, err... maybe for dinner and dancing or whatever."

Frances didn't like the sound of anything he was saying to her. She started to panic. Then she abruptly stood up; she just wanted to get out of there as quickly as possible. With him still gawking at her, she thanked him and said, "I'm sorry, but the job doesn't seem to be exactly what I am looking for, but if I change my mind, I will call you."

With that Frances practically ran out the door without saying a word to the woman at the front desk. She pressed the elevator button incessantly until it finally arrived. Frances was totally exasperated. She'd spent money to come into the city, only to find the job was not what she had hoped for, but instead they were looking for a cheap woman to take care of buyers. *How dare he?* she thought.

Frances decided to walk off her anger and resentment. She found herself walking toward Times Square, even though it was quite cold and, as usual, the streets were filled with people. It seemed to her that there had to be a million people rushing all around her. Everyone seemed to be in a hurry walking to somewhere of great importance—everyone, that is, except her. She had no idea where she was going or what she was going to do next. She was exhausted, not just from the long walk up to Times Square, but also because of the frustration she'd encountered during the job interview. She found herself in front of Schrafft's Restaurant and decided to stop to rest for a few minutes over a hot cup of tea. The restaurant was very crowded, and it seemed as if all the tables were filled. The hostess greeted her, and Frances said she would like to sit at the counter. Schrafft's had a large soda fountain where ladies could sit and feel very comfortable being alone. She walked over to the counter, sat down, and ordered the tea. Schrafft's served ladies tea in pretty little teapots with paper doilies placed under the pot.

A matching cup and saucer accompanied the little pot. She sat there, letting the tea steep for a few minutes. *Now what?* she thought. What was she going to do next? She poured her tea and started to sip it slowly. The soda fountain was a pretty one, and the opposite far wall was covered with an etched mirror. The word *Schrafft's* was etched in it just in front of her. While admiring the mirror, suddenly her eyes widened in disbelief. There, in the mirror's reflection, was Charlie sitting and holding hands with a somewhat older-looking woman. The two were whispering and giggling with each other.

That did it! With all that had happened that day, she just couldn't believe her eyes. Frances decided to leave the counter and walk right over to them both—crowded restaurant or not. She was going to confront her husband.

The look on her husband's face was one of total disbelief. In a city with millions of people around, how could his wife wind up in front of him? The coincidence was almost too much, even for him. Frances stood there in front of the two obvious lovers, not caring if anyone heard her.

She ignored her husband and addressed the woman directly. "Do you know you are out with a married man, a man who has a child with practically nothing to eat? We have been wondering where he has been, and now I know he's been out with you. He is my husband, and we are very much married. What the heck is wrong with you, anyway?"

Before the woman could reply, Charlie got up out of his seat and slapped Frances so hard across the face that she fell back to the ground. He grabbed the arm of the woman and pulled her toward the entrance door.

Frances lay on the floor, stunned at what had just happened. Several people came to her aid. One man helped her to walk back to the counter where she had been sitting. Her face not only stung from her husband's brutal attack, but she could feel the stinging of the tears gliding down her face. The side of her face was now red and beginning to swell. She wasn't sure if it was her husband's attack or the embarrassment and humiliation of it that bothered her more.

The manager came over to her and offered his assistance. He was very kind and compassionate; he whispered to her that there wouldn't be a charge for the tea and she was welcome to stay to pull herself together.

A Matter of Survival

Frances just wanted to get out of the restaurant as soon as possible. Not only was she terribly embarrassed, but her heart was truly broken. She was sure once and for all she had lost her husband for good.

After a while Frances tried to collect herself, thanked the manager for his kindness, and left the restaurant. It was very cold now and snow flurries started to surround her, but she hardly noticed the changing elements as she made her way back to the train. The sadness inside her was overwhelming, and she couldn't shake it from her mind no matter what. How could a man who'd previously declared his undying love for her change so drastically? She never imagined he would strike out at her the way he did. It seemed to be one shock after another. She walked blindly as her thoughts consumed her and almost unexpectedly she found herself at the train station. She was relieved to see it. Her knees were weak, and she felt for sure she was on the verge of collapsing in the middle of the street. It took all her strength not to let her thoughts get the best of her. She made her way to her train, and at last she was on it, heading back toward Flushing.

Once on the train, Frances decided now might be a good time to visit Kay. The more she thought about her friend, the more Frances realized she would like to confide in her. When the subway reached its last stop, Frances got off and headed to the bus that would take her to Kay's apartment. It was a short ride to Kay's; Frances hoped she would find her home. Surely Kay must be wondering what had happened to her good friend, as it had been several months since they had seen each other.

Kay now lived in one of the better apartment houses in an upscale neighborhood, and once Frances reached her address, she rang the security buzzer, hoping Kay would answer. After a few short seconds, Kay answered, sounding excited that Frances had come for a visit. Kay enthusiastically greeted her friend, inviting her into her apartment. She started to speak first. "I'm so glad to see you. Since you didn't answer my letter, I assumed you were still ill."

Frances could hardly get the words out. "Ill—you thought I was ill? I never received a letter from you. Please say you didn't give Charlie money."

Kay turned as white as a sheet. "Why yes, both my mother and I gave him money because he said you and Patricia were sick. Weren't you?"

As it turned out, it was the same story. Frances didn't want to elaborate upon the terrible details. She just wanted to leave, and she did.

She ran as quickly as she could to catch another bus. She just wanted to go home. She couldn't wait to see her little girl, the one good thing that came out of her marriage. Just before reaching the apartment, Frances stopped to buy a newspaper so she could once again check the want ads.

Martha said Patricia was not a bit of trouble and she was sorry things didn't go as well as Frances had hoped, but she would be glad to help her out again if needed. Frances was grateful to have this woman so close by.

She and little Patricia walked up the stairs together. Patricia seemed very happy to now be with her mother. They entered the apartment, and Frances looked around for something for them to eat. There really wasn't much at all. She decided on a can of soup and some crackers, hoping this would satisfy her daughter. Patricia ate it without a problem.

Twenty-Six

THE START OF A NEW LIFE

After getting her daughter into bed, Frances decided to take her shower and get into some comfortable clothes, and then she would gather all her strength to once again go through the want ads. The shower felt soothing against her aching body; it felt as if all the day's troubles were going down the drain with the water. Once out of the shower, she looked in the mirror and noticed her face was still slightly red from where Charlie slapped her. She then realized that both Kay and Martha must have seen her face, but neither mentioned it, and for this she was very grateful.

She sat comfortably in the living room chair and started to comb through the ads. She noticed an ad for help at Sperry's, a defense plant just outside the city line. Since World War II was still raging on with no end in sight, Frances thought, *Why not? I could do the assembly work required and could work many extra hours, as the ad requested. It would take a bit longer time wise to reach the plant, but then again, it might be worth the effort.*

Frances asked Martha to watch Patricia again. Morning came quickly, and Frances's face didn't look quite as bad. If there was still any sign of bruising, she decided to just cover it up with makeup. Then, as arranged, Frances dropped Patricia off with Martha. She hugged her little one goodbye, and it touched Frances's heart the way her child hugged her back and kissed her softly on her cheek. With a sigh and a deep breath, she now headed for the bus. The first bus took about thirty minutes, and then it was necessary for her to transfer to another bus, taking an additional twenty minutes—almost an hour, she figured, but still she was looking forward to the interview and hearing about the job.

The plant was quite big, and as soon as she entered it, she realized it had mostly women working there. The receptionist escorted her to one of the back offices to the personnel manager. He was an older, pleasant-looking man who appeared to be nicely dressed. He extended his hand out to hers and asked her to please sit down. He described the job to Frances. It did not seem to be particularly interesting work, because it was mainly assembly-line work, but the pay was even more than Frances had expected, and for this reason she was anxious for him to offer her the job and even more anxious for the chance to accept it.

After a few minutes, he did offer the job to her and, of course, she accepted it, saying she would like to start as soon as possible. They agreed she would start the following Monday. Today was Wednesday. In a way this was great because it would give her a chance to get Patricia ready for Martha.

Monday came quickly, and Frances was anxious to start her job even though the commute would take just a few minutes short of an hour. Once inside the plant, she was escorted to her work area and introduced to her supervisor.

Her supervisor indicated she was to sit at an empty chair between two other women. The two women would show Frances what was expected of her. Introductions were made, and Frances sat between them. Her coworker on the left was Val, and to the right was Carol. Both women welcomed Frances to their little crew. Val explained to Frances that while the work was not difficult, it must be done accurately and efficiently. Frances decided right then and there she liked both women, especially Val.

After a few weeks, Frances was becoming an expert at her job, and whenever overtime was offered, she would take it. She was able to pay the rent with her salary and managed to buy some food for Patricia and her. More importantly, however, now Frances was able to accomplish one major item on her mental "to do list," and that was to have the locks changed on her apartment door and the mailbox. She couldn't bear the thought of Charlie going there when she wasn't home. Uncle Ralph had been right when he told her to make a plan for her future and not to include her husband.

She and Val started to spend their lunch break together, and Frances enjoyed her company a great deal. Frances learned that both Val's and Carol's husbands were in the service, as were so many men these days. They had assumed Frances's husband must also be in the service and when they inquired where he was, Frances replied she really didn't want to talk about it. Enough said—the women got the message.

Frances wanted all of this nonsense from her husband to stop. The other women's husbands were away fighting for their country, and Charlie was fooling around with another woman, not even giving a thought to his responsibilities as a husband and father. In her desperation, feeling both angry and hurt, she thought of a way that would force Charlie to support her and their child. Together with Patricia, she went to the local recruiting office, and after relating the hardship she was encountering to the recruiting sergeant, she suggested they should consider taking her husband in the army. The sergeant just shook his head and said nothing. Frances left with a feeling of complete despair. However, shortly afterward, she heard that Charlie was drafted into the service. Several months passed, and Frances had not heard anything regarding her husband's service status. Finally she decided to inquire with the Department of the Army only to learn he didn't last long there either. She never did get the family allotment that was given to the other servicemen's families. Finally she decided to give up on Charlie as a lost cause and try to go forward with her life on her own.

Six months passed, and Frances and Val were becoming very close friends. While Val's husband was away, she had opted to live with her mother and father, and many Sundays Val invited Frances and Patricia for Sunday dinner. Val's mother was a great Italian cook as well as a warm and welcoming woman. Val always included Patricia in the room with the grownups, and it was obvious she liked having a child in the house since she herself was childless.

On one such Sunday, Val introduced Frances to the new sophisticated practice that everyone was doing, and that was smoking cigarettes. "Today's women just have to do it."

Frances quickly found she enjoyed it immensely, especially with her coffee. Once she started smoking, she selected Viceroy cigarettes and never changed her brand. She not only felt sophisticated, but Frances actually felt they calmed her nerves.

The two women became the best of friends, and it wasn't long before Frances confided to Val the true story about her husband. Val's heart went out to Frances and her daughter, knowing full well they didn't have anyone now. One Sunday afternoon, Val asked Frances if she would like to move in with them. There was an extra bedroom, which was big enough for Frances and Patricia, and Val would love to have their company while her husband, Al, was away. This would also save Frances the high rent she was paying to keep the apartment. The women agreed that Frances would pay just a small amount each month. The idea appealed to Frances, as it would help her save regularly so that she could pay off some of the debt her husband incurred to people she loved. The best part was that Val had a car, and they could drive to work together every day. Val assured Frances she would inquire in the neighborhood for someone who could watch Frances's three-year-old daughter.

In just a little over a week, Val said she found a neighbor's teenage daughter who would be willing to babysit Patricia. Val told Frances the parents seemed to be nice people and that they would arrange for Frances to meet the young sitter. So it seemed as if after a very long time, things were starting to fall into place.

Frances decided to sell just about everything: the living room furniture, the bedroom set, and the kitchen set. *Funny, this furniture meant so much to the two of us when Charlie and I were just starting out.* Now she was getting rid of almost everything. Unfortunately, Frances discovered that used furniture was not worth nearly as much as when it was new, but still, Frances was glad to sell everything off. She kept only their clothes and a few of Patricia's favorite toys. This was going to be a fresh new start, and she was sure she was going to love living with Val and her parents.

Val helped Frances move her and Patricia's clothes into what was formerly a very large guest bedroom. For the first time in a very long time, Frances was looking forward to the future. She now had a little money in a savings account, and she would be able to add a good portion of her salary to her new bank account. She also loved the area where Val lived and appreciated having a backyard where Patricia could run and play.

Val made arrangements for Frances to meet the neighbors to whom she had spoken previously about their daughter, Marie. They lived nearby, which was very convenient for all concerned. Frances met Marie, who had recently dropped out of school at the age of sixteen and was now looking for work. After speaking with the young girl, Frances decided she seemed pleasant enough, and she offered her the job of watching her daughter. Frances gave the teenager a list of things she would like her to do for Patricia. It included taking the child outside each day for fresh air, giving her lunch, and also reading to her just before putting her down for a short nap in the afternoon. Frances told Marie they would come by each day by five o'clock to pick up Patricia on their way home from work. The girl seemed satisfied with the financial arrangements as well as the list of duties she was to perform.

It was now early spring, and the weather was extremely pleasant. She and Val and Val's family would spend many weekends in the backyard just relaxing in the peaceful surroundings. Some Sundays Val would take Frances and Patricia for a long car ride out to Long Island. They didn't have much money, but they always managed to have fun. They would stop for lunch, which usually consisted of a hot dog and a soda but always ended with each having an ice cream cone. It seemed as if the women looked forward to the ice cream more than little Patricia.

Frances hadn't come in contact with or heard from Charlie at all and was just as glad. For the first time in a very long time, Frances was beginning to feel secure with her life, knowing that she had a decent job, and the new living arrangements were working out quite well. Each day after work, Val would pull up in front of the neighbor's house, and Frances would get out of the car to get Patricia, who invariably would be waiting by the door. She was always excited to see her mother and squealed with delight as soon as she saw the car pull up next to the curb. As soon as her mother exited the car, she would come running down the walkway to her, hugging her arms around Frances's legs. Val and Frances always had big laugh at little Patricia's enthusiasm. Once she was inside the car, she always presented Val with a big kiss and hug as well.

One day after about six weeks of this routine, Val and Frances pulled up in front of the familiar house. Frances exited the car, only this time little Patricia was not at the door, and the entrance seemed unusually quiet. Frances turned to Val with a questioning look and continued to walk up to the door, but somehow she had a feeling something was definitely wrong. Fright started to fill up inside her. Whether it was intuition or something else, Frances felt her knees go weak.

"Marie," Frances called as she opened the unlocked door.

There was no response to her call. She called again as a feeling of real fear came over her.

"Marie, are you here?"

Still there was no answer. Frances ran into the living room, through the small dining room, and then into the kitchen. She looked out into the small backyard, and still no response. Frances couldn't imagine where they were. She walked swiftly to the other end of the house toward the bedrooms. She suddenly stopped, horrified at the view before her.

Her little child was lying on the bed, awake but silent. She was covered with black-and-blue marks. It was obvious she had been severely beaten. Frances went immediately over to her child and held her close to her. The child never said a word to her mother. Frances's heart broke at the sight of her.

All at once Val appeared at the bedroom doorway. She too was horrified at the sight before them. Val went into the bathroom to retrieve a washcloth and ran cold water over the cloth. She brought it into the bedroom, placing it gently on the child's bruises and dabbing it in so many places that it made her feel sick to her stomach. The two women barely said anything to each other. Tears started to run down Frances's face, but she couldn't find her voice to speak.

Val noticed a wooden toilet brush that had apparently been thrown on the floor next to the large metal bed. *Odd,* she thought. *Why would that be there...Oh please, God, don't let me even think she hit this little child with that thing.*

Frances was clinging onto her daughter, holding her with tears now streaming down her face. Finally, Val spoke.

"Frances, let's get out of here right now."

A Matter of Survival

She repeated the words again. "Let's get out of here."

With that, Frances carefully carried her three-year-old daughter out the front door and kept her on her lap as she entered the passenger side of the car. It was just two short blocks to Val's house, but to Frances, the ride seemed to take much longer than it normally did.

Val's parents were dismayed at the sight before them. Val indicated to them to please not ask questions just yet. Frances and Val took the little girl into the bedroom. Frances started to undress her, relieved to see that apparently no bones appeared to be broken, but there were so many bruises all over the little child's body, it sickened her.

Val drew a bath for Patricia. Once the bath was over, Frances got Patricia into her pajamas, and Val's mother prepared a light dinner for the little child. After Patricia ate, Frances gently asked her daughter to please tell them what had happened to her and what had happened to Marie. Now the child started to cry, saying that there was a boy in the house with Marie. Marie had given her some crackers. After eating the crackers, Marie wanted her to go to sleep, but she wasn't tired and didn't want to sleep. It seemed to Frances and Val that Marie wanted to be alone with the young man who was visiting her.

"Mommy, Marie pulled me first into the bathroom and then pulled me into the bedroom and started to hit me with a brush that was in the bathroom. I kept asking her to please stop hitting me, but she kept on doing it. I tried to go to sleep, but I wasn't tired."

Now the child was sobbing. Frances held her close to her, stroking her head and gently telling her Mommy was here and she wouldn't be staying with Marie again. Little Patricia started to close her eyes. It was obvious she was going to drift off to sleep.

Once she was asleep, Frances and Val went into the kitchen with Val's parents. Frances was visibly shaken and couldn't stop crying. A flood of horrific memories came back to her as she recalled the abuse she'd received years ago from her own mother and the physical pain and mental anguish she had suffered. Now the child she loved so much had also undergone dreadful abuse. She kept asking herself, *how could this happen to the child I always protected?* Val was not only upset, but furious that something like this could happen to this child.

"Frances, let's go over to that house and try to find out what happened today."

Val's mother said she would keep an eye on Patricia, and Val and Frances went back to the neighbors' house. The parents were home, but obviously Marie was not. The parents claimed they knew nothing of the story that Frances and Val related to them. They acted as if the women were exaggerating the events. They insisted their teenage daughter was a lovely girl and would not commit an act of such violence. They got absolutely nowhere with those people. Val told them she was going to contact the police and have them question their daughter. The girl's mother angrily replied, saying she would tell the police it was Frances who probably had done this, because her husband had left her and she took it out on her child, and now she was trying to blame Marie. The parents became very defensive and shouted at them to leave immediately.

Frances and Val felt they had no choice but to leave their house. As soon as they returned home, Frances, shaking like a leaf, immediately ran into the bathroom and started to violently throw up. *How could these things happen to me? Is life really supposed to be this hard? If it wasn't for my daughter, I would just give up and end it all. It's all seems to be too much for me—the most precious person in my life had been terribly beaten, and now it's not only me who is horrendously hurting, but my child as well.*

Val tried to speak with Frances, but Frances just couldn't stop crying. She couldn't bring herself to go back to work and leave her young child. It seemed as if Frances cried for days on end, and to make matters worse, her little girl was stuttering with almost every word she said. Frances just didn't know where to turn next.

Several days passed, and Frances and her daughter shared each waking moment together. While Frances was sitting in the living room, watching her daughter play with her toys, there appeared to be someone at the front door. Frances couldn't imagine who would be ringing the bell in the middle of the day. As she answered the door, she was shocked at who stood before her. It was her mother-in-law, Charlie's mother.

"Oh Mom, I'm so surprised to see you. Please do come in," Frances requested.

A Matter of Survival

Charlie's mother had her two youngest children with her. The children immediately seemed to bond with Patricia and kept each other occupied in the center of the room.

Charlie's mother spoke first.

"Frances, I heard what happened to Patricia, and I want to offer my help. I know when we last spoke I defended my son without hesitation, but I know I was wrong. Please, Frances, please let me take care of Patricia for you. You can go to work knowing she is in good hands. I promise I will take good care of her and love her as if she was one of my own. The children will be together, and I'm sure it will be good for your daughter. You can go to work and take her back with you every night if you like."

"Mom, how did you know? Who told you?"

"It really doesn't matter, but what does matter is Patricia will be in a safe home, a home where you will not have to worry." The older woman continued, "Frances, why don't you take a few days and go away someplace not too far from here. Go someplace where you can rest and sort out your thoughts. Then you can decide what to do next."

The offer was a good one, but what if Charlie should appear and want to take his daughter? Mom promised her she would never let him take Patricia. Besides, his mother hadn't seen him for months and also had no idea of his whereabouts. Frances sat silently, her eyes still swollen and red, and thought about what this woman was saying. It was, in fact, the best and only offer she had received. It sounded as if it would be a solution to her problem. Charlie's mother made it very clear that she would not take any money from Frances for the care of her granddaughter. It was her way of trying to make up for some of the hurt her son had caused.

No matter what Frances had been through, she realized she still loved and trusted Charlie's mother very much. Frances invited the woman into the kitchen for a warm cup of tea while the children played nearby. As they sat together at the kitchen table, Charlie's mother placed her hand upon Frances's.

"Frances, I really want to help you. Charlie has also broken my heart too."

The two women sipped the tea at first in silence, but then Frances decided to take the offer and let Patricia stay with her mother-in-law.

"Suppose I bring her to you tomorrow, and we can talk some more?"

When Charlie's mother got up to leave, Frances also rose and put her arms around this woman and thanked her from the bottom of her heart.

"Mom, thank you. I didn't know what else to do or where to turn."

The older woman simply smiled and left with her own children.

Frances did as her mother-in-law suggested. She took a few days and went alone to Atlantic City. She didn't want to spend the little money she'd managed to save on a trip, but it was just what she needed. Frances sat in the sun, read, and tried to sort out her thoughts. She stayed for six days, and this time away, if it did nothing else, did help settle her nerves.

Twenty-Seven

A New Start Again

While she sat on the beach watching the ocean, she thought, *Now for the next plan, but where and how do I start again?*

Frances knew she could continue to live at Val's parents' house, and when she returned, she would also return to work. Val had told the boss a little bit of Frances's problems, and apparently the factory had approved a short-term leave for her.

No matter what, she must see Patricia every night even though she knew that it would be logistically very difficult for her. She and Val typically drove to work and returned home together. Unfortunately, this would now have to change, but if it meant seeing her daughter, it would be worth the extra effort. Perhaps she could drive with Val in the mornings and go back to taking the buses, first to visit her child and then later to go back to Val's house. It would be a lot of commuting, but there didn't seem to be a choice. She had to see her daughter nightly! And she would still have her on the weekends. That meant on Fridays they would drive to her mother-in-law's to pick up Patricia for the weekend.

After five days of rest, Frances started to feel better and was now looking forward to going back to Val's and even more looking forward to seeing her little girl again. She went back to her hotel room, took a shower, and put on a casual dress, deciding to go to dinner in the hotel's dining room.

When Frances arrived in the dining room, she realized she had hardly eaten anything since she arrived five days ago. It seemed as if she had been existing only on coffee and toast, but, finally, tonight she felt like eating. She sat by an open window where there was a soft summer breeze and one could see the ocean's waves pounding the sand. It had been a pleasant visit to the ocean, and now she was glad she made the trip even if the circumstances of her going were not the best. Yes, she needed the rest. She realized otherwise she might really have "lost it." Now she could prepare herself for a new start once again.

The waitress came over to Frances. She decided on a small bowl of soup, a cheese sandwich, and, of course, coffee, lately always coffee. Once Frances started to eat, she didn't stop until she finished every bit of food that was put before her. She was actually surprised at just how hungry she really was.

After dinner she went to the front desk and told the clerk on duty she would be checking out of the hotel in the morning and wanted to make arrangements for getting the bus back to New York. She found there was a bus leaving at ten in the morning and would arrive in the city at around one thirty in the afternoon. The timing was perfect. She would get into the city and take a train to Queens to visit her daughter and mother-in-law. She would probably see her daughter by three or three thirty at the very latest. Frances was now filled with the anticipation of seeing her little girl.

After what seemed like an eternity of traveling from Atlantic City, Frances was now walking toward her mother-in-law's house. She could hardly wait to see her little girl. As she rang the bell, she could hear the sounds of the little girls laughing and playing together. When Patricia realized her mother was at the door, she stopped what she was doing and ran to greet her.

"Mommy, Mommy, I missed you so much!"

With that she wrapped her arms around her mother's legs and held onto her tightly for fear of being separated again. Frances bent down and kissed the little child, holding her so closely that she could feel the tears flowing down her own cheeks.

Her mother-in-law stood back, taking in the scene of how much mother and child had missed each other, even though it was just a few days of

A Matter of Survival

separation. Mom invited Frances to come into the living room with her where the two women could sit and chat a little bit. The older woman related how well the two little girls had gotten along; they seemed to be constant companions for each other. Little Patricia stuck by her mother like glue and refused to leave her side, even though her little playmate kept asking her to come and play in the next room. Frances decided since today was Thursday and she was not due back at work until the following Monday, she would take her daughter home to Val's with her for the weekend and return on Sunday evening to leave her daughter again with her mother-in-law. Little Patricia was excited to be leaving with her mommy and kissed her grandma and her playmate good-bye.

Once they got on the bus heading toward Val's house, Frances explained to the somewhat confused child that she was going to stay with Mommy for only a few days, and then she would go back to her grandmother's. Little Patricia seemed very resistant to the idea of going back to live at Grandma's without her mother. This brought further tears to Frances's eyes, and to make matters even worse, Frances now noticed her daughter was constantly stuttering and could no longer seem to speak normally as she had before being beaten by that dreadful babysitter. *Oh dear God, How is all this going to work out? Now I have no husband and a child who is showing obvious signs of stress, but at least I still have a job and I'm able to support us.* Frances, lost in her thoughts, suddenly realized they were approaching their stop. She signaled to the driver they were getting off. Frances took her child's hand in hers, and they exited the bus. Just two short blocks and she would be at Val's house. It was now nearing six thirty; Val probably would have just arrived home about an hour ago. Frances approached the front door and rang the bell, anxious to get inside and settle down after traveling all day. The day's traveling had really gotten to her. She was exhausted, but happy to have her daughter with her even for just a few days.

The weekend went very quickly, and now it was Sunday evening. It was time to take her little girl back to Grandma's. As they traveled on the bus, Frances could feel the sorrow within her. She wanted to keep her daughter with her, but she knew that was not possible. There was no other choice to be made. It was what it was.

Once they reached Mom's, she got her little girl ready for bed, read her a story, kissed her good night, and said good-bye, adding that she would come back tomorrow night. It meant when she left the house, she would have to walk five blocks, wait for the bus to Flushing, and then wait for another bus to transfer to, and then walk two more blocks to Val's house. Yes, it was a long night, but it was worth it. She just wished it didn't hurt so much.

This routine continued for several months. Frances would go to work with Val but then commute to her mother-in-law's house to tend to her daughter's needs each night. Finally, one Friday night when Frances was preparing to take Patricia to Val's for the weekend, her mother-in-law suggested to her that she didn't need to come every day as she had been doing.

"Frances, I can take care of Patricia for you during the week, and you can take her on the weekends. I know how hard it is for you now. You are exhausted. Patricia will be fine here during the week. Frances, I would like to see you get your own little place; no matter how small it may be, it will be yours. It will be a place you can take Patricia home to. It will be your home—you will make it a home."

"Mom," Frances replied, "Let me think about all that you have suggested. Being able to pay rent might be difficult for me, if almost impossible, and as far as only seeing Patricia on the weekends, I don't want my daughter to think I've abandoned her also."

The older woman listened to her reluctance and just told her to think about it. Frances knew her mother-in-law to be a very wise woman. Then she continued, "Frances, Patricia will be fine. You'll see after a few weeks, she will fall into the routine of going home with you on the weekends, and she will probably even look forward to it. Think about it. You should really have a place of your own. I will protect Patricia as if she was one of my own. Please don't worry about her. She will be in good hands."

All the way back on the bus to Val's, Frances considered her mother-in-law's suggestion. Maybe she could just take Patricia for the weekends, and the idea of having her own place certainly was appealing, but could she

A Matter of Survival

afford it? The idea was scary. However, she promised herself she'd look into the possibility and make a realistic budget, calculating all the expenses.

She got to Val's later than usual, greeted Val and her parents briefly, and decided to take shower and call it a night. Frances found that once in bed, it was impossible to sleep. She had so much on her mind. Her mother-in-law's suggestion was a good one, and if Patricia seemed to adjust to the new routine, then she would try it. The very next day Frances got a local newspaper and found there were several ads for apartments. Furnished apartments were too expensive, but maybe, just maybe, she could afford a small unfurnished apartment. She didn't mention anything to Val just yet, but rather decided to pursue one or two of the ads listed in the paper. The first ad was a good location with a bus stop on the corner. There was also a public park at the end of the block, and she thought it would be nice to take her daughter there. The rent was seventy dollars a month for two and a half rooms. Frances wasn't sure if she could handle this amount of rent, but decided to look at it anyway. She went to look at the apartment that very afternoon.

She reached the address of the superintendent's apartment listed in the ad and rang the bell. The door was answered by a lovely older woman, and once she found out why Frances was there, she called to an older man who seemed rather tired, but very nice. He said he had only one apartment vacant and was willing to show it to her right then and there.

They walked to the apartment's entrance. The unit was on the second floor. There was a long foyer, a large living room, a full kitchen, and a dressing area adjacent to the bathroom. Frances liked it immediately and decided if she was ever going to have a place of her own, this would be it. She turned to the man and told him the truth: she did like the apartment, but she was afraid she might not be able to pay the rent on the first of each month and asked him if he would take half on the first and the second half on the fifteenth. He thought about it for a little bit, and then answered affirmatively. Frances couldn't believe it—he actually said yes to her proposal. It was now the twentieth of the month, and he said he would hold the apartment for her until the first of the following month. He smiled and said not to worry about a deposit for now—he would just hold it for her. Years later Frances realized he must have sensed she was a woman who was desperate for help, and since he was obligated to turn all the rents into his management company the first week every month, he must have been putting in her second half for her. Somehow he felt she was going to be a good tenant and went by his instincts to help this young woman.

Frances was excited with the prospect of having her own place, a place that she and her daughter would now have as theirs. She couldn't wait to tell her mother-in-law and, of course, Val. She knew her mother-in-law would be pleased that she took her advice. Val was very understanding, saying the war would eventually be over and her beloved husband would be returning to her. Frances would sooner or later have to find a place anyway, and now was as good a time as any. The two friends would only be a short bus ride away from each other.

Val had a spare couch and a small kitchen set that was just being stored in the garage and offered to give it to her. Frances thought this was a very generous gesture and felt this was going to be a great new start. Val got one of the young men in the neighborhood to help move the small pieces of furniture to Frances's new apartment. Frances loved her little place, even though it was almost empty. Mom was right; it was fantastic to have her own place at last.

She searched the "for sale" signs on the company bulletin board and found little odd bits of furniture that she could use, and it wasn't long before she managed to turn her little place into a home. Even though she was on a tight budget, she managed to be very selective and only bought quality items. She also took great pleasure in keeping her apartment very clean. She felt proud of what she had accomplished on her own!

It didn't take long for the new routine to settle in. On the weekends, she brought Patricia to their little apartment. She would save as much as possible all week so they would be able to do something special on most Sundays. Usually it would involve taking in a movie and eating out. Sometimes Frances would even manage for them to go into the city for a really special treat. The hardest part was bringing her daughter to her mother-in-law on Sunday nights and taking the return trip back to the empty apartment. When she got home, she felt the absence of her daughter and missed her so very much. It was at times like this when she wondered how

A Matter of Survival

Charlie could leave without caring—maybe not so much about her, but to totally abandon his daughter was something she couldn't comprehend. This she would never understand. It was astonishing how much he had changed from those wonderful early days. Again she had to suppress the hurt.

Enough, Frances said to herself, *I'm not going to let myself get upset all over again thinking of him.* Once and for all, she promised herself not to look back and just look forward to whatever the future would bring. Now, at last, she was able to make a life for herself and her daughter, and this was what she was going to concentrate on from now on.

Twenty-Eight

A Time to Celebrate

More than two years passed, and now Frances had settled into her new life, which mainly consisted of working and looking forward to seeing her daughter on weekends. She made sure the days that they were to spend together were extra special for the both of them. Frances had no desire to see anyone else on the days that she was scheduled to have time with her daughter. This was their time together. Her little daughter also seemed to look forward to seeing her mother and showed her excitement when Mommy came for her.

During the week Frances worked long, hard hours at the defense plant and took advantage of the many hours of overtime that were offered. She tried, but not always successfully, to pay back some of the money Charlie had taken from so many people. Her in-laws absolutely refused to take any money from her. They were just as heartbroken over their son as she was.

The year was now 1945, and she celebrated little Patricia's fifth birthday in their small apartment. Frances had made a cake just for Patricia, and her daughter was delighted to share this happy occasion with her mother. Although money was tight, Frances managed to buy a doll and a little coach carriage for her daughter, which Patricia clearly loved. It was very special for them both!

The summer arrived, and Frances was now entitled to a week's paid vacation. Her vacation commenced in the middle of August, and it seemed

A Matter of Survival

to be a marvelous opportunity to take Patricia home to the apartment for a week. Frances was excited about planning many different activities with her daughter. On Sunday they went to the Bronx to visit with her father and Jenny. Frances wanted Patricia to know her other grandfather as well as the one she lived with. Her father always seemed pleased to see them. Jenny was just as wonderful and became a good friend to Frances. On this particular visit, Frances's father told her he'd been keeping in touch with her brother for the past year and continued to ask him to return to the United States. As far as he knew, Peter would be returning within the next year or maybe two.

Frances could hardly believe her ears. Her brother was returning to New York. She hadn't seen him since she was six years old. A flashback came to her mind immediately of that horrible Easter Sunday. She recalled her father grabbing her brother's arm and pulling him out the window and climbing down the fire escape. Frances thought back to how she missed him and of the lonely days living in the convent, wondering what had happened to her brother. She suddenly trembled, thinking of these unhappy memories.

Her father was still talking. "Frances, Frances, are you all right? Frances, are you listening to me?"

Frances replied, "Oh, yes."

There was a deafening silence between the two. Finally, Frances asked, "How is he? What does he do? Did he ever get married?"

Her father replied he was fine, having grown up with his uncle in Italy. He had graduated from the university in Naples after studying engineering. He also told Frances her brother was planning to get married the following year, and after the marriage, they would further discuss coming to the United States. Frances's father explained to his daughter that he felt, since he was getting older, he needed his son, a son that could look out for him in his old age.

Frances was horrified that her father was still, after all these years, only thinking of himself and never seemed to consider for even a second what he had done to the lives of his children. As a matter of fact, he never asked Frances too much about her childhood or what her life was like after she left the children's home. Frances assumed he really didn't care much about her, and her assumption was correct.

After this conversation, the rest of the day went fairly well as Frances purposely avoided the subject of her brother. Jenny was in the kitchen putting the finishing touches on the lunch she prepared. As they ate, the conversation was pleasant enough, still somewhat strained between her and her father, but he didn't even seem to be aware of it.

It occurred to Frances that Jenny knew very little of her father's past life. She thought Frances grew up living with her mother, and Frank, because of his illness, asked relatives in Italy to look after Peter. Jenny never questioned his relationship with his children and did not press the issue about them.

It was now approaching early evening, and Frances decided it was best to start to head back home to her apartment with her daughter.

They made better time than usual and she made it back to Flushing in just a little over an hour. Once in their apartment, she prepared the tub for Patricia and let her have some play time in it. When bath time was over, she read her a story and tucked her in to sleep.

Frances went into the kitchen and prepared water for tea. She just sat there, thinking of the conversation she had earlier with her father. Yes, she would be most anxious to see her brother again and hoped he would remember her. No matter what had transpired in the past, the bond they held would always be special to her. She wondered if he too still felt the connection they had as children.

Frances was very tired and decided to go to bed. The day's outing had exhausted her, or to be more correct, the conversation with her father had exhausted her! She got into the pullout couch with her daughter and cuddled up next to her. Frances decided the next two days would be leisurely spent; maybe they would visit the park after breakfast and do some needed grocery shopping. It would be nice to just spend the days together, not doing anything special. Besides, she had planned to take Patricia into the city on Wednesday for a movie and dinner. This would be their most special day together. Frances loved the city and it was obvious her daughter liked it as much as she did. It was always exciting for them both.

Monday and Tuesday were as Frances had hoped for—two days of leisure. Each day she made breakfast, did the dishes, and straightened up the living room. She thought, *It may be small, but it's ours.*

A Matter of Survival

On Monday she dressed her daughter in a pretty pink dress and fixed her hair in neat braids. Frances added matching ribbons tied into perfect bows at the end of each braid. She also dressed herself in a lovely green-and-white casual summer dress. As they walked to the park, the two females looked very pretty together. They spent over two hours in the park. It was a warm August day, and the sun felt good. Patricia was having a great time playing with her doll, talking to it as if the doll understood each and every word she said.

After the park Frances and her daughter walked to the local store to purchase something to prepare for dinner. Without her realizing it, several shopkeepers gave admiring glances at the pretty lady with the pretty daughter. Frances decided to stop at the local candy store to buy ice cream cones for the two of them, but as usual Patricia only ate a small portion of her cone and then wanted her mother to finish the rest of it. There was Frances, trying to juggle groceries and two ice cream cones at the same time. She laughed out loud, saying to her daughter, "You are the only child I know of who doesn't like ice cream." This was the usual scenario each time she bought ice cream for her daughter, but she continued to buy it just the same—she was supposed to like it!

It felt good to arrive at the apartment. It looked bright and pretty. *Mom was right to talk me into getting a place of my own.* It was so good to bring Patricia to their home. The only thing that still was a concern to Frances was that her daughter was still stuttering, sometimes constantly. She tried not to make an issue of it, hoping it would eventually stop and go away. Frances had consulted a doctor about it, but the doctor would only say perhaps someday it would disappear and she should just try to give her child as much love and guidance as she possibly could. The love and guidance must have worked, because together with speech classes in the public school system, the stuttering did eventually stop, although not completely until her daughter was almost thirteen years old.

Tuesday was another relaxing day of mother and daughter just appreciating each other's company. Wednesday came, and it was a perfect day to travel into New York. Frances planned to see a stage show, to be followed by a movie.

Once they arrived in the city, the two walked hand in hand, each wearing pretty little white gloves. They stopped to share a quick sandwich before arriving at the theatre. Frances planned to stop at a nice restaurant later, where they would have dinner before heading back to Flushing on the railroad.

The stage show was wonderfully entertaining, and the movie was very enjoyable. It was almost over when a big commotion was heard coming from outside the theatre. People started to laugh and scream and began pouring out of the theatre, heading from the back rows first, into the streets of Times Square. When Frances and Patricia finally got out into the street, she too discovered the reason. There, zipping around the building towering over Times Square was the announcement that the war was finally over. It seemed as if everyone inside of the buildings poured into the street. In a matter of minutes, Times Square resembled New Year's Eve. Frances could never stand crowds. She could barely hold onto her daughter's hand in the melee. Her only thought was to get out of the street as soon as possible. She tried to head toward the subway station across the street, but it was almost impossible to get through the crowd of people who were laughing and cheering. There was so much jubilation and celebration that Frances was dreadfully afraid she might lose her daughter in the massive crowd. She kept telling her child to hold onto her hand tightly. She just kept saying over and over, "Please let me through," and as if by some miracle, people actually did let her through. When she'd almost reached the subway entrance, a young sailor reached out, stopping her, and said, "It's okay, Mom. Your hubby will be coming home soon!"

Little did he know her husband would never be coming home. She gave him a slight smile and continued toward the downward stairs. As she entered the train and sat down, she realized her heart was racing furiously. She was glad to have left the crowds behind. There was hardly anyone on the train, and she felt greatly relieved. She needed to just be alone with her daughter and make her way back to Flushing to the safe haven of their little apartment.

Once she reached Flushing, again, many people were cheering in the streets. However, it was nowhere near the chaotic scene she had left in New

York. It was good to breathe the fresh air again. Frances decided she and her daughter would still eat out today and have their own private celebration.

The rest of the week passed all too quickly, and soon it was Sunday. Frances knew she would have to take Patricia back to her grandmother. She felt her heart was going to break, but she didn't want to upset her child, so she tried to sound as positive as possible.

Finally they were back at her in-laws' home. After greeting her mother-in-law, she took Patricia upstairs to get her ready for bed. She read her a story and told her to look forward to the following week, when Mommy would return again. She kissed her and held her tight, telling her how much she loved her. After she was satisfied that her daughter was sleeping, Frances returned downstairs, said her good-byes, and started the journey back to her apartment. She always left with a heavy heart. She thought of the man she had married, asking the same questions to herself. *How could he leave without caring for his child? If he didn't love me anymore, he had to have some love for his daughter, didn't he? I suppose not.* It was just too much for her to understand.

What Frances didn't know was that her child woke up after she left, looking for Mommy, and, of course, Mommy wasn't there anymore. Little Patricia cried and cried for her mother, but to no avail. She cried herself to sleep many Sunday nights.

Twenty-Nine

MAKING CHANGES

The war was over; that was true. Frances now found herself in a new and even more frightening situation. She was told she was going to be laid off at the defense plant in two weeks. Her supervisor informed her they were going to give her a few weeks' pay as a severance package. Even if she spent sparingly, she knew this money was only going to last a short time, so the next step was to look for another job as quickly as possible.

Frances decided to try applying at Abramson's, the local department store in Flushing. Taking a chance, she groomed herself to look her very best and went apprehensively to their personnel department. She was sure she was going to be turned away, but much to her surprise, she was granted an interview. After a rather extensive interview, in what was even more of a surprise, she received a job offer to work in the ladies' dress department, starting the following week. At least this would give her time to give notice at the defense plant.

Frances was happy as she left the store. She realized the salary at the department store was not going to be as much as she made at the defense plant, but still it would be enough for now, and there were promises of periodic increases based on her performance. The next day she informed her supervisor she would be leaving almost immediately. Luckily, she still received her severance pay, which was a relief.

A Matter of Survival

Frances was eager to start her new job, and when Monday came she got up extra early, wanting to make sure she would get to work on time. It was a nice day so she decided to walk the ten blocks or so to the store. The walk only took about twenty minutes, and she was happy to have saved the bus fare.

The days flew by, and she learned very quickly everything that was expected of her. Much to her delight, she discovered she loved working in retailing, particularly in women's fashions, and within just a few months, Frances gained a following of wealthy women who loved to have her take care of their fashion needs. It appeared she had a natural knack for choosing the right dress for the right woman. It wasn't too long before she made departmental assistant. Frances was happy working for the store, and, moreover, she made friends with a number of female coworkers. There was one coworker Frances bonded with almost immediately. Her name was Florence, and she worked in women's accessories. It wasn't long before the two women became the best of friends.

Florence also lived in Flushing, and the women would often eat dinner together at an inexpensive local restaurant. There were other times when Florence would visit Frances at her apartment, and Frances would prepare dinner for them both. Florence was an attractive blonde who wore the best clothes and always looked stunning. She apparently grew up in a well-to-do family and still lived at home with her parents. Currently she was dating an attorney, although future plans with him were a bit vague. She apparently liked visiting Frances's little apartment as it gave her a sense of freedom from her parents.

One of the things Frances liked best about Florence was that she respected her privacy. Florence knew Frances had a young daughter who only lived with her on the weekends. Still she never pried or asked questions regarding the circumstances of her failed marriage or what caused her to be separated from her husband. Florence felt if Frances wanted to confide in her she would, but, of course, she didn't, and that was okay too.

After her recent promotion, Frances saved for almost two years and was able to purchase a new sleeper couch and chair for her little apartment. The couch and chair had a pretty floral print and went nicely with the coffee table Val's mother had given her when she first moved in. She was still able to keep the little couch she had been using, placing it on the opposite wall, and together with the new furniture it made the room appear to be a much cozier arrangement in the rather large room. She also managed to purchase pretty sheer crisscross curtains and hung them carefully on the windows. Frances took pride in the pleasant setting she had created and enjoyed it immensely.

With her additional income she also was now able to order a telephone of her own, as so many people were doing in 1947. All at once, or so it seemed, everyone was getting a telephone installed: first her mother-in-law, then her father and Jenny, and then her good friend Val, to name just a few. Prior to having a telephone, she would correspond with her father, her friends, and even her mother-in-law through letters. Now all she had to do was pick up the telephone and dial a number. It was an exciting time to have this indulgence, even though when the telephone was installed, she had what was known as a "party line." A party line meant the telephone line was not exclusively hers, and she would have to share it with several unknown strangers. Apparently this was not uncommon; more and more people were having telephones installed in their homes, and almost everyone started out with a party line.

Frances felt that even if she was not completely happy, she was satisfied that she was making a go of her life. She had put the heartbreak of the past behind her. The only thing that still bothered her was when she had to leave her daughter every Sunday night and go home alone.

Frances had been living in her little apartment for almost two and half years, and she remembered how terrified she was in the beginning to get a place of her own. Now she loved having it and kept it as neat as a pin. Every Saturday, she would spend a good portion of the morning cleaning since it gave her a feeling of satisfaction to see everything shine. She'd never thought much about her attitude toward cleanliness, assuming it was because she had been raised in the convent where everything was perfect, and this was just the way it was supposed to be. The apartment obviously reflected her efforts. Even her little daughter would pitch in and help her mother as best she could. Frances would smile at her young child and think of how happy she was just to have her.

A Matter of Survival

She often thought if it wasn't for her mother-in-law's advice and encouragement, not to mention her offer to care for her child, she would never have had the nerve to get a place of her own, but here she was, in her own little apartment, a place she could bring her daughter home to, and it looked prettier than ever.

Things were looking up.

Thirty

WE'RE LOOKING FOR YOUR HUSBAND

One day in late October, while Florence and Frances were having lunch together, Florence mentioned an employment ad she had read in the *New York Times*. Macy's in the city was starting to interview for help for their busy Christmas season. The offered salary and eventual benefits seemed to be much better than what Frances was presently making. She read the ad and then read it again, thinking about the possibility of changing jobs. After all, she had more than three years of retail experience and felt confident enough to go for an interview. It was a big decision as she knew it was only a seasonal job, but the ad did state they would be retaining the best holiday workers once the Christmas season was over.

Frances decided to take a chance and go for an interview. She knew if they did not keep her on their permanent payroll, the outcome would be disastrous, but still she felt it was worth the risk. She would do her utmost to be the very best seasonal employee; they would just have to offer her a permanent position working for them. Florence, however, was undecided about leaving the store where they now worked. She didn't need to make more than she was earning now. She lived comfortably with her parents and even had the possibility of marrying an attorney. Frances decided to go for the interview, and Florence decided to stay just where she was.

With Frances's prior retail experience, the personnel person at Macy's didn't hesitate to hire her on the spot. They agreed to let Frances give two weeks' notice at the Flushing store, and then she would start working for Macy's immediately after. Florence was happy for her friend to have been hired so quickly by such an important store as Macy's, but she also realized she would miss seeing her almost every day. The women decided to celebrate Frances's new opportunity and planned to spend the evening together at Frances's apartment.

The weather was turning colder. Florence stopped at one of the local grocers to purchase some delicious homemade soup and a roast chicken. Frances stopped on her way home as well, buying wonderful-looking bread and something scrumptious for dessert. The women also decided Florence would spend the night, and the two would go to work together the next day.

When Florence arrived at Frances's apartment, she handed the package to her friend. Frances immediately poured the soup from its container into a pot, placing it on the old-fashioned stove. She then took the chicken and placed it in a pan, putting it into the oven on very low heat—just enough to keep it warm. There was also a variety of seasoned vegetables in another container in the bag, and Frances also placed these in the oven as well. In the meantime Frances poured coffee for each of them from a pot she had on the stove.

As usual, Frances had the table set very prettily with a yellow cloth and matching napkins, and even though she had modest dishes and glasses, there was still an air of elegance about the table setting. Frances had even managed to pick up a small bouquet of fall flowers, placing them in the center of the table. As Frances set the dinner on the table, the two women settled down to a very pleasant evening, looking forward to the meal and each other's company. They talked mostly about the day's events and, of course, the latest fashions. Once dinner was finished, the women cleared the table and washed the dishes together. Frances suggested they have their coffee and dessert in the living room. She placed a fresh pot of coffee, together with cups and saucers and cake plates containing pieces of chocolate cake, on a tray. She decided it would also be nice to bring the flowers into the living room as well, and then she carried everything into the other room. Frances thought, *Even if we don't see each other every day, I am not going to let this friendship end.* She liked having Florence as another very good friend. Their conversations were not only interesting, but always contained laughter, lots and lots of laughter, usually about oddball customers—like the lady who wore a size sixteen and insisted she was only a ten and would become angry with the sales help when the dress didn't fit. This was what Frances needed the most.

Just as the two women settled down to have their coffee and dessert, the sound of the doorbell pierced the room. The women suddenly stopped their conversation and wondered who could possibly be ringing the bell at this hour as it was just a little after eight o'clock. Frances kept mostly to herself and didn't even know the people who lived next door. Very apprehensively Frances rose and walked to the door. She uneasily opened the "peeper" to see who was on the other side. Florence was watching her friend carefully and never took her eyes off her. She was just as nervous as Frances.

When she looked through the "peeper," she saw a gold police shield being held up by one of the two men.

"May I help you?" she hesitantly asked.

"We are looking for Charles and understand he lives here."

"No, he does not live here," Frances quickly replied.

"If you are his wife, we would like to talk to you anyway even if Charles is not here now. Please be good enough to open the door, as we would like to ask you some questions," one of the men asked very matter-of-factly.

Frances opened the door, keeping the chain in place. She observed two very large men who were both very well groomed and nattily dressed. She whispered to them that she had company, but this didn't seem to deter either of the two. They persisted, saying they just needed to speak to her briefly.

"Just a minute," she replied.

Frances's fears started to race through her mind. Florence was in her apartment, and she had never confided in Florence about her problems. It also occurred to her that if she were to tell the police to come back at another time, she didn't want to be alone with them either. So Frances shrugged her shoulders and shook her head, looking toward Florence almost as if to say *be prepared*, and unlocked the door to let the men into her apartment.

She turned to Florence and said, "I don't know what you are about to hear, but please try not to let it influence our friendship."

Florence stared at her friend blankly, not sure of what was going to happen next.

The two men entered the room and introduced themselves as New York State Detectives Tom and Nels. Then Frances made the introduction of her friend to them. She asked if they would like to sit down, but both men declined. "So what is it that I can help you with?" Frances asked.

Detective Tom spoke first. He took out a small leather-bound pad from his inside breast pocket, obviously prepared to jot down notes.

"You are Charles's wife, correct? And do you expect him back tonight?"

"Tonight?" Frances repeated.

She could feel herself begin to visibly shake with fright and tried desperately to conceal the tears that were welling up in her eyes. She told the men she had not seen or heard from her husband in over four years and, moreover, did not care to see him anyway. She proceeded to explain that her husband had left her and his two-year-old daughter and took up with an older woman.

"Moreover, he never inquired as to how we were doing. He just left. He never cared if we could pay the rent, or pay any of the bills for that matter, or even if we had food to eat, or anything else that normal men are supposed to do. My daughter is now seven years old and doesn't even know her father. Detectives, I can almost guess why you are looking for him. What I don't understand is why are you coming around now? All this happened a few years ago, and I am just now almost getting back on my feet. So why now?"

With that the detectives looked at each other. They asked if they could take off their coats and then decided to sit down after all.

"I am sorry to inform you that your husband borrowed a great deal of money from a friend of ours, just about all of his life savings. My friend is not connected with the police department, but he asked if we could help locate your husband. He apparently borrowed the money about two years ago, but he has not contacted him since or made any attempt to pay our friend back. He claimed that his wife and daughter were very sick, and he needed the money to get them medical care with some top doctors in New York."

Frances couldn't believe what she was hearing. She assumed she had heard the last of Charlie taking money from people years ago, and now it was still haunting her. Frances had been so absorbed in speaking with the detectives, she almost forgot Florence was in the room listening to all this. Florence sat there in disbelief, not wanting to say anything.

Frances looked at the two men and shook her head.

"Unfortunately, your friend is not the only one who gave Charlie money and never saw it again. Many others did also. He even stole my wedding rings and my fur coat, just to name a few of the things he took from me. There were days when I didn't know how I was going to feed my child or myself. I would visit people in the afternoon, hoping they would invite us for dinner. Not a pretty picture, is it, Detective, but it is what it is."

Her voice started to crack and she could feel herself filling up with tears, but she stopped, turning away from their eyes. She wouldn't allow herself to cry in front of these two strangers. The men looked at each other and felt genuinely sorry for this nice woman, who'd obviously gotten a raw deal from her husband.

"I worked all kind of hours and tried to pay back several people, but just couldn't. I had many creditors also hounding me for back bills. I paid those off as best as I could until I finally gave up. I tried very hard to make amends to many people for my husband's dishonesty, but the bills and debts just never seemed to have an ending."

Florence finally decided to speak up and asked the detectives if they would like coffee, and they answered affirmatively. She then went into the kitchen, retrieving two cups and saucers and bringing them into the living room. After they started drinking the coffee, Tom asked Frances if Charlie had relatives nearby as they may like to contact them as well.

"Yes," she replied. "His parents live in Bayside, but please, don't bother them. They also do not know their son's whereabouts, and even more they're the ones who take care of my child during the week."

She continued. "Charlie broke their hearts as much as mine and it would do no good to contact them. As far as I know, he cleaned them

A Matter of Survival

out of all their savings also. I am very grateful to my mother-in-law, because if it weren't for her, I don't know what I would have done with my daughter. She has been my strength and has guided me throughout this whole mess."

After a brief silence to digest what they had just been told, they inquired as to how Frances was now supporting herself, and she told them she worked for the local department store, but was due to change jobs within two weeks to work for Macy's in the city.

As the evening wore on, it was obvious both men felt sympathy for this woman who had apparently been through so much. Before they realized it, almost two and half hours had passed, and it was now close to ten thirty. The men rose to their feet and said they were satisfied that Frances was telling them the truth. Leaving their business cards with her, they said they would appreciate a call from her just in case she ever heard of her husband's whereabouts. They shook hands with the two women and left.

Frances locked the door, and then leaning against it, she took a deep breath. She was exhausted, and Florence looked stunned. Florence had had no idea what her friend had been through before they met at work. Frances apologized to her friend for what had transpired. Florence simply said she was sorry her friend had been through so much, but added no one in her family had ever been through anything like the stories she had heard tonight.

"Didn't you try to stop him from leaving?" she asked.

Frances didn't answer her question and sensed uneasiness in her friend.

Florence finally tried to make light of the situation, saying she didn't think either of the detectives were married, because neither wore a wedding ring, adding they were both quite handsome and impeccably dressed.

"Did you notice the striking diamond pinkie ring on Tom's right hand? I wish I had a ring with that diamond in it," she exclaimed. "I bet they're both single."

Frances said the very last thing she wanted was to get involved with anyone, much less one of the detectives who had just left. Florence just laughed at her.

Frances suggested she would clean up the dishes and they should get ready to retire for the evening. The women didn't speak again about the evening's events.

In the meantime the two detectives drove back toward their office, discussing their conversation with Charles's wife. Surprise, surprise—as far as they'd known, the man they were looking for was still living with his wife. Tom stated very emphatically he'd expected to find this man's wife to be a real "tomato," but instead found her to be a very decent and apparently hard-working woman.

"Wow, what a story. Looks like our friend might be out of luck, but then again, we'll keep trying to help him."

After that there was nothing but silence between them.

In the morning, the two women were quiet and hardly spoke to each other. Frances sensed uneasiness from Florence, and a feeling of separation between the two was very evident. There was definitely coolness on Florence's part. Frances wasn't quite sure what to say, so decided to say nothing.

The next two weeks passed quickly. Frances was anxious to start her new job.

She definitely saw a change in Florence's attitude toward her. On several occasions she tried to make a lunch date with her, but Florence always had an excuse. On her next to last day at work, Frances confronted her friend, asking her to be honest and to tell her what was going on.

Florence admitted that the night at her apartment did upset her and she did not want to get involved in Frances's problems. She felt it would be best to step away from her and her problems and hoped she would understand. Frances simply shook her head as she turned away from her former friend. *How easy it is for people to hurt you,* she thought. *I guess it's just another*

A Matter of Survival

bump in the road of life. She shrugged her shoulders and walked toward the dress department. *How it is that so many people can be so cruel?*

Frances was glad the job was over and now was looking forward to starting fresh at Macy's on Monday. She knew the Christmas season was fast approaching and silently said a little prayer to help her do her best. Wherever the personnel people decided to put her, she would make it work, but she hoped it would be in a department that wouldn't be too difficult to handle. The dress department would be perfect!

That Sunday night after she put her daughter to bed in her mother-in-law's house, she sat with Mom and told her about the new job. As usual, the wise woman gave her great encouragement and told her she would also say a special prayer for her. They talked for a few minutes, and then Frances left, kissing Mom good night before starting the journey back to her apartment.

Thirty-One

A New Christmas Season

Although Frances could hardly sleep that night with the anticipation of starting her new job, she still managed to get up extra early. She was well prepared for her first day of work at Macy's. She had chosen her clothes carefully the night before after she got back to her apartment.

Frances looked at herself in the full-length mirror that hung inside her closet door, approving the selection she had made, which was a smart little black dress. The only jewelry she wore was a string of costume pearls with matching earrings as well as a simple watch. She gulped down a small glass of juice and a piece of toast, washed the few dishes, and placed them in the drain board next to the sink.

When she finished the quick cleanup, she put on a plain black coat adorned with a colorful scarf and black leather gloves. With one quick last glance in the mirror, she grabbed her pocketbook and left the apartment, locking the door behind her.

Somehow the excitement within her must have shone through because people were smiling at her, even the bus driver. Frances decided she would travel to work via the Long Island Railroad, even though it meant paying a little extra carfare. She never could stand crowds and definitely hated the subway. The bus deposited its passengers at the subway entrance, and it was only a short walk to the railroad. Frances stopped by the little coffee shop

A Matter of Survival

near the train entrance to buy the paper and a cup of coffee. The ride into the city was somewhat crowded, but still much better than the subway. She was able to sit down, read the paper, and drink her coffee.

When she arrived a little before nine, she felt strange going into the employee entrance. The store, of course, was not open to the public yet. Frances headed right to the personnel department. There, the waiting room held a number of people, all of whom were anticipating their name to be called. After only a few minutes of giving her name to the receptionist, she was called into the personnel office by the woman who had hired her. The woman, who was probably in her late thirties, extended her hand to Frances, at the same time indicating for her to sit down in front of the desk. She was a very well-groomed and attractive woman and handled herself in a very professional manner.

She held only one folder in front of her and started to speak in a firm, businesslike manner.

"Frances, after careful consideration and going over your work history, we have decided to place you in one of our most difficult and busiest departments, the toy department. With your retail experience, we feel you will be able to handle the many demands this department requires. The toy department is our top-selling department of the Christmas season, and we are sure you will able to meet all its challenges. Do you have any questions?"

Frances hoped her surprise did not show on her face. *The toy department. They're placing me in the toy department? I can't believe it.* She finally answered the woman seated across her.

"No, I do not have any questions right now. I think the assignment you have given me will be just fine."

The personnel manager replied, "Okay then, you will have two days of training, one in our training room and one in the toy department. Good luck."

The two days of training went very quickly. The toy department was already filled with customers hoping to get a head start on their Christmas shopping. There was a tremendous assortment of dolls, doll carriages, trucks, skates; the inventory of stock went on and on, but Frances was determined to learn it all and work as hard as she possibly could. As the days passed, the store got more and more busy. Soon Thanksgiving came, and, of course, the store was closed.

Mom had asked her to have Thanksgiving dinner with the family; this way she needn't take her daughter out and back for just one day. Frances gladly accepted the kind invite. Her daughter barely left her side the entire day. Neither she nor Patricia seemed to eat very much, but still Frances was pleased just to be able to share the day with her child. Frances sensed an awkwardness from Charlie's family since no one could comprehend the change in their brother. The laughter and teasing of past times seemed to have vanished. As early evening came, Frances decided it was time to go back to her apartment. She thanked her mother-in-law for, as usual, being so kind. When she turned to her little girl, the child started to cry, pleading, "Mommy, Mommy, please don't leave. Please stay with me."

It was all Frances could do to hold back her own tears.

"Honey, Mommy will come back tomorrow, and we will go home. Tomorrow Mommy has to go to work, but I will be back right after work, I promise."

The young child hugged her mother as if to say she understood and said she would be waiting for her. Frances put her child to bed, kissing and hugging her tightly, and shortly afterward left the house.

The walk to the bus stop seemed to take her longer than usual, but Frances knew it only meant she had a very heavy heart. It was difficult for her to leave her daughter, but she had no choice. She would just look forward to returning to her tomorrow night.

Returning to work on Friday, Frances could not believe the crowds that made their way to the toy department, and they all seemed to surround her like flies. Of course, all the other salespeople were surrounded as well. Frances worked as hard as humanly possible. She met all their requests, and if she found they did not have a particular item, Frances was sure to offer a replacement. If necessary, she took the customer's name and made a list in her book to call if the stock was replenished.

Frances was glad when the evening came. She took the train directly to Bayside and then took the short bus ride to her mother-in-law's home. Once she walked up the path to the front door, she saw in the window her daughter, smiling and happy to see her mommy. Frances didn't care how

A Matter of Survival

hard she had to work, just as long as at the end of the day she could come to get her daughter and take her for the weekend.

Her routine continued throughout the holiday season. Soon it was the day before Christmas Eve, and Frances had not been given any word if she would be retained to continue to work for the store after Christmas. Her heart was now in her mouth. She started thinking, *Oh my, if they don't keep me, I'm really in trouble. Maybe I shouldn't have left my job in Flushing. I don't know where I'll turn if I have to look for another job. Everything slows down after the holidays and doesn't get any better until the anticipation of Easter sometime in March.* Frances's heart was beating faster and faster. She tried desperately not to let her thoughts get the best of her and tried to just keep busy.

The next day was Christmas Eve, and it was now two o'clock in the afternoon. Frances was scheduled to work until six, and all employees would be going home at this time. She had managed to buy an adorable baby doll and toy crib for her daughter, and for this she was glad she worked in this department. She knew her little girl would love it. As she was finishing up with one of her harried last-minute customers, her supervisor asked her to come into his office as soon as possible.

"Yes, sir, as soon as I complete this sale," she replied, hoping he wasn't going to say good-bye and let her go home.

Frances, obviously shaken, walked into her boss's tiny office, which was located just inside the stockroom. Funny, she now noticed the shelves in the stockroom were almost empty; she must have sold everything in sight. Frances almost laughed out loud as she said to herself, *of course, I'm not the only one who worked in this department. We all worked very hard and put in long hours as well.*

Her supervisor asked her to sit down, which she did immediately.

"Frances, we have been very pleased with your performance and would like to offer you the opportunity to continue on after Christmas working for Macy's. Are you interested in staying on?"

Frances could hardly talk and nodded her head affirmatively. After taking a deep breath, she thanked him and said yes, she would love to stay on with the store. She could hardly contain her emotions. She wanted to throw her arms around her supervisor, but, of course, she didn't. He told her to go to the personnel department, where they would give her the necessary paperwork and further instructions of where and when to report for work as a full-time permanent employee. She simply thanked him again and headed straight to personnel.

The people in personnel were fantastic. She was told that not only would she have Christmas off, but she wouldn't have to report for work until after the New Year.

"Consider it a Christmas bonus," they said.

Frances was ecstatic; this meant she would have seven days with her daughter. She made plans to pick up Patricia after work. They would spend Christmas morning at the apartment and then visit her father and Jenny for Christmas dinner. She had managed to buy a little tree, which she placed in the living room. The tree had a minimum of ornaments on it, but still it was their tree. She hid the gifts for Patricia in her closet. The little crib hardly fit. She also bought her a pretty red velvet dress with white lace on the collar and sleeves, as well as a navy coat with a matching hat, and to complete the outfit, a little white rabbit-fur muff. When her little girl was asleep, she carefully placed everything under the tree. The next morning Patricia squealed with delight at the magnificent presents Santa and her mommy had given her. It turned out to be a wonderful Christmas after all.

On Frances's last day off, she planned to take her daughter into the city. She wanted just the two of them to celebrate her new job. First they went to Radio City to see a movie and a marvelous Christmas stage show. Once the show was over, Frances and her daughter took a short walk, holding hands all the way, to view the biggest and most fabulous Christmas tree at Rockefeller Center. Her little one was delighted. Yes, there were what seemed like thousands of people crowding in to get a look at all the amazing decorations, and even though normally Frances didn't like crowds, today they didn't seem to bother her. She wanted her child to see all the beauty the city had to offer. After all, this was a day of celebration! After viewing the tree and the holiday decorations, Frances told her daughter they were going someplace very special for dinner.

As it turned out, Frances took her daughter to the Candlelight Room at the Hotel Victoria. It was very elegant and, surprisingly, Patricia felt very comfortable just as if she had always belonged there. Both mother and daughter were stylishly dressed, and several heads turned as they walked hand in hand through the reception area. Even the maître d' gave them an approving glance and smiled at the two as he escorted them to a very pretty table in the center of the room. The room was beautiful with shiny, embossed gold satin fabric covering the walls. There was an enormous chandelier with endless sparkling crystals hanging down from the center of an ornately carved ceiling. As young Patricia glanced around, she observed the elaborate matching crystal sconces holding dimly lit electric candles on the walls as well. Even as a young child, she was mesmerized by the ambiance that filled the room. She was thrilled that her mother had taken her to such an elegant restaurant. She could hardly eat her dinner—she was just happy to be in the atmosphere.

As the two rode back to Flushing via the railroad, little Patricia cuddled with her head comfortably snuggled into her mother's chest and fell fast asleep. Frances felt good knowing, it had been a wonderful day. It was a day that neither mother nor daughter would ever forget. She knew Patricia had loved it, and once more Frances was happy to have made the sacrifice to save as much as possible so that they could share this festive outing together.

The bonus vacation was over. Frances brought her daughter back to her in-laws' home. Even though the vacation was done, Frances felt it had been truly a wonderful Christmas. A feeling of satisfaction spread throughout her, knowing mother and daughter had both enjoyed her time off. It couldn't have been planned any better. It was a perfect few days.

The next morning Frances reported to personnel and was told she was going to be placed in the women's dress department. Frances said a silent *thank goodness* to herself and was happy she did not have to report back to the toy department. It was evident based on the way Frances dressed and carried herself that the higher echelon felt she would be an asset to them and had decided to place this person, who obviously loved fashion, to work where she could do them the most good. This was the wise way management chose to match people within various departments of the store. They were sure to increase sales with this logic.

Two months passed, and during that time Frances tried to learn everything there was to learn about the latest trends in fashion. She sold numerous dresses to many wealthy women, both from out of town and also to those who lived within commuting distance. She proved to management their decision was correct to place her in this department. Already there were some repeat customers who insisted they only wanted to be taken care of by Frances. Frances loved her new job and looked forward to coming into work every day with the anticipation of selling fashionable clothes to some very nice ladies.

One afternoon while Frances was writing up a rather large sale and making arrangements for its delivery, she noticed a familiar tall and well-dressed man walking toward her. *Oh no,* she thought. *It can't be.* But yes, of course, it was. It was one of the detectives who'd came to question her at her apartment several months ago. She couldn't believe it. *How dare he! Now he's coming to ask me more questions at my job. I've already answered his questions.*

Frances completed her paperwork and stepped aside to a quiet area of the department, and he followed.

"What is it now?" she inquired. "Haven't you asked me everything you wanted to? I'm sure there is nothing more I can add to what I have already told you."

She hardly gave the good-looking man a chance to answer since she was so angered by his sudden appearance.

"Wait, wait a minute," he said. "I didn't come here to ask you more questions. I was just in the area and thought I would stop by to see you and find out how the new job was turning out."

Frances was rather surprised and simply said, "Oh?" She then somewhat angrily continued, "How did you know where in the store I was working? I hope you didn't go to the personnel department flashing your badge around."

He smiled and replied no, but then he told her he did have his ways but he would rather not elaborate on them right now.

Frances again asked, "So why did you come here?"

"As I said, I just wanted to see how you were doing with the new job and thought maybe you would like to talk about it over dinner this evening."

Frances looked surprised and simply replied, "Thank you, but no, absolutely not." She paused and then continued. "Look, Detective, you seem like a very nice person, but I usually just keep to myself, and I prefer to keep it that way. I don't date."

"Okay," he replied, "but you can't fault a guy for trying. Would you mind if I stopped by again, er—just to say hello?"

Frances hesitated, not really sure what this guy wanted from her.

"I guess not, but remember, I do not want to go out with you, or anyone else for that matter."

He just smiled and tried to enter into small talk with her, but the department was getting busy, and Frances excused herself to continue with her job.

Tom left feeling somewhat stunned that she had declined his offer. It was rather unusual for a woman to refuse a date with him. Still, for some unknown reason, he was attracted to her and even more so now that she'd refused to have dinner with him. Another month passed by, and sure enough, Tom appeared again. This time Frances smiled as he approached. He again asked her out to dinner, and again she refused, citing the same reasons that she had previously outlined to him.

"Look, I told you the last time, I don't go out with men. I would just rather be by myself," she reiterated.

After a little small talk, Tom left her area. Frances felt relieved that he'd left, but even so, she later found herself thinking about him. She did think he seemed very nice and always looked so good, but this was silly, as dating was not in her plans, at least for now.

This continued on and off for almost a year. Tom would show up at her job, chitchat for a little while, and then invite her to dinner, but her answer was always no.

On several occasions, her coworkers asked her who was this man who kept showing up and asking her out, but Frances did not answer too many of their questions. She just said she would rather not discuss it and that she definitely did not want to go out with him. They laughed and said she should introduce him to them. They would go out with him if the opportunity arose.

One day during the summer months, Tom came into the department and again asked her out. Only this time Frances hesitated and then spontaneously decided to accept his offer. She was just as stunned as he that she finally said yes. He made arrangements to meet her by the employee entrance at seven o'clock and left. Frances immediately regretted her decision. *What did I do? Maybe I should have declined as I usually do.*

She was wearing a pretty two-piece navy-blue dress. *Hmm, this may be okay for work, but not to go out on a date with a man like Tom.* Then she remembered a lovely black cocktail dress that was on sale. It was a dress Frances loved but had never considered buying, because it was so expensive and she would never have a place to wear it to anyway. But now she had a place to go, and since it was on sale, together with her employee discount, it seemed like a real bargain. It had a delicate sheer fabric covering a black crepe strapless dress and had an attractive scoop neckline. Once she tried the dress on, she immediately knew it looked fantastic. It was definitely a luxury for her to buy it, but she loved how it looked on her. Then too, she repeated to herself, it was already reduced. She talked herself into buying it. She also purchased a pair of black dress pumps and a little black evening handbag.

When six o'clock came, Frances went into her locker and retrieved her makeup case, taking it into the ladies' room. First she washed her face and applied fresh makeup and then combed her hair. She looked into the mirror and as a last-minute decision, she decided to pull her hair up and pile it high on her head in an upsweep. This made her feel very glamorous. She was wearing a minimum of jewelry, only small pearl earrings and a little gold watch. She placed all her work clothes neatly into her locker and headed slowly toward the employee entrance, trembling a little. *I must be crazy, but here goes nothing.* She walked out of the door.

Tom was standing on the street directly across the doorway waiting for her. He almost didn't recognize the woman who exited the store. He took an absolute double take as she walked toward him.

"Well, it looks as if there will be no ordinary place for you tonight," he said.

Frances was very nervous and hoped it wasn't obvious. It had been a very long time since she was out with a man. She wasn't even sure what to do or say.

A Matter of Survival

Tom spoke again and simply said, "Frances, you look beautiful. Thank you for going to so much trouble for me."

Frances smiled but didn't answer. They walked to the corner, and Tom indicated they were going to take a taxi to their destination. Frances thought, *A taxi? I hope he can afford this.*

After a very short wait, he hailed a cab and gave directions to the driver. Frances was not exactly sure where their destination was, because it was an unfamiliar address. However, even with Manhattan traffic, the ride was brief, and within just a few minutes, they pulled up in front of the Astor Hotel.

"Here for dinner?" Frances inquired.

"Dinner and a show I'm sure you will like, Frances," Tom replied.

Frances and Tom walked silently through the lobby and into an elevator where Tom indicated to the elevator attendant that they were going to the roof. Frances could not believe her eyes as the elevator doors opened. It was the most elegant restaurant and nightclub she had ever seen. In the past she could only have dreamed of going to a place like this. She'd seen places like this in society magazines. It was called "The Astor Roof." A sign posted just outside the restaurant announced Harry James and His Orchestra would be performing that evening. Frances could hardly believe her eyes. She was a big fan of Harry James. She would often listen to his orchestra on the radio, but never did she ever expect to see him in person. Frances wasn't exactly sure, but she was almost certain Tom slipped something into the hand of the maître d'. After a very brief wait the maître d' escorted the couple to a front-row table. He then pulled a chair out and indicated for Frances to sit down. Frances felt like that proverbial kid in a candy store.

She finally spoke. "Tom, this is so beautiful. I'm speechless. I really don't know what to say, except it's so nice of you to take me to such an elegant place."

He just smiled and said he was glad to do so, adding the only thing he was sorry about was that she'd obviously purchased a very expensive dress just to go out with him. He knew full well it probably had exceeded her budget and must have cost her a week's pay. Frances just smiled and didn't answer him regarding her budget or share the fact that her dress was really a bargain. When he asked her what she would like to drink, Frances hadn't a clue as to how to answer him. The only beverage she might have ordered out was coffee or perhaps a Coke, but now she wasn't sure.

Tom said, "I know, I'll order you a Pink Lady, because you look like such a lady tonight, a lady that I am very proud to be with."

Frances's eyes almost welled up with tears; she hadn't received a compliment like this from a man in years. He then placed his hand on hers, indicating everything was fine.

"Tom," Frances explained, "I don't drink, and I don't even know how."

He was very reassuring; he simply said she would like this drink and he wanted her to just enjoy their evening together. Frances did like the cocktail and felt very sophisticated drinking it. The drink helped her nervousness dwindle, and now she was beginning to feel more comfortable with him. He asked if she wanted him to order dinner, and she nodded affirmatively. Tom told her a little about his job and also that he still lived at home with his parents. His mother was quite ill, and his father, who was still working, had an excellent job with the railroad. Apparently his father was well respected, as he was one of the very first engineers to work with air conditioning in passenger railroad cars for long-distance travel. Frances was not too familiar with air conditioning, as very few places had it installed in their offices or stores.

After a while, Frances felt more relaxed and confided in Tom the details about the circumstances of her daughter and how she, of course, did not live with her, but lived with her former in-laws. Tom noted immediately the sadness in her voice when she spoke of her child and the fact that she was not able to have her child live with her. She did, however, praise her former mother-in-law and said she didn't know what she would do without her. It was obvious Frances loved and respected this woman a great deal. Frances didn't want to go into too much more detail and let the subject of her failed marriage drop since she didn't feel comfortable in discussing it with Tom or anyone else for that matter.

After a splendid dinner, the orchestra began to perform. Harry James played the trumpet superbly, and the orchestra sounded marvelous. Tom asked Frances to dance, and she hoped she remembered how to do so. She surprised herself, because she did manage quite well.

It was now about ten o'clock, and Tom suggested he better see her home, because they both had to go to work the following day. He paid the check, and they exited the nightclub, riding in the elevator that took them swiftly down to the street level. Once again Tom hailed a cab and directed the driver to take them to Queens near the railroad yards. They exited the taxi, and Tom showed Frances to his car, which was parked adjacent to the yards. It was a luxurious dark-blue Buick and probably one of the biggest cars Frances had ever seen, much less been in.

There was very little traffic, and in less than a half hour, they reached the block of Frances's apartment. Tom parked the car on the street and walked over to her side to open the door. Frances thought, *Now what does he expect from me? I hope he doesn't want me to ask him up to my place, because that is out of the question.* She started to say good night to him on the street, but he said he wanted to see that she got into her apartment safely. Once they reached the second floor, Frances took her key from her purse, and then Tom took it from her. Unlocking the door, he said he was glad she finally accepted his invitation to go out with him and he hoped they would see each other again very soon. Frances nodded her head and thanked him for a wonderful evening. He kissed her lightly on her cheek, saying good night and telling her she should be sure to lock the door as soon as she was inside.

Once inside Frances flipped on the light switch and she did double-lock the door as usual, only this time she leaned back against it and smiled to herself thinking of the evening that had just passed. She heard Tom's footsteps go down the stairs and out the front door. With a deep breath, she decided it was time to get ready for tomorrow. It had been a fabulous evening. One of many she found herself hoping to share with him in the future.

Thirty-Two

FRANCES MEETS HER BROTHER

Tom and Frances were now dating almost on a regular basis, but Frances still looked forward to having her daughter each weekend. Dates with Tom were always limited to weekdays.

Frances found she was managing her money well, budgeting very carefully so that she and Patricia could have their special outings, which often included visiting her father and Jenny. On one such visit her father told her that her brother Peter would be coming to America in just a few weeks. Frances was excited to learn of his pending arrival to the United States and made arrangements with her father for them to meet. It had now been well over two years since he'd first told her that her brother would be returning to the United States, and finally the time was here.

The next weeks quickly passed, and Frances was getting most anxious for her brother's arrival in New York. Her father told Frances that Peter was sailing from Europe and would be arriving on the following Tuesday. He said he was going to meet him at the boat in New York and then take him to his apartment in the Bronx. Frances made arrangements to take Tuesday off and planned to travel to the Bronx for the long-anticipated meeting of the brother she hadn't seen for over twenty-five years. Frances desperately hoped he would remember her. But how could he? She was six years old and he was only three when they had been separated. She didn't know what to expect at their meeting.

A Matter of Survival

Frances traveled to the Bronx Tuesday morning, and all the time while she traveled the familiar bus route, she could feel nervous butterflies within her. Finally, she reached her destination and stopped in front of the apartment building. She adjusted her clothing and powdered her face and put on fresh lipstick. Frances took a deep breath and proceeded into the building, walking anxiously up the stairs to the second floor. As she gathered her courage to ring the bell, she could hear voices coming from behind the apartment door. Jenny answered almost immediately and greeted Frances with a big smile and a kiss on her cheek. She took Frances's hand and led her into the living room. There in the room was her father and a younger man. Ironically, she instantly recognized him as her brother even after all the years of separation.

"Peter!" Frances exclaimed, going right to him.

He too was relieved and delighted to see her. Her father made the introduction, which really wasn't necessary. Frances and Peter immediately embraced and held onto each other for what seemed like a very long time. Tears started to flow down Frances's face, and Peter's eyes also were filling up, only this time they were tears of joy. It was wonderful to be together again. Frances quickly discovered her brother did not speak English and, of course, Frances, having grown up in the convent, did not speak Italian. It really didn't matter to Frances, because at last they were together again.

Unfortunately, Frances's father had written to Peter telling him it would be very easy for him to get a job in New York, because after all, he did have a degree in engineering and they were always looking for engineers in New York. What he failed to tell him, however, was that he needed to speak English, and speak it fluently. Without speaking English, his prospects of getting a job were nil. After just a few days of Peter arriving in the United States, his father made it very clear he would have to contribute toward the rent while staying with him, and soon he would need to find a place of his own. His father further suggested he could get him a job through one his friends who worked in a construction company and made arrangements for his son to meet him.

Peter did meet the friend and did get the job. He then found himself digging ditches in the streets of the Bronx where a new subway station was going to be built. The hours were long and the work was extremely hard, especially for a man such as Peter, who, with his education and background, was used to finer living conditions.

Peter found he had no choice but to continue working with the construction company, and soon he found himself a small one-room apartment not too far from where his father lived. Eventually he learned how to travel to Flushing to meet with his beloved sister. Peter started to learn the English language, mostly from working with his coworkers on the construction crew, although most spoke broken English.

A few months later, Peter was able to get a job in a paper cup factory in College Point, which was not too far from where Frances lived. He worked the midnight-to-eight shift and would stop by to visit with Frances on her days off every week. Even though they could not converse well, it was enough that they could make themselves understood. There was a bond between the two that existed even without words. Frances was now the happiest she had been in a very long time, and it was all due to having a brother and a daughter. This was her family, and no matter how small it was, it was her family nonetheless. Of course, another important contributing factor to her happiness was that there was a new man in her life.

Peter was quite ambitious and was not going to be satisfied to work in a paper cup factory. After just a few weeks of working in the factory, he enrolled in Queens College, taking English courses during the day. Even with his hectic schedule, he made sure to stop to see his sister at every possible time available for them both.

Peter told Frances he was saving as much as possible so that he would be able to send for his wife and bring her to America. He spoke often of her, and Frances could see the sadness in him because he missed his wife very much. There were many times when Frances went to work that she would insist her brother stay at her apartment rather than have him make the exhausting trip back to the Bronx. She would often buy him the cigarettes he liked and leave him something to eat. Frances was afraid if she didn't leave food for him, he simply would go without.

Frances and her brother continued on with their lives. They became even closer to each other, even more than she thought was possible. The plan to bring Peter's wife to New York was now becoming a reality; Peter said Wilma would be arriving in just four months. Not only was Peter

A Matter of Survival

anxious to see his wife, Frances felt she was just as anxious to meet her sister-in-law. They had had so many conversations about her during the past two years, Frances felt as if she already knew her. She could hardly wait to spend time with the woman who was not really a stranger to her, even though they had yet to meet.

During one of Peter's recent visits, he confided to his sister that his wife was not a well woman. It seemed while they were engaged, Wilma had apparently developed rheumatic fever, and although she eventually recovered, it had left her with a serious heart problem. They knew she would require great care, but the doctor said with the proper attention, Wilma could live a full and normal life. Frances was a little concerned for her brother and sister-in-law, but Peter seemed to be okay with his wife's health issues and was well prepared to help her in any way he could. He did not seem overly concerned, saying it was nothing that they couldn't handle. Frances was glad he'd confided in her and told her brother if she was needed, she could also be of help to them.

On the weekends, when Frances would bring her daughter to the apartment, many times Peter would also be there, as he adored his niece immensely. He always looked forward to seeing the young child. He would hide a bit of candy in his shirt pocket for her. Peter would never stay over when Frances had her daughter for the weekend. As much as he loved his sister and his niece, he believed it was best to let them have their time alone so mother and daughter could have their treasured days together.

The next four months flew by, and finally Peter, together with his sister, went to meet the boat, which was scheduled to arrive in the early afternoon. Frances again made arrangements to change her day off for this special occasion. Both she and Peter could hardly contain themselves while making the trip into the city to greet the boat.

Frances tried to picture her sister-in-law. The only Italian women she knew were very short, pulled their hair back severely in a bun placed neatly on the back of their head, and were always dressed in black—oh yes, and they wore god-awful shoes. Moreover, they never wore makeup. This image really didn't bother Frances, because she didn't care what Peter's wife looked like. She was just happy that her brother and his wife were going to be together again. Since Frances worked in the fashion industry, she was well prepared to show Wilma how women in the United States dressed, especially in New York. She would not only teach her how women dressed, but also how they cared for themselves. After all, Wilma was coming from a country that had been ravaged by war, and she was sure it must have been very difficult living through this. She was certain that fashion was the last thing they needed, or even cared to know about. It wouldn't bother Frances how Wilma was dressed. She was just anxious to have her with them. Wilma was one more person to add to the small group that she called her family.

Finally the boat docked. Peter was so excited that he could hardly contain himself. His eyes were going back and forth, scanning the many passengers lined up against the railing waiting for their chance to disembark. The crowds were enormous, both on the ship and on the dock. Frances made sure to stay right next to her brother for fear they might get separated in the crowd.

Passengers started down the gangplank, and strange as it may have seemed, the giant crowds were extremely orderly while disembarking the huge ship. All of a sudden, Peter exclaimed, "There's Wilma; there is my wife."

Frances's eyes searched ahead. She could only ask, "Where is she? Where is Wilma?"

Peter held Frances close to himself and pointed straight ahead.

Frances was dumbfounded to say the least. She was astonished to see before her a very elegant lady dressed in the latest fashion. Wilma was wearing a dark navy-blue suit and wore a exquisite large white picture hat. She had on gorgeous leather high-heeled pumps and carried not only a beautiful handbag, but also held a sleek blue-and-white umbrella as well. She looked as if she stepped off the cover of *Vogue*. Frances chuckled to herself. *So this is the woman I was going to teach fashion to—that's quite a laugh.* She smiled, and even though they had never met before, somehow Frances was very proud of her and even more so because she was her sister-in-law.

Peter and his wife embraced and could hardly let go of each other. He hugged her and kissed her so hard that her gorgeous hat fell to the ground, which Frances quickly retrieved. This was the happiest she had seen Peter since his arrival in America. Frances just stood there smiling, ecstatic to see

A Matter of Survival

what a wonderful couple they made. It was obvious to her that they were very much in love.

Finally Peter let go of his wife and introduced the women. Frances and Wilma embraced, just as if they had always known each other. There was an unspoken bond between the women. Frances then handed the hat back to her new sister-in-law but not before very carefully brushing it off. Again, Frances discovered communication was going to be difficult, as Wilma did not speak English at all, and Frances had picked up only a few Italian words.

Once the luggage was collected, the three of them boarded a taxi and headed to Peter's apartment in the Bronx. Wilma seemed to be well rested and told her husband the voyage was a pleasant one. Peter hated taking his wife to his little apartment, but he was planning to move as soon as possible. In the meantime, his father and Jenny were preparing a celebration party for Wilma's arrival in the United States.

Wilma freshened up a little, and the three headed to their father's apartment. The gathering was a very festive one and, of course, Jenny had prepared one of her fantastic meals for them all. After spending a few hours together, it now was time to leave. Peter and his wife put Frances on her bus, knowing she would be home before dark. It was obvious they were all now exhausted from the day's events. Frances left them feeling happy. It was fantastic to see her brother happily contented at last, just being with his wife.

It was just about six o'clock when Frances arrived at her apartment. She had made arrangements with Peter for them to come visit the following Saturday. She would have Wilma meet her daughter, as well as her uncle Ralph and aunt Jean and their now three children. Frances, of course, extended an invitation to her father and Jenny for the occasion. It was a time for celebration indeed. Saturday soon came, and Frances found herself surrounded by the people she loved the most.

Frances prepared a large meal for everyone and set up a table in her living room. Uncle Ralph and his wife, Jean, and their children were anxiously anticipating meeting Peter's wife. When Peter and Wilma walked into the room, the greetings were obviously very warm and celebratory.

Wilma had brought gifts for everyone, but it was strange and confusing to little Patricia. Wilma gave her several gifts—a sewing set and hoop, a baby doll, a puzzle, and a pop-up book depicting the story of Snow White, although it was written in Italian. Patricia couldn't believe all these gifts were for her. She could not recall ever getting so many presents all at once just for her and from someone she didn't even know. She was sure some of the gifts must have been meant for her cousins, but not so.

Wilma seemed to have an enjoyable time conversing with Aunt Jean and Uncle Ralph, who helped Peter with translating the Italian into English for Frances. Even little Patricia was caught up with the excitement and started repeating some of the Italian words she heard, which made everyone laugh.

After dinner, the women decided to go for a walk in the neighborhood before dessert was served. They walked perhaps ten or so blocks before turning around and heading back to Frances's apartment. It was obvious Wilma loved Flushing. When the women returned, Wilma asked Peter since they were planning to move, could it please be to Flushing? Peter agreed. Frances was delighted to hear this and promised to help them find a place to live in the area. They all had a delightful time and thanked Frances for her hospitality. It truly was a happy day!

Frances tidied up the apartment and got little Patricia off to bed. She herself couldn't wait to get into bed as well. It was always good to cuddle up with her child. Drifting off to sleep together was a treasured time for both of them. It didn't matter to either that they slept on a pull-out couch. They were just happy being together.

Frances and Patricia spent Sunday together quietly. They had breakfast, went to church, and spent some time in the park. Afterward, Frances prepared dinner for the two of them, and sadly then it was time to take Patricia back to her grandmother. There was always that ache in her heart when she prepared her daughter to make the journey back to Bayside. She loved her child so very much, but unfortunately there was nothing she could do now to change their situation. She was very grateful to her mother-in-law for keeping Patricia safe, and she would look forward to the following weekend.

That night Frances, as usual, got Patricia washed up and into pajamas. She always read a story to her daughter, and once she was in bed, she kissed her good night and tucked her in. For some unknown reason, Patricia didn't go right off to sleep and heard the front door closing downstairs. She desperately cried out for her mother, but of course, her mother was gone.

Wilma and Peter did find a place in Flushing and moved into an adorable three-room apartment that was just a short bus ride away from Frances. The only drawback was that it was on the third floor of a three-floor walk-up. On the day they moved from the Bronx, Frances helped them set up their new apartment. Peter still needed to go work that night and excused himself so that he could get some rest before leaving for work. Before he went into the bedroom, he asked Frances if she would please be good enough to stay with Wilma for the night. It was going to be her first night alone in the new apartment, and he would feel better if she would stay overnight.

Frances was quite reluctant to stay, because there would be no one to translate the language for them. How would they be able to communicate with each other? How would they make themselves understood? But Peter pleaded with his sister to please do this for him and, of course, she said yes, she would. Peter then went to the bedroom to rest and later got ready for work, leaving the women alone for the remainder of the night.

Strangely, once the women were alone, they discovered they could, in fact, communicate. They stayed up all night laughing and talking, making themselves very much understood.

Peter and Wilma settled into their new life quite comfortably and seemed to be very happy although Frances got the feeling Wilma missed her family, especially her mother, a great deal. Never having had love from a mother, Frances's heart broke for Wilma, but still she never wanted to confide in her about her and Peter's own mother.

During the past several years, Frances had made a few friends in Flushing and often would see them during the week after work. She decided it would be good for Wilma to have a little outside companionship and made arrangements to introduce them all to her sister-in-law, knowing it would be good for her to have the company.

Peter continued to go to work and school and did not have the free time that he had in the early days when he first arrived in the United States. Frances missed seeing him as often as she used to, but she understood, and they made arrangements to see each other as often as possible. One thing

Frances observed about her brother was he too was extremely neat and organized. Frances knew they were very similar in this respect, but she wasn't sure if it was the way they were raised, or maybe it was a trait they'd inherited. It really didn't matter; Frances was happy they were so much alike.

Peter developed an excellent command of the English language, and within a year he spoke it fluently. Wilma learned English quite well also, not only from her husband, but from the local shopkeepers in the neighborhood as well as conversing with her sister-in-law.

Thirty-Three

INTRODUCING THE NEW MAN

Since Frances and Tom were seeing each other steadily now, Frances thought it was finally time for him to meet her family. She had invited her brother and Wilma as well as her father and Jenny to come for Sunday dinner. After picking up Patricia on Friday evening, Frances took great pains to prepare a menu for the dinner on Sunday. They got up early the next day, and together with the list, mother and daughter went to the local shops to buy the necessary items. While they were out, Frances told her daughter she had made friends with a gentleman by the name of Tom, and she would have the opportunity to meet him as well. The young child was excited that her mother and she were going to have a party and somehow sensed the man she was going to meet would be someone very special.

After shopping Patricia helped her mother put away the groceries, and Frances prepared as much food as possible for dinner the next day.

The two went to bed feeling excited with the anticipation of having company. They awoke early, dressed, and went to church. As soon as they got home, Frances opened up the table in the living room and set it for her company. The kitchen had an older but dependable stove, and Frances prepared a pork roast with all the trimmings. Her family would be arriving about two thirty in the afternoon. Now everything was done and she could sit and relax for a few minutes with her cigarette before getting busy again.

The doorbell rang at two fifteen; Frances had asked Tom to come a few minutes early to meet her daughter before everyone else arrived. As usual, he was impeccably dressed and made a terrific impression.

Since Tom had not been around children very much, he was very taken with the young girl who stood before him. She smiled, saying it was nice to meet him when introduced, and Frances was very proud as her daughter displayed her very best manners to her friend. Tom took an immediate liking to the young child and presented her with a pretty little doll dressed in a pink dress with a matching coat and hat. Needless to say, Patricia loved it, and without being prompted, she thanked the kind man who stood before her. Frances just smiled and kissed her daughter on top of her head. He then handed Frances an enormous bouquet of yellow roses. Thanking him, she placed the flowers in a vase of water and brought them into the living room, taking care to put the vase in just the right spot.

The bell rang again, and her father together with Jenny entered the apartment. Just at about the same time, her brother and Wilma came to the door. Everyone greeted each other, and Frances introduced Tom to her family. Patricia showered everyone with hugs and kisses and then showed them all her new gift, holding the little doll up proudly for everyone to see.

The dinner turned out perfectly; everything was delicious. It was a wonderful afternoon, and everyone seemed to be enjoying themselves. After dinner the women cleared the table and helped Frances put out the desserts, which she and her company had provided. It made for a very nice display of scrumptious confections. As Frances poured the coffee, Peter said he had an announcement to make. Frances thought, *He must have gotten a new job.*

"I think today would the perfect day to let everyone know Wilma and I are expecting a baby, and the doctor said she will be having our baby sometime in early June," Peter continued.

Everyone stood up and excitedly offered their congratulations to the young couple with lots of hugs and kisses. Peter looked as proud as could be, and Wilma could not stop smiling. Although Frances was ecstatic knowing she was going to be an aunt, inside she was a little concerned about her sister-in-law's serious heart condition, but she didn't want to make an issue of this, at least for now. She was sure her brother and his wife had fully discussed her medical problems with the doctor.

Everyone sat back down at the table, only now they all were very excited and full of smiles. What a joy it was to hear the happy news. Our little family was growing.

Patricia asked her mother, "Mommy, will I be related to the baby?"

Her mother, smiling, told her in simple words that she was going to have a little baby cousin.

After everyone had made and eaten their selection from the huge assortment of desserts, the ladies again cleared the table, and once the dishes were washed and dried, it was time to leave. Yes, it had been an especially pleasant day. Everyone seemed genuinely fond of Tom, and he too had seemed to enjoy meeting Frances's family.

Frances's father and Jenny were the first to leave. The bus stop was just a block away, and they were very familiar with the schedule. Tom offered to drive Frances and her daughter to Bayside and at the same time also offered to drive Peter and Wilma to their apartment, since it was on the way, and Frances was glad he did this. He certainly was a thoughtful man. Tom went downstairs to start up his car and indicated he would meet everyone outside.

Peter whispered to his sister, "I like your friend, Frances. I want to see you happy. I love you."

He then kissed Frances on her cheek and proceeded downstairs. Frances, little Patricia, and Wilma walked together and met the men outside. The weather was starting to turn colder, and Frances was very glad she didn't have to take the bus to Bayside tonight.

They dropped Peter and Wilma off at their apartment. Frances kissed and hugged her brother and sister-in-law good night, telling them how happy she was that she was going to be an "Auntie."

Once back inside the car, Frances told Tom she rather he didn't bring her directly to her in-laws' house, but would prefer it if he could wait for her a short distance away. She decided this was best as she didn't want them to feel bad now that she was seeing someone else beside their son. She even instructed her daughter not to mention Mommy's new friend to her grandparents. Frances hated herself for being "sneaky," but right now she

Arleen Patricia Mercorella

just couldn't handle a lot of questions. She tried to rationalize her requests to herself. *After all it has been six years since I have last seen Charlie. I guess it's time to get on with my life, but I still don't want my in-laws to know that I'm seeing someone.*

Tom broke the silence by saying good night to Frances's daughter and said he hoped they would see each other again soon. As Frances exited the car, she told Tom she may be a while and walked toward her in-laws' house. She held her daughter's hand, secretly never wanting to let go.

As usual she got her young child ready for bed and read her a quick story. They hugged and kissed tightly, and Frances reminded her she would be there again on Friday.

"Mommy," Patricia said, "I think your friend looks like Daddy."

"Oh no, don't say that," she answered.

Little Patricia smiled at her mother, saying, "Mommy, just one more thing."

Frances replied, "And that is?"

Her young child then simply said, "Mommy, I love you more than tonkin tell."

With that she turned over and went immediately to sleep. Surprised by her daughter's words, Frances smiled. Patricia hadn't said that in a very long time. She thought back, remembering the earlier days when Charlie had taught their two-year-old child to say, "I love you more than tongue can tell." It always made them laugh. Remembering the happier times gave her a lump in her throat. She then quickly decided to let the memories go and not dwell on them.

Frances must have been in the house for almost an hour, but she was sure Tom would understand why she just couldn't get up and leave. Her first priority was to attend to her daughter. Once she finally got her to go to sleep, she was able to say good night to her in-laws and walked toward Tom's car.

Once inside the car, she thanked him but otherwise stayed very quiet. When he asked if she was all right, Frances started to cry. Now she was embarrassed. She thought maybe it was better to take the bus, because no one on the bus asked if she was all right. He simply leaned over, held her

A Matter of Survival

in his arms saying he was there for her and understood completely how she must feel. *Yes,* she said to herself, *he really is a special man.*

Once they reached her apartment, Tom parked the car and walked Frances to her door, telling her to be sure to double-lock it before he left. He kissed her gently, holding her ever so tightly. Frances smiled and thanked him again for being so sweet.

Now that she was alone in her apartment, Frances tidied up a little more, putting the few things that had been left out in their right place. She thought how delightful it had been to have the family together, especially hearing the good news about a baby that was on the way. Still, somehow, even though she was happy for her brother and sister-in-law, she couldn't shake the feeling of depression. She didn't have to think too hard to know this was a common feeling every Sunday when she took her daughter to her in-laws and came back to the apartment by herself. Nevertheless, she didn't want to think about it anymore, so Frances got herself ready for bed and prepared her clothes for work for the following day.

Thirty-Four

The New Arrival

The next day while Frances was on the train heading into the city, she started to smile to herself at the prospect of becoming an "Auntie." Then Frances got an idea. She loved entertaining and thought it would be nice to plan a baby shower for Wilma. It would be so much fun, and the baby gifts would be a big help to them. She got out a pad and pencil from her handbag and started writing down notes detailing what she would need to do.

She checked her small pocket calendar and decided to have the shower early, perhaps the end of January. This would give Wilma plenty of time to make storage arrangements for the gifts she would receive and also arrange the baby furniture in her room.

On her lunch hour, Frances started to shop for the party. First she bought the invitations and matching paper goods. Each week when she got paid, she would buy something else for the shower.

Thanksgiving was quickly approaching, and Tom thought that it was about time he took Frances to meet his parents. He also thought it would be nice if Frances were to meet his sisters and their families at Thanksgiving.

A Matter of Survival

He decided he would bring up the subject on the following Wednesday, which had now become their regular date night. While they talked almost every night on the phone, Wednesday was their night.

As usual, when Frances opened the door, she looked lovely. One of the things he liked most about Frances was that she always paid particular attention to the way she was groomed. She looked so fresh, and her taste in clothes was always in the best of fashion. Tonight she was dressed in a soft beige dress with dark brown accessories including a brown-and-beige scarf placed casually around her neck. Yes, she looked stunning.

Tom was also dressed impeccably. He loved good clothes as well and made a terrific impression on whomever he met. It's no wonder that when the two entered the restaurant together, it seemed as if all heads turned, admiring the handsome couple. They usually had dinner at the same cozy place known as the Pilgrim Inn. It was a small, but very elegant restaurant and the maître d' knew them well. Every Wednesday, he would reserve the front booth by the window for their arrival. Now that they were comfortably seated in the luxurious leather booth, Frances admired the small ring of fresh seasonal flowers placed in the center of the table. The flowers were surrounded by what appeared to be a tiny lamp which housed a flickering candle. It made for a very romantic setting. Tom ordered a cocktail for Frances and a scotch and soda for himself.

"Frances, I would like to take you to meet my parents, perhaps next week, if that's okay with you. I have told them about you, and they are most anxious to meet you as well."

Frances was taken aback by his request.

"Tom, I'm not sure whether I'm ready to meet them. Do they know I'm separated from my husband and moreover, I have a young child? I'm not sure how they would accept these facts. You have never been married, and now you want them to accept me?"

Tom replied, "I have already told them about your past, and they are fine with it. Please, Frances, I'm sure they will like you as much as I do, so let me take you to meet them next week."

Frances sat silently and finally nodded her head affirmatively.

The week flew by, and Frances took great care in choosing what she was going to wear to meet Tom's parents. She decided on a simple navy dress with a little scoop neckline and white cuffs on the three-quarter sleeves. The only jewelry she wore was small pearl earrings and a single strand of matching pearls around her neck. It was conservative, but very flattering.

Frances had nervous butterflies in her stomach, but Tom held her hand and she felt better just to have his strength to support her emotionally. As they pulled up in front of the house, Frances drew a deep breath and decided, *What will be, will be.* Tom opened the front door and held it for Frances to enter. Inside she noted a very well-kept and nicely furnished living room. She did not have to be told the furniture was among the very best.

Tom's parents were seated in the room watching the television, which happened to be one of the largest Frances had ever seen. It was housed in a large, dark mahogany cabinet, and the television screen itself was probably a huge ten inches. In 1950 some families were now purchasing television sets, although Frances had never seen one as large as the one that was in their living room.

Tom immediately took Frances over to his mother and father and introduced her to them. His dad stood up and offered his hand to the pretty woman who stood before him. He asked her to sit down, and they exchanged pleasantries. Tom spoke first deciding to put Frances's mind at ease straightaway.

"Mom, Pop, didn't I tell you Frances was married and is separated from her husband and she has a young child?"

They both nodded their heads, and his mother answered, "Yes, of course, you explained this all to us."

Their conversation continued to be very pleasant, and after about an hour or so, Tom suggested they leave for dinner.

The four said their "good nights," and Frances and Tom left to go to dinner. Frances found Tom's parents were very pleasant, and she liked them instantly. Yes, Tom was right—it was better to get everything out in the open. Her life didn't change, but still it was good to know they accepted her. Back in the early fifties, there were not many divorced or separated women.

"Now that you have met my folks, Frances, we want to invite you and your daughter for Thanksgiving," Tom said. "My sisters and their families will be there, and I would like you to be with us as well."

A Matter of Survival

"Yes, I would like that, very much," she replied.

Thanksgiving came, and it was incredible to be with a family like Tom's. They were obviously well-educated and affluent people, but still exhibited no airs whatsoever. Tom's one brother-in-law, in particular, had a great sense of humor and made everyone laugh, making Frances feel very at ease. They all genuinely welcomed both her and her daughter into their family's holiday celebration.

What turned out to be the biggest surprise to Frances was to learn that Tom cooked most of the Thanksgiving dinner. She could never recall him ever saying that he even knew how to cook. He said he felt cooking was more like a hobby rather than a chore. Frances learned he had been good friends with a few executive chefs who had taught him a great deal. He quoted them, saying that not only the actual cooking was important, but presentation was a very big part of preparing a meal. It was very obvious Tom had been an excellent student as he carried through with everything he had learned.

Frances was now preparing for the Christmas season at Macy's, which was almost overwhelming, but still she continued to make plans for her sister-in-law's baby shower. She had sent out the invitations for the shower which would take place in the middle of January. As soon as the holiday season was over, the baby shower would be upon them.

However, one night while Frances was wrapping some gifts, the phone rang. It was her brother telling her Wilma had been placed in the hospital and would have to remain in bed for the next six months until she had the baby. Her doctor was not going to take any chances with Wilma's or the baby's life. Wilma's heart condition was extremely serious. Frances laughed ruefully as she told her brother her plans to give the shower. She never expected her sister-in-law to go into the hospital six months early. He thanked his sister for her good intentions and said that perhaps she could host the shower after the birth of the baby. *So much for well-laid plans,* she thought.

Frances visited Wilma at the hospital often, and even though she was confined to bed, it was still exciting for both of them to plan for the birth of the baby together. They had become the best of friends since Wilma first arrived in this country. Frances would tell Wilma about work and how

Arleen Patricia Mercorella

she loved her job, and they apparently were very pleased with her since she recently had been told she was being groomed to be promoted to an "executive." Wilma was just as excited for her as she was for herself.

Tom also came to visit Wilma, and the three would sit and talk together. Tom's job was becoming more and more demanding, and his supervisory capacities were becoming larger and larger. After all this time, Nels and Tom were still partners, and they not only worked together, but they were also the best of friends. Many times Nels's wife and Frances would spend an afternoon together. Sometimes the four would go out together.

Strange as it may seem, Tom didn't like talking about his job, even when they were out with Nels and his wife. He valued privacy when it came to police work, never elaborating about his position. Then one day when a new issue of *Life* magazine came out on the newsstands, Tom's picture appeared in it. There, on a full page, was a picture of Tom standing directly behind the current president, which was President Truman. It was obvious he had been one of the president's bodyguards while the president was visiting in New York. Even then, when Frances questioned him, he simply did not want to talk about it, much less brag about his position. Later on after Tom retired from the force, he admitted he had been bodyguard to many presidents and other dignitaries when they visited New York City by train. Furthermore, whenever President Truman came to visit, he always requested Tom be at his side.

Spring came to New York showing the miracle of rebirth everywhere. The trees were starting to bud, and flowers were popping up all over. Yes, May was a beautiful month, and it was almost time for the new baby to be born.

Then one night in early June, Frances received the awaited phone call from her brother. His wife had been taken into the delivery room. Frances simply said, "I'll be right there with you, Peter. I'll meet you at the hospital, and we will wait for the baby together."

Frances quickly grabbed her coat and handbag and ran to the corner. This was very rare for her, but she decided there couldn't have been a better time than now as she hailed a passing taxi. She instructed the driver to take her to Flushing Hospital as quickly as he could, for she was about to become an auntie.

A Matter of Survival

Within fifteen minutes, she was at the hospital's front entrance. After inquiring where the maternity delivery area was, she took the elevator and joined her brother and other expectant fathers in the fathers' waiting room. As odd as it may have seemed to some, she was the only woman in the room. They both waited for hours until finally the doctor came in the room and announced Peter was the proud father of a healthy baby daughter. Peter immediately asked about his wife, and the doctor told him she was quite weak, but with the proper rest, she should be fine. He would have to wait for at least an hour before he would be allowed to see his wife.

Peter was so happy. Both he and Frances were oblivious to the other fathers in the waiting room. It must have been a tender sight—brother and sister hugging and holding on to each other for what seemed like a very long time. When they finally broke their hold on each other, Peter looked at his sister, and for the first time spoke about their separation as children.

"Frances, I'm so happy that we have been reunited with each other after so many years. I'm especially happy you are able to share my joy with Wilma and me now, with our child. It was cruel what happened to us, and although I will never discuss it with our father, I know deep down I will never forgive him for separating us. I promise you, we will never be separated again."

Frances smiled and nodded her head in agreement. She simply said, "Peter, I always loved you, even when we were apart."

Although others in the room observed Peter and Frances with curiosity, they knew it had to be a very exceptional moment between these two young people.

The two continued to sit in the waiting room in silence. It was now very late, but still Frances did not want to leave until they could see mother and child. After almost an hour and a half, a nurse entered the room and called for Peter. Both Peter and Frances simultaneously rose to their feet. The nurse told them his baby daughter was now in the nursery, and they would be able to see her. She also said Peter could have a few minutes with his wife, but she made him promise not to stay too long as his wife was exhausted and needed to rest.

Peter and Frances followed the nurse toward the nursery. Frances was almost giddy with excitement. She could hardly contain herself with the anticipation of seeing her new niece. As they reached the nursery, they observed there was a closed curtain over the viewing window. The nurse, without actually speaking, indicated for them to stay just where they were and proceeded to enter a closed door adjacent to the room. Peter and Frances just stood there, looking at the window with the curtain closed. As funny as it may seem now, all Frances could think of while they were waiting was that the hospital should really change the curtain. It was starting to look worn and frayed. Her thoughts were broken as the curtain was suddenly drawn open. The nurse then placed a little bassinet on wheels near the window. She then proceeded to take the infant out of the tiny crib and held the baby up to the window for both of them to see. Peter looked as if he was going to cry when he saw his daughter. She was the tiniest baby Frances had seen in a long time, but she looked absolutely perfect. They had her wrapped in a little pink blanket, and there was a tiny pink cap on her head. After a few minutes, the nurse placed the infant back in the little crib.

"Peter, your little girl is just perfect," Frances said, and with that the nurse indicated she was about to close the curtain again.

After a few short moments, she came out into the hall and told Peter he could visit with his wife, and again reminded him it could be only for a minute. Frances stayed behind and waited for her brother.

When he came back, he looked very concerned.

"Frances, Wilma looks awful, just awful, and she could hardly talk to me."

"Peter, she just had a baby. Please don't expect too much; I'm sure when you come back tomorrow, she'll be a lot better," Frances said, trying to reassure him.

He just answered, "I hope so."

The two walked down the corridor toward the elevator. Peter told Frances he was parked in back of the hospital and he would drive her home before going home himself. Frances suggested he spend the night rather than have to drive back to an empty apartment. After thinking about this, he agreed. He kept a few spare clothes at his sister's place, so this might not be a bad idea. Frances did keep the spare couch, so it wasn't a problem for him to sleep overnight. It was now close to three in the morning, and when the two finally got to bed, they both fell asleep instantly.

A Matter of Survival

Frances rose first, put on the coffee, and quickly grabbed her clothes and headed for the bathroom to shower before her brother woke up. She got partly dressed, planning to put on something nicer to wear to work. Peter heard his sister in her little kitchen preparing something for them. She made some toast and served it along with some orange juice and coffee. She told Peter she had to leave in about a half hour, but that he was welcome to stay as long as he wanted. They talked about the new baby and his wife. He was anxious to see his wife again today and hoped she would look better than the night before.

"I'm sure you will find a big change in her today," she replied.

Frances finished getting dressed for work and told Peter to take his time. He turned on the radio, as he always liked listening to the news every morning. Frances kissed him good-bye, saying that she would join him tonight at the hospital.

She was exhausted at work because she had had such little sleep the night before, but felt it was well worth it. She was anxious to join her brother and sister-in-law at the hospital that evening. Tom had called her at work; she told him what had transpired the night before, and he was happy for all of them.

That evening, when Frances got off the train at Flushing, she decided to grab a hot dog and an orange drink at the local eatery and then take a bus to the hospital. She gulped down the food and caught the bus just as it was leaving. It was only a fifteen-minute ride to the hospital. At work today she was able to pick up some dusting powder for her sister-in-law and had it wrapped in the prettiest of paper.

When she got off the bus and walked up the hospital walk, she was surprised to find Tom waiting by the entrance door for her arrival. He was holding a large bouquet of pink and white flowers. It was just like him to surprise her. She smiled at him, and he kissed her hello, saying he wanted to surprise her. He would have met her at the train station, but he wasn't sure what train she would be taking and was afraid he would miss her. Frances was pleased that he was there to share in this time of happiness. After obtaining the hospital room pass, they rode the elevator together. Wilma's room was not too far from where she remembered, and as they walked into the room, she noted Peter was already there. Wilma was sitting up in bed, and although she still appeared somewhat tired, Peter said she looked better than the night before.

She kissed her brother hello and went over to Wilma, kissing her also. Frances told Wilma she had seen the baby the night before and thought she was just beautiful. Wilma smiled, and although she was very weak, she was happy both of them were there with Peter and her. She loved the flowers and asked the nurse to please put them in water and place them next to her bed.

Peter explained to his sister that the doctor had indicated he wanted Wilma to stay in the hospital for at least another month, as he felt it would be necessary to monitor her very carefully. Since the four of them were together talking about the new baby, and since Peter and Wilma had already decided to ask Frances and Tom to be the baby's godparents, this seemed the perfect time to do so. They were both delighted and accepted with great pleasure.

Once Wilma was discharged from the hospital, plans were set in motion for the christening of Frances's niece and soon-to-be godchild.

On the day the new baby was to be baptized, the weather turned out to be extremely hot and very uncomfortable. The plan was that everyone would go back to Wilma and Peter's apartment for dinner after the christening. The christening went smoothly and was over quickly. Tom suggested he would like to take everyone out for a drink at a delightful little place just over the Queens/Nassau County border. It was just the four of them and Patricia. So now there were five, plus a little baby. They all sat together in a large booth, and Tom ordered champagne for everyone, except, of course, Patricia. He ordered her a Shirley Temple. Afterward, as planned, everyone had dinner together at Wilma and Peter's home. It was a wonderful afternoon. It was so wonderful, in fact, that every year on the baby's birthday, they would all go together to the same small little place to celebrate.

Thirty-Five

DECISIONS, DECISIONS

Time was passing quickly. Frances would try to visit with her brother and sister-in-law as much as time would permit. It was fun to watch how much the baby grew from week to week. Now the baby was almost two years old.

Frances and Tom continued to have dinner together once a week, usually on Wednesdays. During one of their conversations, Frances told Tom she had received a call from the school where her daughter attended. Apparently Patricia longed to live with her mother so much so that it was starting to affect her schoolwork. She explained to Tom that she'd visited Patricia's teacher, and the teacher told Frances her daughter did not seem happy. As a matter of fact, the teacher encouraged Frances to take her daughter to live with her, since Patricia was now twelve-years old and mature for her years. She explained to Frances that many other children of the same age, so called "latch key" children, who stayed by themselves until their parents got home from work, seemed to do just as well as the other children whose mothers were at home.

As Frances left the school, her heart sank. She had to admit that because her daughter was being taken care of very well, it had never occurred to her to take her child back to live with her. After thinking it over, Frances decided she needed to talk this over with her daughter, and especially her mother-in-law.

Frances admitted to Tom that she was scared and very apprehensive, wondering whether she could continue to work and still be a full-time mother. She wanted to try to make a go of this, but needed encouragement. Tom listened very carefully and finally decided it was time for him to speak.

"Frances, your daughter should be with you. I also think it is time she left her grandmother's home, as her place now belongs with you. I know you are afraid, but I honestly think Patricia is the type of kid when you outline what would be expected of her, she would obey and listen to you. I don't think you have much to worry about, and, as a matter of fact, you may like having her around you on a permanent basis and not just weekends. Give it a try and don't be afraid. I'm sure it will work out."

Frances slept on the proposed change. To say that she was afraid was truly an understatement. Could she go to work and also be a full-time mother? Could she afford to provide for both of them? There were so many questions going around in her head that it was difficult to fall asleep. However, once the morning came, she knew she had decided. It probably would be the best thing for both of them.

Frances knew she didn't want to even discuss this with her daughter until she had had a chance to speak to her mother-in-law. As soon as she arrived at her in-laws' the next Friday night, she apprehensively explained her feelings, and unexpectedly her mother-in-law did not seemed surprised at all. She even said she had expected this would happen one day soon.

"Yes, Frances I think it is time she lives with you, and if it doesn't work out, there will always be a place for Patricia here. Don't be afraid, just tell her and take it from there."

Frances immediately felt better after talking to Mom. The funny thing was that whenever she needed to talk over something important, she would turn to her former mother-in-law. She always gave the wisest advice of anyone she knew. It was at times such as these when Frances could hardly believe her mother-in-law had gone no higher than the third grade in formal education. Yet she was excellent with spelling, grammar, math, and even more importantly, she had "good old common sense." Frances had a very deep sense of gratitude to this woman, a woman who she realized she loved a great deal and owed a great deal of appreciation. She had taken Patricia

A Matter of Survival

in to live with them from the age of three, and now that she was twelve she still wanted nothing but for Frances and her child to be happy. In all the years that her daughter was being cared for by her in-laws, Mom would never take even a dime from her. Instead Frances would always bring her something on Friday. Sometimes it might be a housedress, dusting powder, or some personal item, as Frances knew the woman would never spend money on herself. This was the only way she felt she could say thank you to this extraordinary woman.

That night while Frances and Patricia were traveling to the apartment, Frances told her daughter she wanted to talk to her about something very important and very special. So special that it was to be discussed between only the two of them once they got home. Her daughter was somewhat curious, to say the least. She just shook her head and cuddled next to her mother. The young girl loved her mother very much and was happy just to be with her. She was absolutely devoted to her mother and looked forward to being together with her every weekend. Her mother never disappointed her. She was always there. Every Friday she would be there without fail. Sometimes while she was growing up, she would ask her mother, "Why did Daddy leave?" Frances always answered that Daddy left Mommy because he didn't love her anymore, but she was sure even though he wasn't around, he still loved his daughter. Young Patricia just accepted what her mother said and didn't question it any further.

Once the two got home, Frances prepared something for them to eat and asked her young daughter to set the table for them. They sat down to dinner. Her daughter was happy, and that was obvious to Frances. She thought her daughter was very special and at the same time thought how very blessed she was to have her.

Frances said, "Patricia, how would you like to move from your grandmother's house and in with me? Since you are getting older now, I feel you would be responsible enough to be alone after school. I feel you can handle it. What do you think?"

Patricia jumped up and hugged her mother. This was the best news she could have been told.

"Oh Mom, I promise I will do everything you ask me. This is the best. Yes, yes, I would love to live with you. When can we start? Soon, I hope."

Frances never expected her daughter to be quite so jubilant and knew immediately from her child's reaction she definitely had made the right decision.

"You know, honey," Frances continued, "I don't make a lot of money, but I think we will be able to survive and we'll do okay. You won't be living in a house, but we have our apartment, and it is definitely ours. You will have full responsibility of locking the apartment door when you leave each day. I will also need for you to help with some small chores and errands. So now how do you feel about all this?"

Her daughter smiled and said she didn't need a lot; she was just happy to be with her. They talked for what seemed like hours about the pending change in their lives. They knew Grandma and her aunt would miss her, so they both decided Patricia would continue to spend one night a week at her grandma's house, probably every Wednesday. This seemed perfect. They discussed Patricia changing schools, and Frances told her daughter she would see to it that all the necessary arrangements would be made. It was exciting for both mother and daughter to discuss their future together. Frances realized that she herself hadn't been this happy in a very long time. As usual her mother-in-law was right again.

The very next day, Patricia actually ran through the streets exclaiming, "I can live with my mother! I can live with my mother!"

Some people stopped and stared at the young girl, but she didn't care. She was just happy to be able to live with her mother and to take on such an adult role in her young life.

Thirty-Six

LIFE WITH MOTHER

On Frances's first day off from work, she walked to what would become her daughter's new school. As she walked, she thought, *This is really a very far walk, much farther than the three blocks Patricia is used to walking each day.* She only hoped that her daughter could adjust to the newness of everything. As she walked, she counted the blocks, and it was twelve good-size blocks. Frances said a prayer to herself, hoping her daughter would be safe walking this distance by herself.

Once she got to the school, she made all the necessary arrangements, and it was all set. In exactly two weeks from today, Patricia would be starting in her new school. The next weekend, Patricia started taking her little possessions to her new home, anxious to get on with everything. This was an exciting time for her. On Friday night Tom came to visit and wished her luck. He assured her if there was anything she needed, she could count on him. He said the first thing he was going to do was to help buy her new school supplies. Tom, being a typical detective, warned Patricia when she started the new school not to give out any information to anyone.

"Just stay to yourself," he said, "and don't tell anyone your business."

This frightened Patricia somewhat, but she decided she could handle any questions that were asked. She just wanted to get on with her new surroundings.

The following week Frances made arrangements to go into work later than usual. Now both mother and daughter walked to the new school together. It was a nice-looking school, newer than the one Patricia had been attending. They first stopped at the office for the necessary paperwork and were given instructions to go to the second floor to find Patricia's classroom. Just then Patricia's mother did something Patricia would never forget. As they approached the second floor and before opening the corridor door, Frances stopped and said to her daughter, "Let me kiss you good-bye now and wish you good luck. I don't want you to feel awkward in front of the other children. Patricia, I want you to be happy."

"I am already happy," her daughter replied.

Then the two kissed good-bye in the stairwell and proceeded to Mrs. Roberts's seventh-grade classroom.

Frances knocked on the classroom door, and a somewhat matronly looking lady came over and said she was expecting them. Frances thanked her, handing the teacher the paperwork from the office.

"Patricia, I will see you tonight. Have a good day." With that Frances left the room and hurried off to work.

The teacher brought Patricia with her to the front of the room and introduced her to the class, stating, "Children, we have a new girl with us who transferred from a nearby town, and I would like all of you to make her to feel welcome."

The teacher then indicated for Patricia to follow her. She assigned her a desk and chair where she was to sit for the rest of the school year. Patricia felt so shy that she didn't really look at anyone, just the teacher.

After about an hour or so, the new teacher announced it was time for them to spend an hour in the auditorium for their study hall period. Lining up, the class followed her to the very large auditorium. The children piled into the aisle where they usually sat. Patricia was glad she was on the end and didn't have to speak to anyone. The seats behind her were empty, and the aisle in front of her was only a third of the way full with students. She took out one of her books and started to look through it.

Suddenly, Patricia realized she was surrounded by what appeared to be a gang of girls. One of them spoke.

A Matter of Survival

"Okay, Sister—where do you live, and how come you came to our school just now?"

Patricia remembered what Tom had told her, not to tell anyone her business, but she didn't think that was going to work just now. She shrugged her shoulders and simply said, "I live on Thirty-Fourth Road, and I just moved here to live with my mother." Before she could finish her sentence, the girls jumped up with lots of smiles and laughter.

"Wow!" one of them exclaimed. "We all live on Thirty-Fourth Road! What is your address?"

Patricia was stunned as she immediately felt accepted by the group. After giving them her address, one of them said, pointing to another girl, "She lives in your building."

After comparing notes, Patricia was told that one of the girls lived across the hall on the same floor.

"Patricia, you can join us walking to and from school. We can all walk home together today."

After study hall the class went into the lunchroom, and the group made room for the newcomer. All in all there were about ten girls who lived on the same block. Patricia was just one more to be added to the group. She was very happy now and already felt a sense of belonging. She couldn't wait to tell her mother about the day's events.

After school the girls gathered together and walked the many blocks home. The whole time there was lots of laughter and lots of talk about the latest clothes, which apparently none of them could afford, and of course, they talked about who liked which boy, which only created more laughter and good-natured teasing. When they arrived at their destination, the twelve blocks did not seem like such a big distance. Patricia could already sense she would develop a close relationship with these girls and was pleased to be a part of the group. One surprising thing she learned was that most of the girls lived with their mothers, and only their mothers. Apparently, all the mothers worked during the day, and each girl was responsible for school and their chores. They all seemed to be living the same life that Patricia now had. *Yes,* Patricia thought, *this is going to be even better than I ever imagined.*

Frances arrived home at the scheduled time of seven o'clock. She was very anxious to find out how Patricia's first day at school had gone and hoped she got home safe and sound. As soon as she walked in the door, Patricia threw her arms around her mother, at the same time kissing her on the cheek. She started to talk nonstop about her day, and Frances was both very pleased and relieved. She was happy to find she had made friends so quickly and had company to walk back and forth to school with, knowing there was safety in numbers. Frances did remember seeing an older girl leaving the apartment across the hall. The girl locked her apartment door with a key on a chain around her neck. She recalled that the girl had seemed so much bigger than Patricia.

As Patricia continued explaining the day's events to her mother, Frances realized the girl her daughter was telling her about must have been the same girl Frances had observed previously. This was too good to be true.

All the time Frances was preparing something for dinner, Patricia went on and on about her new school and more importantly, her new friends. Frances thought how odd it was, after living here for so many years, she knew no one—except, of course, for the super—and now she finds out that there must be many other women in her same situation.

Frances taught her daughter how to start to prepare some of the food for their dinner. She found Patricia was eager to learn and help as much as possible. Patricia started with peeling potatoes and placing them in a pot of cold water. She was also responsible for setting the table for the two of them. Everything was working out quite well.

Eventually, the two young neighbors, who were now good friends, decided it was time to introduce their mothers. The girls giggled over this; they were certain their mothers needed company and hoped they would "hit it off." When the arrangements were made, Patricia pulled her reluctant mother across the hall. The other girl was anxiously waiting, and as soon as the doorbell rang, she opened the door instantly.

"Mom," Patricia said. "Please meet my friend, Carolyn, and Carolyn, this is my mom."

Patricia was so proud of her mother. She was still dressed from work and, as usual, looked great. Then Carolyn's mother, Mildred, appeared, and Patricia thought she was one of the prettiest women she had ever seen, outside of her own mother, of course. The two older women went into the living room while the girls stayed in the kitchen finishing their homework.

A Matter of Survival

Together they enjoyed what they had accomplished in introducing their mothers.

Their mothers seemed to like talking to each other, and after about two hours, Patricia decided she had better leave and get ready for bed. Excusing herself as she entered the living room, Patricia asked her mother if she could go home and get her clothes ready for the next day and wash up.

Her mother said, "Sure, honey, I'll be in a little later. I have my key, so don't worry; if you get tired, just go to bed."

She kissed her mother and said good-bye to her friend's mother and left.

As things turned out, Frances and Mildred stayed together talking for about another hour and a half, something only women can do. The two found they had a lot in common. Both were single mothers, raising their daughters by themselves, each was a professional working woman, and more importantly, each had a gentleman friend. Unfortunately, Mildred's story was not a pretty one. It seems she had been very happily married when her husband took seriously ill and died; her daughter was only two years old at the time. It was quite a different story than Frances's, but tragic nonetheless.

Yes, this was the start of a wonderful friendship. A friendship that would last for many, many years.

It had now been five months since Frances had decided to have her daughter move in with her, and the arrangement was working out much better than she had ever expected. She not only had her daughter, but now she also had a very close friend.

One afternoon, without telling anyone—even her daughter—Mildred decided to buy a good used car and surprised all of them with it. The car enabled them the freedom to go to new and out-of-the ordinary places.

Patricia's thirteenth birthday was approaching, and Frances decided she wanted to treat her daughter to something extraordinary. She decided to purchase tickets to see a play, Patricia's first Broadway play. She hoped that after introducing Broadway theatre to her, she would want to see many more. Frances saved as much as she possibly could for this special day in March. After discussing it with Mildred, they decided why not plan for the four good friends to spend the entire day out together? First they'd go to the play and then afterward have dinner at a nice restaurant.

A week before her birthday, Frances surprised her daughter, saying she was taking her to see a delightful new play entitled *The King and I* and that Carolyn and Mildred were also going with them. Patricia loved these exciting times in the city with her mother and their friends, and she looked forward to celebrating her birthday this way. As it turned out, this was the perfect birthday present! They all had a fantastic time. Patricia loved every bit of it, and so did Frances.

Time quickly passed, and Frances and her daughter often visited her brother and sister-in-law. It was wonderful to have her little family together. She adored her brother and loved her sister-in-law just as if she was a sister.

After a while Frances introduced her friend, Mildred, to her brother and sister-in-law, and everyone got along splendidly. They even planned for all of them to vacation together somewhere in upstate New York. The arrangement was that they would use two cars and follow each other to their destination. They were all to meet at Frances's apartment and take off from there.

Just before they were about to leave, Wilma and Peter said they wanted to speak with them. The group all looked at them, curious, waiting for them to continue. Peter spoke first.

"We wanted you all to know that we are expecting our second child, and we are just thrilled. The baby will be born in February."

Everyone was very happy to hear this news. The two young girls were elated to be a witness to this marvelous announcement. Only Frances was a little apprehensive. She remembered full well how sickly Wilma had been when she gave birth to their first child and couldn't help but feel somewhat troubled by this news. She decided not to say anything negative, but instead congratulated them both, putting her arms first around her beloved brother and then her just-as-beloved sister-in-law. She offered to give them whatever help she could. Frances had to turn away since she didn't want

A Matter of Survival

it to be obvious that she was somewhat upset by the news. *Dear God,* she prayed. *Please take good care of Wilma and watch over her and please help her to have a healthy baby.*

The vacation was fantastic. Peter took the two young girls under his wing, and after a huge breakfast, the three would go for long hikes, playing challenging verbal games along the way. The three woman, together with Frances's little niece, would spend the mornings exploring the local shops and finding a special restaurant to go for dinner. The hotel had a small pool behind it, but its size didn't seem to matter, because they considered it an incredible luxury to have this for their outdoor recreation. They would all gather around it for an afternoon of fun. As it turned out, this was a vacation that would never be forgotten by any of them.

Soon the vacation was over. Everyone had a great time, but Frances was somewhat concerned because since their return, Wilma looked tired and a very peaked. She was thankful Wilma had mentioned they had a doctor's appointment two days after their return.

It was no surprise to Frances when the doctor put Wilma directly in the hospital from his office. He was very concerned as he had told her previously if she was to become pregnant again, it would be extremely dangerous for both mother and child. Again she would need constant supervision. Peter had to make all sorts of arrangements for his first child. Along with others, they all took turns watching her when they had days off, but still it was difficult for him to be driving his daughter from place to place to see that she would be cared for properly. They all worried, and it seemed like an eternity to everyone, with seven months still to go. Actually, the only one who seemed calm and not as worried—or at least didn't show it—was Wilma. She said her faith would see her through, and it did.

Everyone would visit with Wilma in the hospital, as she was required to stay in bed for her entire pregnancy. Even Patricia would stop by after school to spend some time with her aunt. She admired the baby items her aunt sewed for the new baby. Wilma was very gifted at sewing and she was able to make lovely outfits, sewing them all by hand. Wilma kept busy with her sewing and her devotion to God. Sometimes she would read magazines and books, both in Italian and in English. Peter had gone to school to learn English, but Wilma was self-taught and excelled at it. The nurses loved her as well as the other members of the staff.

Finally, February came, and it was time. Wilma was going into labor. Frances, again, was at Peter's side in the fathers' waiting room.

The doctor was summoned immediately, as he had instructed the staff, and upon his arrival, it only took one glance for them to realize that he was very worried. Frances and Peter sat together, holding on to each other without saying a word. After many hours the doctor came into the room.

"Wilma had a baby girl. The baby is fine, but I'm afraid that we're not out of the woods with Wilma. She is very, very weak, and we almost lost her on the delivery table. Through the grace of God and our perseverance and determination, she came back to us. I'm afraid she cannot see you tonight, as I insist she must rest."

Peter broke down and cried with fear and worry. Frances held him and assured him God would hear their prayers and she just knew Wilma was going to be fine. They stayed for a few minutes to view his new daughter. She was absolutely beautiful, but Peter couldn't stop worrying about his wife.

Peter saw his sister home, and she insisted he stay the night. Even though it might be a little uncomfortable for him, she didn't want him to be alone. His daughter was with close friends, so there was no reason for him to go home tonight. The single couch was situated against one of the walls, and with the sofa bed pulled out, the room was crowded, but it was still better to have Peter stay with her. They would make do. Patricia was already in bed and could see from her mother's and uncle's expression things were not going as well as they may have hoped for.

In the morning Frances got up extra early, making coffee and a little breakfast for her brother and daughter. Her brother was also up and said he wasn't able to sleep at all. He just wanted to go back to the hospital to see his wife and new baby. They called the hospital and were told that Wilma showed some slight improvement from the night before, and the doctor had left word saying Wilma's husband could visit later that morning.

He gulped some coffee down and had a bit of toast, but said he really didn't want to eat anything. Patricia was up and got ready for school. Upon entering the kitchen, she knew for sure something must be wrong. All she

A Matter of Survival

had to do was to look at her mother and uncle and the expressions on their faces.

"Mom, what is going on? Is Aunt Wilma okay?"

Frances sighed and told her daughter that her aunt did have a rough time, but the doctor assured them that with a good portion of rest, she should recover just fine. Patricia went to her uncle and kissed him tenderly on the cheek and put her arms around his neck.

"Uncle Peter," she said, "I'm sure Aunt Wilma will be fine. I am so anxious to see the new baby, and I also miss seeing my other cousin. As soon as we can, please may I go to the hospital to visit my aunt and new baby?"

Peter smiled and thanked his young niece for her concern and caring. He simply said, "I love you for that, Patricia." He hugged her back at the same time.

Frances quickly tidied up the kitchen and told Peter he could take his time, but right now she needed to get ready for work. After about a half hour, Frances was ready to leave for her job in New York. She had on a stunning dark-brown fitted dress with a V neckline. The dress had three-quarter sleeves and looked perfect with her short white gloves. It was a conservative dress, but still it showed off her attractive figure. Even though Peter was distressed, he looked at his sister and said, "Frances, you look so elegant—you always look elegant."

She smiled and thanked him. She gently kissed him on the cheek and said she would call later and wished him luck at the hospital. With that she was out the door.

As Frances hurriedly walked toward the bus stop, she prayed for her sister-in-law and her brother. She loved them both, but the bond between her and her brother was inseparable. If he was hurt, she was hurt. She was thankful to be able to give him whatever support he needed and was glad he'd accepted her offer to stay the night. Aside from the latest worry concerning her sister-in-law, Frances was happy. She knew she had a lot to be thankful for: She now had her daughter whom she dearly loved living with her. She had been reunited with her brother and also gained a wonderful sister-in-law, plus two young nieces. Aside from all these blessings, she also had a remarkable gentleman friend who was very good to her and her family. She had a great job, having recently been promoted to an executive with a major department store. Wilma just had to get better, and that's all there was to that!

Wilma did recover, but understandably it took a long, long time before she felt back to normal. Once she finally was discharged from the hospital, Peter was told it would be necessary to hire someone to assist in not only the care of his two children, but also his wife. Peter knew money was going to be tight, especially on his small salary, but if sacrifices had to be made, he would see to it that they would be made. He immediately decided to get a second job. Anything that was required of him, he would do without hesitation.

Already financially things were not easy for Peter and his wife, not only because of Wilma's severe health problems, but also because his father made it very clear—one could say even somewhat demanded—he would have to help support him as he was reaching his older years. He would whimper, saying his small amount of Social Security wasn't enough. (It should be noted that back in the 1950s, male children were expected to contribute to the financial well-being of their parents.) Now, on top of all this, his wife needed extra help at home. Peter took a second job; at the same time, he continued to look for engineering work, for which he had been educated.

After the birth of her second child, Wilma recovered but knew she would have to stay on a strict regimen in her daily routine. Doctor's orders were for Wilma to rest in bed every afternoon for at least an hour. This was not easy for her as she loved being active and taking care of her husband, her children, and her home. She was an excellent wife and mother. She taught her girls to do small tasks, which were a big help to her, and at the same time taught them to speak Italian as well. It was also necessary for her to see the doctor frequently to make sure her heart was not failing and she was doing all that was required to maintain her health, no matter how frail she was.

Eventually, Frances's father passed away. Upon his death, Frances, Peter, and Jenny started to make the necessary funeral arrangements. While doing this, they were shocked to discover among Frank's papers, that while anticipating his death, he had prepared his burial arrangements and had taken care of the financial obligations as well. He never discussed this with any of them. It was almost as if he was trying to make up for his negligence of his earlier years. Peter was no longer responsible for giving him financial aid.

In time Peter was finally able to get a good job using his engineering skills and eventually worked his way up into a management position. His new position required him to travel a great deal, and sometimes he was able to take his family with him, which would turn into a vacation for all of them. His wife's health was steady now, as she always followed the doctor's orders. She rested daily and took the prescribed medications. Her health would always be a concern.

Thirty-Seven

MAKING IT ALL WORK

Patricia was preparing for her grade school graduation and looking forward to attending high school the following fall. Now, at thirteen, she was not only allowed to take the bus alone to visit her grandmother every week, but very often she would also visit her aunt Wilma. Often her mother would meet her there after work, and later in the evening, the two would travel home to their apartment together. Things were working out marvelously.

Since Patricia was graduating elementary school, Frances and Tom thought maybe it would be good for her to attend camp during the summer months and presented this idea to her.

"Camp? Camp? Absolutely no way. Camp is for children, and I do not want to go to camp. Absolutely not. I am not a child. Please, please don't treat me like one."

Well, needless to say, that was the end of that idea.

Frances was proud watching her daughter grow into a responsible young woman. Even though she was just a young teenager, her daughter loved the independence and responsibility that was given to her. Frances would leave a list of chores and errands her daughter would be responsible for, and for the most part, they got done. It seemed to work out well, as most of Patricia's friends had similar errands and responsibilities. Sometimes the girls would accomplish their errands together. Once a week the girls would pull a cartful of soiled laundry, drop it off at the Laundromat before school, and retrieve it at the end of the school day. The girls actually thought doing these chores together was fun; knowing it was a help to their mothers was a bonus. The girls felt very grown up to have so much responsibility for taking care of their homes and also attending school. Of course, there were many times when chores would be put off to the last minute, and Patricia would run around the apartment dusting, carpet sweeping, setting the table, and taking care of other routine tasks at a furious pace. Usually she made sure everything was completed just as her mother got home from work. When their friends got together and compared notes, they would have a good laugh at how quickly they could work to make up for their frivolity.

When Patricia started high school, Frances had a day off in the middle of the week as well as Sundays. She would spend her day off cleaning their little apartment until it was spotless and making a terrific dinner for the two of them. Of course, Sunday was still a special day for her and her daughter. Occasionally, they would deviate from their normal Sunday routine since Patricia was getting older. Some Sundays Patricia would spend the day with her friends. A few of the girls would take the subway into New York just to walk around for the afternoon and then come home before dark. They always had good, clean fun just being together. Although none of them had a boyfriend, the subject of boys always occupied a large part of their conversations, giving them an opportunity for more laughter. The young girls loved their independent lifestyle. They would go into the city with a minimal amount of money in their pockets, which didn't seem to bother them at all. They all had the trust of their mothers, and none of them wanted to violate that trust.

When the young girls got together on these Sundays, Frances would spend her day with Mildred, who was now her best friend. Sometimes Frances, Mildred, Carolyn, and Patricia would go out together and have a terrific time. Once summer arrived, the four would jump into Mildred's car and spend hot weekend days at the beach on the north shore of Long Island. Sometimes the girls would be allowed to bring an additional friend along. Patricia thought this was a terrific way to grow up.

Patricia looked forward to Saturdays, when Frances went to work. Almost every week Tom would come by early before his shift would start.

He and Patricia would go shopping on Main Street. The day always included a light lunch, which usually consisted of a hot dog and orange drink at Nedick's. This was one of Patricia's favorite spots for a quick lunch. Today it might be called "fast food," but in the 1950s this was one of the most popular quick places to eat.

The two would shop in the early afternoon together. Tom loved clothes and always looked the part of a very well-groomed gentleman. He would ask Patricia to help him pick out shirts and ties. He was particularly aware that the wealthier kids at Patricia's school had many things she did not, and he would find out whether there might be something she needed or even wanted. It gave him great pleasure to act as a substitute father. He would always treat her to some fabulous item, even though she would never ask for it. Sometimes it was a type of pocketbook the young girls were carrying, or perhaps shoes which were the latest fad. As they shopped they talked about music. Early Saturday mornings there was a radio show announcing the top ten recording artists and the top hits of the week. Tom and Patricia would bet each other which hit was going to be number one. Tom was extremely good to Patricia, and she loved him for it. Frances would say he was spoiling her, but he only replied, "She deserves to be spoiled."

Tom found enormous pleasure in acting as a father figure to this young girl who he knew had been abandoned by her father. It made him angry. How the father of this blossoming teenage girl could just forget her was something he couldn't understand or accept. How was it possible for a man to shirk his responsibilities and not care if his child was provided for? He never even sent her a birthday or Christmas card. Since Tom was a bachelor and didn't have children of his own, he treated Patricia as a daughter and loved doing it.

Needless to say Patricia relished the attention and the love he displayed on her. She admired Tom; he seemed to be capable of doing anything he set out to do. She remembered observing him one day at his parents' home arranging a large bouquet of flowers, setting it off with an enormous handmade bow, marvelously preparing hors d'oeuvres for company that evening, and then going outside and pulling himself under the car on a dolly to make a repair. He was the most amazing man she knew!

A Matter of Survival

Patricia also treasured the fact that Tom always included her when making plans with Frances. He told Frances she had a very special child and she deserved a lot of credit for raising her so well: "Patricia is a good kid." His words made Frances very proud, to say the least.

Tom's heart and admiration went out to Frances, and he supposed this was one of the reasons why he loved her so much. She was a strong woman. Patricia knew how hard her mother worked to provide for them both and therefore would never ask for anything. She appreciated everything that was given to her and felt extremely lucky to have this wonderful woman for a mother.

Frances could hardly believe the years were passing by so quickly. Her daughter would soon be graduating high school. Was this possible?

During her daughter's teenage years, even though Frances was on a limited budget, she tried to give Patricia the best quality of clothing, although most was bought at the end of the season. This enabled her to buy beautiful clothes at great prices. Frances learned early on to be a wise shopper. She would watch when the better clothes were being reduced, which was usually when the new season's stock was put out to the public. Frances would buy the reduced items and hold them in a closet for the following year. During the 1950s women wore beautiful fashions and dressed exquisitely. Frances and her daughter were no exception. They both looked as if they'd stepped out of a fashion magazine.

Since Patricia's high school had such a large population of students, the classes were held in what were called "split sessions." The freshmen and sophomore grades started school at one o'clock in the afternoon and would be released at five, but the upperclassmen got the better schedule of seven thirty in the morning to twelve thirty in the afternoon. Patricia got a part-time job after school, working a few afternoons in the office at Flushing Hospital, which alleviated the need for Frances to give any spending money to her daughter. Often Patricia would finish school for the day and go into the city to meet up with her mother.

Patricia loved visiting her mother at Macy's and sometimes would spend hours going from floor to floor, admiring all the good-looking clothes and other merchandise. She particularly loved visiting the pet department. There were always some cute little puppies or kittens who seemed to appreciate her attention. After Frances got off from work, the two would have dinner in the city and travel home together.

Frances loved her job, especially now that she had obtained executive status as a supervisor. During the Christmas season, she was given the responsibility of supervising the main floor of this huge department store. This involved a great many details, not only in supervising and scheduling numerous personnel, but she was also responsible for constantly replenishing the always-depleting inventory of merchandise. The pace was hectic, but Frances loved it anyway. Frances did all she could to assure the higher-ups they would have a profitable holiday season. Frances was consistently complimented on her ability to handle detail and lead others. At the conclusion of the holiday season, her current boss, who was a senior buyer, confided in Frances that she was being observed for the possibility of another promotion, perhaps to a junior buyer. She admired her skilled boss and considered this the ultimate compliment. Not only would this mean a substantial monetary reward, but also her efforts and hard work were being recognized.

Thirty-Eight

ANOTHER COINCIDENCE

During Patricia's senior year and just a month after her seventeenth birthday, Tom had arranged through a good friend for Patricia to be interviewed for a position at Pan American Airways whose headquarters were in Long Island City. The position was for a junior girl reporting to one of the higher-level executives.

After completing the necessary tests and paperwork, Patricia got the job. Since her school day was over at twelve thirty, her new boss offered for her to work part time until she graduated, and then she could start to work full time afterward. What an exciting time this was for both mother and daughter. Patricia would not only be eligible for flight benefits, but her mother would also be entitled to these benefits as well. Frances was proud of her daughter as she knew the values she had instilled in her were now very obvious. She gave herself a mental "pat on the back" for raising her daughter with all the challenging obstacles that had been placed before her. Frances thought it was quite ironic her daughter would land her first real job at Pan American. It was an unbelievable coincidence!

Both Patricia and Frances were looking forward to graduation. Frances was especially happy for her daughter, since she herself was never able to finish high school. She wanted to treat her daughter to something extraordinarily different. Finally she came up with an idea she knew would make her daughter feel exceptionally loved. In a way, she not only wanted to reward her daughter, but herself also for a job well done. She decided they should have a very special celebration.

After careful contemplation and much deliberation, Frances chose to take her daughter into New York to see one of the latest Broadway plays and then afterward onto the Hawaiian Room at the Hotel Lexington for a dinner show. Frances knew this was going to be a very expensive outing. Having dinner at this exclusive restaurant was more than extravagant on her salary, but Frances decided what could be a better time than now to indulge in such a luxury? She thought, *Yes, money may be tight, but she was not one to accumulate bills.* She managed to support them both by making sure all the bills were paid on time and working overtime whenever it was offered to her. She was very selective about spending on extras. After the experience she'd had with her former husband, Frances did not like spending money foolishly, and because of this, she had developed good budgetary skills.

As it turned out, it poured rain on Patricia's graduation day, but the rain did not dampen the spirits of either mother or daughter. After the graduation ceremonies, the two went back to their apartment, freshened up a bit, and headed to the city. She hoped her daughter would remember this day forever, and she did!

As arranged, the next day Patricia starting working full time. Even though she didn't go on to college, she always felt she didn't miss anything. She loved working for Pan American and loved her new job enormously. It was very exciting for a young woman to work in the atmosphere of a major airline. The company was filled with stimulating young adults who were always traveling to or from someplace in the world. Patricia now relished buying her own clothes and contributing a small portion of her income to her mother. It also gave her great pleasure to buy pretty things for her mother, surprising her with something she was sure she would like. She would still periodically meet her mother in the city, only now she would sometimes be the one to pay for dinner.

Even though she was working full time, Patricia faithfully continued to visit her grandmother every Wednesday. She lived in a simple home located in an unpretentious middle-class neighborhood in Queens, but it was a place Patricia loved visiting. She felt comfortable with what she now considered to be her second home. She loved her grandmother and her young aunt. Over the years the two girls had developed a bond, a bond that was even closer than any sisters might have. When they were together, they were inseparable, acting more like twins than aunt and niece. It was a bond that would last forever.

They both were attractive and well-groomed young women who constantly turned the heads of young men when they were out together. Even though they were mature young women, Patricia's grandmother would remind them they were "descendants of royalty" and as such they must demonstrate a demeanor of ladylikeness and "class." The girls were never quite sure if this tale was true, but whether it was family lore or not, it worked. Deep down they really wanted to believe this story. There always seemed to be a boy or two who vied for the girls' attention. The young women would just laugh at the interest that was frequently being displayed.

After Patricia had been working less than a year, another position opened up in Pan American's New York executive offices in the Chrysler Building. The position was for a receptionist working on the fifty-seventh floor, where many of the vice presidents and higher-ranking executives had their offices. Moreover, the position would be reporting to Patricia's boss. Patricia immediately suggested that her young aunt come for an interview. Needless to say, she got the job, and now they both felt they were taking New York "by storm." They often would meet after work and walk around the city, thankful for all the benefits of living and working there. At nineteen Patricia felt life couldn't get much better than this; she felt like a woman of the world. She had also met a young man at Pan American that she fairly liked, but didn't take too seriously. Before long she was seeing him steadily. Patricia thought it was so much fun living with her mother. As strange as it may seem, she never missed her natural father. Even with the hardships her mother and she endured, she was always able to overcome them. Patricia just shrugged them off. After all she had her mother and, of course, Tom, who acted as a father figure to her.

On one recent visit to her grandmother, a terrible argument ensued between her grandparents. From what Patricia gathered, her father still kept in contact with her grandfather, usually only when he was desperate for money. He often needed large sums to get him out of trouble that his now-heavy gambling habits had gotten him into. When Patricia's grandmother discovered her husband had been helping to get their son out of debt even to the point where he had taken out bank loans to feed their son's irresponsibility, this was too much for her to bear. This issue became a constant source of friction between the two grandparents.

Thirty-Nine

WHEN ALL IS GOING WELL, LOOK OUT

Things were going very smoothly at home for Patricia and her mother. Since Frances did get her promotion, they were able to move into larger apartment on the same floor of their building. They went from two and a half rooms to three and a half rooms, the main difference being they now had a large bedroom. This might not seem like much to most people, but to Frances and her daughter, this was a very big accomplishment. As soon as they moved into their new home, Frances managed to buy a nice bedroom suite with two twin beds and had it delivered to the new apartment. With her mother's decorating talents and her keen way of managing finances, she was able to make it a marvelous place for the two of them. They both loved their new home.

Frances was still dating Tom, and now Patricia was regularly dating the young man from work. Her former mother-in-law eventually met Tom and took an instant liking to him. Odd as the situation was, Tom seemed to take the place of the son she had lost so many years ago. Tom liked "Mom" a great deal and respected her even more so for all that she had done for Frances. On the holidays, he would bring her something special for her alone to savor. Usually he would make up a large serving tray or cutting board with an assortment of gourmet cheeses and treats. Frances was pleased her mother-in-law liked Tom so much, but then again, so many people seemed to take an instant liking to him.

While Frances's nieces were still young, Peter and Wilma bought a home and moved to Long Island. Many weekends Frances and Patricia would visit Frances's brother and his family at their new home. Frances was very proud of Peter's success and was extremely happy for him. To say that they still maintained a strong bond of togetherness was an understatement. It was obvious to everyone their bond was an extraordinary one. The attachment they had for each other could never be broken.

Peter was now an engineering executive for a large company, traveling all over the United States speaking at conferences on behalf of his company. It was wonderful to see him succeed after all his hard work and the difficult start he had from childhood. Holidays would come and go, but they always included fantastic times together with her brother and his family.

If Frances learned anything from her past, it was that when things are going well, look out. Life doesn't stay wonderful all the time. She confided to her daughter that her boss, whom she greatly admired and respected, was going to be transferred out of her department, and soon she would be reporting to a new manager. Although she had already met her new supervisor, she was concerned. As soon as she was introduced, she had a feeling of uneasiness. Sometimes women's intuition does play out correctly.

Frances could not believe what was happening to the job she loved so much. Her new boss had a very odd attitude toward her. He was not only demanding but also demeaning, not only to her but her staff as well. It was obvious that he did not like working with a woman. She continued to perform anything that was required of her in her usual efficient manner, but he criticized her constantly. Frances couldn't seem to please him no matter how hard she tried. At one point she decided to discuss the situation with the people in personnel, asking for some guidance because she could never seemed to please her new boss. Frances felt they were very noncommittal and actually very vague about giving her support. She was only told to be patient with him. However, one of the women she knew quite well in personnel confided to her that there were rumors her new boss had very strong connections higher up and to be very careful of him. Frances was horrified. How could she even compete after hearing something like that? All she knew was hard work and dedication to her job. She even tried to reach her former boss for

A Matter of Survival

his input, only to find he had been transferred to an out-of-state store, and it would be difficult, if not impossible, to even reach him, much less discuss her new predicament with him.

It wasn't long before Frances discovered her new boss had a gentleman friend who also worked in the store and his friend was vying for a promotion, preferably working with her new boss. Frances decided no matter what rumors she heard, she would work harder than ever. She needed her job, and she was not going to be deterred by this individual. She would remain respectful and hardworking, no matter what.

Finally almost a year passed, and Frances realized her new boss had very little to say to her except to criticize her for some little something all the time. Then it was job review time, and Frances discovered her performance evaluation working for this man was awful. He didn't have one good thing to say about her and suggested to personnel that Frances should be placed somewhere else in the store, as he didn't want to work with her anymore. When the personnel representative summoned her to his office, Frances discovered she was being demoted to a sales position on the first floor, which would mean starting all over at the bottom again. This was totally unacceptable to her. She had been wronged, and it was apparent no one was going to help her. Considering this to be a tremendous insult, Frances decided to leave the store entirely. Back in the late 1950s, women didn't have much recourse in the business world; they just had to accept things as they were given. Yes, she left the store, but it took its toll on her. There was nothing Frances could do.

Patricia was heartsick for her mother, and for the first time since she'd started working for Pan American, she took a day off to spend with her mother. She decided to take her mother into the city, because in the past, it had always seemed like a "cure all." The two women didn't talk much about what had happened, but instead did some shopping, and at Patricia's suggestion they would see a new movie that just arrived at the Capitol Theatre called *Vertigo*. Since she knew her mother was a big movie fan and loved Jimmy Stewart, Patricia thought this would take her mother's mind off her problems, or so she hoped.

It was a Tuesday afternoon, and the theatre was practically empty. Patricia suggested they take two seats in the balcony. This would enable her mother to relax and smoke her Viceroy cigarettes if she wanted. It appeared no one else was sitting in the balcony. Once they were comfortably seated, Patricia placed her packages and handbag on the seat next to her. She made sure her mother was comfortable and, in the darkness of the theater, placed her hand on top of her mother's. Without saying a word, Patricia gave her mother the reassurance that she was there for her.

The movie also stared Kim Novak. The actors played exceptional parts, turning out what were to be among their best performances. It was an engrossing and absorbing film, full of suspense and intrigue. During the course of the film, Patricia had noticed someone coming in and sitting down right in back of them. *Oh well,* she thought *guess we won't have too much privacy now.* Feeling somewhat awkward, she removed her hand from her mother's.

At the conclusion of the movie, Frances appeared to have gotten her mind off her troubles. Patricia suggested they have a bite to eat while in the city and then go straight home. Frances nodded her head, and as they got up to leave, Patricia discovered her handbag had vanished. She looked all over, even checking under the seat on the floor, but her handbag was not there. *Oh no, can anything else go wrong?* It was true. Her purse had vanished. Then she recalled the man who'd sat in back of them while they were watching the show. She remembered thinking at the time it was strange—with all the seats around, why was he sitting there? Now she had her answer.

The two women gathered their packages and proceeded down to the office to report the stolen handbag. While the manager didn't admit anything, Frances got the feeling this was not the first time this had happened in this theatre.

Fortunately, Frances did have money on her, and the two just decided to take the train and go directly home. As soon as they arrived at their apartment, Frances telephoned the superintendent, who was good enough to change the lock on the apartment door after she'd explained to him what had happened. Frances and Patricia prepared a light dinner, which consisted of only bacon and eggs since they didn't have much else available to them.

Tom telephoned that evening, first speaking to Patricia. He thanked her for being so supportive to her mother. He was concerned for this woman for whom he cared so much. After a rather lengthy conversation with Frances, she said she wanted to go to bed early and forget the horrible problems that had started the day before.

The next morning Patricia got up for work, deciding to let her mother sleep. Once she was dressed, she looked in on her mother, who appeared to be resting comfortably. Not wanting to disturb her, she simply kissed her lightly on her cheek and left a note on the kitchen table saying if she should need her to just call her at work and she looked forward to seeing her later after work.

It was about three o'clock in the afternoon when Patricia received a call from Tom. He said he didn't want to alarm her, but since he wasn't able to reach her mother by telephone, he decided to stop by the apartment, only to find Frances with hives all over her body and almost hysterical because the hives seemed to be causing unbearable itching. He immediately took her to the emergency room, where the doctor on duty said the hives and the severe itching were probably a reaction to the recent stress she'd endured. He prescribed tranquillizing medication and sent her home. Patricia rushed home, anxious to speak with her mother.

"Mom," she said. "We will get through this. I just know you will be fine. Tom is here with us, and I'm sure the medication you were given will help. I know in the morning you will be just fine."

Her mother could only simply look up at her. It was obvious she was heavily sedated with medication. Even though Patricia was not really sure her mother was going to be fine, she wouldn't allow herself to show her apprehension and worry. Tom had left to get some take-out food for Patricia and him, saying he would stay the night and perhaps they should take turns watching over her mother. He returned with some simple Chinese food consisting of soup and lo mein. Neither one felt like eating, but they sat there together in the kitchen nonetheless, hoping Frances would be better by the time morning came.

During the night Frances developed a low grade fever. The hives were still all over her. Patricia took a cool cloth and placed it on her forehead, hoping to reduce her fever somewhat. By the time the morning came, Frances did not look any better. As a matter of fact, she looked worse. This almost panicked them both. Tom called Patricia into the kitchen.

"Patricia," he said, "I know some very fine doctors in the city who are personal friends of mine, and I think I better call on them. Perhaps they might have some suggestions as to how we can take care of your mother."

Patricia was glad he was there with her and was grateful to him for making this suggestion. He indicated to her not to speak as he picked up the telephone in the kitchen. After a somewhat abbreviated conversation with his doctor friend, he related the story of what had recently transpired. At first there was a short silence, and then she heard Tom say, "Okay, we will meet you there within the hour."

Patricia felt her eyes filling with tears, which were more from fright than sadness.

"Tom, what is it? Please tell me."

He replied his doctor friend was very concerned, not only because of the severity of the hives, but even more so because she had been showing signs of delirium through the night.

"He wants us to get her into New York Hospital immediately," Tom continued, trying not to show his concern.

Patricia just shook her head, acknowledging what she had just been told. Without saying another word, she went into the bedroom and prepared a small suitcase with the necessary items her mother would need. Just before leaving the apartment, Patricia thought it best to call her uncle and let him know his sister was very ill. He was grateful she had called and understood she was not able to stay on the telephone with him. Peter said he would wait to hear from her, and if they were to actually admit his sister into the hospital, to please call him and he would get into New York as soon as possible.

Once they reached the hospital, Tom's doctor friend was already in the emergency room awaiting their arrival. He asked them both to stay outside in the waiting room, giving him a chance to examine the patient and administer whatever care he deemed necessary. Finally after what seemed like an eternity to Patricia, the doctor came out into the waiting room and asked them both to step into one of the empty rooms, as he wanted to speak with them privately.

"Please, I don't want to alarm you, but I think it would be best if I admitted Frances into the hospital. She has developed one of the worst cases of giant hives I have ever seen. She will need to be monitored carefully, especially with the medication I have prescribed. Hopefully this medication will give her some relief from the horrible itching and discomfort she is experiencing, but right now I'm not giving any guarantees."

Both Patricia and Tom were obviously very anxious and wanted to visit with her as soon as possible. The doctor asked them to wait. He said he would have one of the nurses advise them as to what room Frances would be in.

After about another hour, a nurse escorted them to a bank of elevators that led to the upper floors, giving them Frances's assigned room number. Patricia could hardly wait to see her mother; she was almost sick with worry.

She looked up and said, "Oh Tom, I don't know what I would have done without you. I'm so thankful that you are here with me and for all you have already done. Thank you so very much."

Tom just smiled, putting his arm around this young woman who he genuinely cared for, leading her into the room to see her mother. The two of them stood there looking at Frances. She was sleeping soundly, but her face looked very distorted and swollen. When Patricia questioned the nurse, she was told it was due to a reaction to the medication, as well as the hives themselves.

Frances stayed in the hospital for almost two weeks, after which the doctor said he was going to release her, but she must be constantly supervised. The hives had subsided somewhat, but could flare up again at any unpredicted time. She would need to continue on a lesser dosage of medication. After the doctor left them, Tom said he wanted to take Patricia upstairs to a restaurant on one of the upper floors. During the past two weeks, Patricia never even knew there was a fine-dining restaurant in the hospital. She had come after work every day to visit her mother, hoping to find her feeling better. Sometimes Frances would acknowledge her daughter's presence; other times she was out of it. Patricia herself was getting sick with worry and didn't know what to do next. Tom took her by the arm, escorting her to their table while following the hostess. Once they sat down, Patricia spoke first.

"I know you have brought me here to give me bad news, haven't you?"

Tom replied, "No, not at all. As you know the doctor wants your mother to be constantly supervised. Neither you nor I will be able to watch her daily. I have spoken to my parents, who as you know are retired, and asked them if I could bring your mother to my home for the necessary care. They are both very fond of her and wholeheartedly agreed to do so, providing that this arrangement would be satisfactory to both you and your mother. You would also be welcome to stay with us, although I will tell you, it will be very crowded and might not be as comfortable for you. So what do you think?"

Before Patricia had a chance to answer, the waitress came over to take their order. Tom ordered for both of them. Patricia didn't feel much like eating. After silently digesting all that had been proposed, she said she thought it would be a good idea and was glad his parents wanted to help.

"I think I would like to keep the apartment going until my mother gets better, so I think I'll just stay there and visit as often as I can."

Now that this was settled, Patricia suddenly realized she was, in fact, hungry and was glad Tom not only took her to dinner, but also ordered it for her. He always seemed to have the foresight to handle whatever was needed. The meal was quite good, consisting of slices of veal with a delicate lemon sauce drizzled over it. It was the first good meal she had eaten since this whole ordeal began.

Peter visited the hospital and called constantly. He was very concerned for his sister. He also agreed that the new arrangements would be the best solution for everyone concerned.

Earlier, Patricia had telephoned her grandmother, explaining why she wouldn't be visiting. She didn't plan to visit anyone until her mother was discharged from the hospital. After speaking with Tom, she called her grandmother again, outlining the proposed new living arrangements. The wise, older woman told her not to worry; she had the utmost trust in Tom and knew if he recommended it, it was probably the best solution to their problem. Moreover, her grandmother assured her anytime she wanted to, she could spend time with them. Patricia was grateful for the invitation and decided she would take advantage of her offer as soon as things settled down. If she couldn't be with her mother, there was no other place she'd rather be than with her paternal grandmother and her best friend, her aunt.

Forty

ROAD TO RECOVERY

Frances was discharged from the hospital and went to live with Tom's parents as planned. They lived in a typical two-story city house in Queens, which had one spare bedroom that was not being used. Tom and his parents decided they would give this room to Frances and make her as comfortable as possible. His mother prepared nutritious meals, saying good food would make her strong again. They were very kind to her and kept a vigilant watch, hoping she would recover quickly. Fortunately the weather was still warm enough for Frances to spend hours outside, reclining in a chaise lounge and reading. The hives were still there, but the doctor assured her that with the proper rest and medication, they should disappear.

Several months passed, and while the hives did get better, there were still periods of reoccurrence. Late one night, Tom went to check on Frances and discovered she was not in her room. Glancing at the clock, he noted it was two thirty in the morning. At first he thought perhaps she'd gone downstairs to read, but he did not find her in the living room. However, he did notice the kitchen light was on and discovered Frances was outside in the driveway, scraping the bottoms of her feet on the concrete, hoping to alleviate the itching that had awakened her earlier. He was horrified at what he witnessed. She was scratching her feet so hard she didn't even notice her feet were bleeding. Not only were her feet covered in blood, but the ground was also covered with blood. Tom immediately called to her to come inside.

Arleen Patricia Mercorella

He took her by the hand and led her into the kitchen. She was in tears; she said she could not control the itchiness and this was the only way she could think of to relieve it. He quickly took a basin of cool water and had her place her feet into it. He found some soothing ointment, and once her feet were dry, he applied the cream to her dreadfully bruised and cut-up feet. He also prepared some warm milk on the stove and obtained some of her prescribed medication for her. Hopefully, all of this would help Frances.

Tom decided to call the doctor in the morning. It had now been over six months since Frances had lost her job, and he had hoped this whole ordeal would be over by now. Tom helped Frances up to her room and put her into bed. Finally she seemed calmer. Somewhat relieved, he hoped she would be better by the time he left for work at five thirty. After seeing that she was comfortably resting, he went downstairs and cleaned up the blood that had been tracked into the room. It looked as if blood was everywhere. After quite some time, all appeared to be cleaned and everything was put away. Tom decided not to go back to bed since it was almost four o'clock and he would normally get up in a half hour.

Patricia came to visit her mother often, especially on Wednesdays. Funny, she thought, ever since she was a young girl, it looked as if Wednesday was her traveling day. Usually, she would spend the night at Tom's house, which meant she would have to sleep on the couch in the living room, but Patricia didn't mind as long as her mother showed signs of recovery. Slowly, each week, she would find her mother's spirits were getting better. She certainly was a strong person. Patricia wondered if she could ever be as strong as her mother. Her mother had endured so many hardships in her life, and yet she always seemed to be able to pick herself up and start over again. It's sad how cruel life could be at times.

She remembered her mother often saying, "When life seems to be going too good, look out—something will be sure to happen to mess it up." Patricia thought, *I guess she was right.* Life had certainly been hard for her unfortunate mother. How she remained so sweet and nice was a mystery to her. She never seemed to want sympathy, saying that life was a lot worse for so many others and "we should be grateful for the good things we do have."

Most other nights Patricia spent at the apartment, but often she would go to her grandmother's and stay there. She was lonely, but found comfort in spending time with her grandmother and especially her aunt. The two young women were still inseparable, and anyone who didn't know them would never believe they were aunt and niece. Even people they worked with assumed they were sisters or even twins since they very much resembled each other.

Almost a year had passed and Frances appeared to be doing much better. She accepted the fact the even though she had lost her job unfairly, there was nothing she could have done to avoid it. She just needed to get on with her life as she had done so many times in the past. The only thing good that came out of Frances's episode of illness was the fact that she had quit smoking and never went back to it.

Patricia was thrilled when one afternoon at work she received a phone call from her mother saying she would be at the apartment when she got home. She just said she needed to talk with her. She hoped her mother would be moving home for good and they could finally get back to living as they had before she lost her job. Patricia was sure her mother was going to tell her she was coming back home. Anxious to speak with her mother, Patricia rushed home from work, stopping only to buy a small bouquet of flowers from the subway florist. As soon as she entered the apartment, she threw her arms around her mother, at the same time presenting her with the welcome-home flowers.

Apparently her mother had been home for a few hours, and she'd prepared something for them to eat. However, Patricia sensed something was wrong. Once her mother put dinner on the table and the two women sat down together, Patricia waited apprehensively for her mother to tell her whatever it was that she wanted to talk to her about.

"So, Mom, you are feeling better, aren't you? Is everything okay? I'm so glad you are home. You are home for good now, aren't you?"

Frances hesitated. "No, honey, this is what I wanted to speak to you about. Tom has asked me to marry him, and since we have been together so long now, living in his parents' home, I think I am going to say yes."

Patricia sat there, not sure how to reply to this new development. She wanted her mother to be happy, but at the same time, she wanted her to come home and restart their lives together.

Frances continued, "You would be welcome to come live with us, but I know there wouldn't be much room for both of us to live in their small home. We have been discussing maybe selling the house and finding a bigger place so all of us could be comfortable. Unfortunately, Tom's parents are not in the best of health, so we know we will have to take them with us no matter where we live. Tom and his parents were very good to me during this past year, and for this reason alone, I would not like to say no to him. One other thing I failed to mention is that while I was recuperating, Tom spoke to a lawyer friend of his, and I am now officially getting divorced from your father. The divorce is actually being filed on grounds of desertion." She paused. "So, what do you think of all this?"

Finally Patricia broke the silence in the room after digesting everything she'd just heard.

"Mom, Tom is a good man, and I'm sure you will be happy with him. After all, you two have been seeing each other for years now, and it's about time you made some definite plans for the future. As for me, I thank you for the offer, but I don't think I would be happy living at his parents' home, even if it was only a temporary setup. I think I would probably like to move back with my grandmother, if it's okay with her. I know I would be comfortable living there. Besides, as you know, I have been seeing the same boy for quite some time now, and while we are still young, I think we may also be planning for marriage in the future. So, I say, go for it."

The rest of the night was quiet, as the two women didn't know what else to say to each other. Patricia was happy for her mother, but at the same time, felt disheartened to know their wonderful life together was coming to an end. Once the traumatic experience of Mom losing her job was over, it seemed as if everything else was also over.

The next day Patricia called her grandmother and told her she would be coming by later that day as she needed to speak with her. Upon her arrival, her grandmother had dinner waiting for her, and both she and her aunt were sitting in the kitchen, wondering why she needed to talk. After telling her grandmother about her mother getting married, somehow she didn't seem too surprised and said, of course, Patricia could move back with them, if that was what she wanted to do.

In less than two months Frances and Patricia decided to pack up the apartment. Most things were being placed in storage until her mother and Tom could find a larger home to move into. Frances married Tom, and Patricia moved back in with her paternal grandparents.

Forty-One

UNFORESEEN OPPOSITION

Strange as it may seem, once Frances and Tom got married, Tom's parents turned on her. It was totally unexpected because she believed they had a marvelous relationship, but she was wrong. Now his parents felt threatened and wanted the constant attention of their son. There was a great amount of arguing and tension between Tom and his parents. During all the arguments Frances remained silent; she didn't want to get involved for fear the awful hives would return. Tom was just as upset with his parents, but knew he couldn't abandon them. Before she knew it, she and Tom were arguing as well.

Frances now hated living with the old folks since it caused considerable strain on her marriage. No matter how hard she tried, she simply couldn't please them. It was obvious they didn't want to share their son with anyone. They may have liked her before, but now that she was their son's wife, she was totally unacceptable to them. Frances couldn't understand why they had changed. Perhaps they were afraid now that their son had a wife, he would abandon them. No matter how Frances and Tom reassured them, their attitude didn't change.

There were times when Frances wondered if getting married had been the right thing to do. Yes, she loved Tom, but perhaps it was all a mistake. With the constant quarrelling, sometimes she wished she had just stayed living at her apartment with Patricia. Deep down she knew she had

Arleen Patricia Mercorella

panicked at the thought of being left alone once her daughter married. Since she was a young child, being left alone frightened her and brought up bitter memories. Now she just had to live with the decision she had made. She and her husband would just have to stick it out and hope for things to get better, but Frances knew it wasn't likely.

Frances and Tom went out many weekends looking for a new house for them to buy, a home where Tom could live peacefully with his parents now that he was married. Even with all the careful planning, it took well over a year to find the perfect home where everyone could live comfortably together. After many, many months, they finally found a builder on the north shore of Long Island who could build the type of house both Frances and Tom thought would be ideal. It was a lovely high ranch, which would allow his parents to have the downstairs living area, and they could have the upper level.

At this point, Frances and Tom decided to invite Patricia to live with them. There were two extra upstairs bedrooms that were not being used. They were sure she would like to live with them. It was a very beautiful home in a beautiful area, but Patricia, thanking them, decided to decline their offer. She confided to her mother that she and the young man she was dating were now seriously talking about marriage and probably would get married in a year or two. Patricia felt it was best to just keep living with her grandmother as she was content with her current situation. Moreover, she had decided she would just as soon get married from there.

Frances felt badly because the arrangements she had hoped for did not work out. She wanted her daughter back with her, but still she had no choice but to understand her daughter's feelings and accept them.

Once the house was built, Frances used her all creative talents decorating it, and now it looked like a home that belonged in a magazine. It was a real showplace and a great source of pride to both Frances and Tom. They kept it picture-perfect.

What's next? Frances thought. Now that the house was finished, she decided she might like to return to work, only this time she did not want an executive position, but rather an ordinary sales position whereby she could do her job well and leave at the end of the day with little responsibility. She already had enough to do with taking care of the house and the old folks.

A Matter of Survival

After finding a job at one of the better department stores on the north shore, each day she woke up extra early to prepare breakfast as well as lunch for her in-laws. Even though the house was a large one and the living arrangements were suitable, it was difficult for Frances to live there since it was very obvious they still resented her. This, of course, caused tension between Frances and Tom, but somehow they managed to overcome their problems and stayed together.

Patricia came often to visit as well as Peter and his family. Frances, with her culinary skills, would make elaborate dinners for everyone. She still loved to entertain, and even with all their problems, she was always sure to include Tom's parents in the family gatherings. During one such visit, Patricia announced she would be getting married in the spring. She already knew exactly what kind of a wedding she wanted and had made all the arrangements to pay for it herself. She knew how to stay within her budget.

Patricia invited her mother to help pick out her wedding gown, and Frances enjoyed going to various bridal shops with her daughter. She wanted her daughter to be happy and offered any assistance she may need from her. Even though mother and daughter didn't live together any longer, they were as close as any mother and daughter could be. Patricia asked Tom to escort her down the aisle on her wedding day, and this pleased him enormously. Patricia did get married from her grandmother's home, and everything worked out quite well.

Just two weeks before her wedding, Patricia was surprised when she received a telephone call from her natural father, asking for her to see him. Patricia could recall seeing her natural father only twice while she was growing up. He showed up at his parents' home once when Patricia was only six years old, and she could remember him staying for maybe just a day. She left for school in the morning, and he was gone before she got home. Years later when she was fifteen, he suddenly appeared again and just as before suddenly left. During these brief encounters, Charlie was pleasant enough toward Patricia, but then again didn't make any great fuss over her either, or even try to explain his absence as a father. Although the subject of her father's whereabouts was not discussed with Patricia by her grandparents, she gathered from whispered conversations that her father was heavily into debt because of his gambling habits, and it was apparent someone was always searching for him. Needless to say, it was a source of constant conflict between his parents.

Apparently Charlie had heard through the family grapevine that she was getting married and was planning to honeymoon in Hawaii, which would necessitate a stop in California, where he was now living. It didn't take much for her to figure out it had no doubt been her paternal grandfather who had told him about her plans. After much persuasion, to see him in California, Patricia finally agreed

Charlie met the newlyweds at the airport in Los Angeles and insisted on taking them to dinner. He wasn't alone and introduced a woman to them, saying she was his wife. To say it was a rather strained evening would be an understatement. Patricia was glad when she and her new husband boarded the plane later that night for Hawaii and left California and her father.

After only two years of living in their new home, Tom's mother became very ill. It became necessary to place her in a nursing home where Tom thought she would receive the proper medical care, but she lived in the home for only two months before passing away. Within a month of her passing, his father also died.

Frances and Tom were now living in this rather large home by themselves. For the first time in their married life, they were able to go out to dinner or a movie without worrying or rushing home. They even took a vacation or two.

Occasionally they would go out with their good friends. They would often get together with Tom's partner, Nels, and his wife, Katie, as the four had remained very close friends. However, as often happens in police work, after many years of working together, Nels was transferred to another division and started pulling weekend shifts. As a result, it became difficult for the four to get together as much as they used to.

Everyday life seemed to settle into normalcy with both Frances and Tom going to work every day. Then one night Tom received a frantic telephone call from one of Nels's relatives. Nels had been shot and killed in the line of duty during a robbery. Tom was devastated.

Forty-Two

THE HONEYMOON IS OVER

Soon after Patricia returned from her honeymoon and set up her new apartment, there in the mailbox came the news that Uncle Sam wanted her husband. Even though it was only a "pre-induction" notice, it became a firm reality, and within eight months of married life, Patricia's husband was drafted into the US Army. After much discussion, they decided once his basic training was completed, she would join him if at all possible. As it was, he was assigned to a base in the South, and they moved away for two years.

While Patricia was living away from New York, shocking news came over the airwaves—President Kennedy had been shot and killed in Dallas, Texas. The entire country seemed to be first in a state of panic and then just sadness. Tom was extremely upset as he had served as a bodyguard for so many presidents, and he wondered how this possibly could have happened. Frances found it was difficult to console her husband during this time of crisis. There was nothing she could say, since she and everyone else felt the sorrow for what had happened to their beloved president.

Frances missed her daughter more than ever. She wanted the comfort of being surrounded by family at this tragic time, and even though she knew her daughter's move away was only a temporary one, she anxiously looked forward to the day when she would return to New York.

Arleen Patricia Mercorella

A year passed, and Frances's daughter finally returned to New York, now being married almost three years. The young couple settled into a small apartment in Queens that enabled them to live near their families as well as the city.

Frances and Tom would visit often, and sometimes they would make arrangements for all of them to go out together. It was on one such occasion the four of them went to a football game at Shea Stadium in Flushing. Since neither Frances nor Patricia was a football fan, the men bribed them, saying if they would join them, they would all go out afterward for a special dinner. Not being ones to refuse a good meal, they agreed. They met at Patricia's apartment, and when it was time to leave for the game, the men surprised the ladies, presenting each one with a large yellow chrysanthemum corsage. They claimed it was because the women were being such good sports about going to the game. If the truth was really to be known, it was because both men loved giving surprises to their spouses.

The team the men were cheering for did, in fact, win. After the game, they had dinner at a typical neighborhood Italian restaurant in Bayside, which wasn't too far from where Patricia's paternal grandparents lived. While having dinner, someone suggested why not stop by and say hello to Patricia's grandmother. Frances hadn't seen her former mother-in-law in quite some time and agreed that it was a good idea. Tom also said he would enjoy seeing her.

"Good," Patricia said. "That settles it. While we are waiting for coffee, I'll telephone her to make sure it's okay if we all stop by for a visit."

So far it had been a fun day that had included lots of kidding and much laughter among the four of them. However, when Patricia telephoned her grandmother, this all changed.

Her grandmother said, "You are more than welcome to come over, but I have to tell you, your father is here. Right now he is sitting with me in the living room, and I'm not sure how your mother and Tom may feel about seeing him."

After an awkward silence, Patricia said she would discuss this with the others and if they still wanted to come by, they would just show up. As soon as Patricia returned to the table, the laughter suddenly stopped. Everyone knew something was wrong. She sat back down at the table,

A Matter of Survival

and the three others seemed to hang onto the silence in the air waiting for Patricia to say something.

Patricia started, "I don't know how to tell you this, but I guess I'll just tell you what I was told. After I told my grandmother that we wanted to stop by, she told me my father was sitting with her in the living room. It seems he just showed up this afternoon from California."

There was more silence with everyone now looking at Frances. Tom spoke first.

"Frances, you have nothing to worry about and certainly should not be intimidated by seeing your former husband. I say let's go for it and visit your mother-in-law. To hell with him!"

Patricia and her husband also agreed and just waited for a reaction from Frances.

"Oh well, why not? Let's make the visit," she said.

Then the laughter started up again with Patricia saying maybe she would have her mother ask him for all the back money he never gave them.

"Oh sure," Frances said, "I'm sure he is just waiting to do exactly that, and that's what brought him here."

More laughter continued. Patricia had thought the news was going to upset her mother, but instead it made everyone laugh even more. Maybe it was the wine, or maybe it was just the climax to a great day, but everyone was in such good spirits, nothing was going to dampen them.

With the bill paid, they all proceeded to the car. Frances dabbed on a little makeup and fresh lipstick. Silently she said to herself, *I wonder if he will have anything to say to me. We'll see.*

As soon as they rang the doorbell, Frances's former mother-in-law greeted the four of them with smiles and welcoming kisses. She was very glad to see Tom and told him that he looked wonderful, as he usually did, and told Frances she also looked fantastic. She walked them into the living room, and there, sitting in an armchair in the corner of the room, was Frances's ex-husband pretending to be reading the newspaper. Frances thought, *Twenty-four years have passed since he last saw me. He left when Patricia was only two and he has no idea what a difficult road it was for his daughter and me. Moreover, I'm sure he doesn't care.*

Arleen Patricia Mercorella

It was obvious the four had been out having a great day together. The girls were still wearing the pretty yellow corsages and excitedly telling "Mom" all about their outing to the game and then dinner. It must have been very apparent to Charlie the man who sat next to Frances had taken his place, not only with her, but his daughter as well.

As the conversation continued, directed to only the older woman, they asked how she was feeling, and she replied she was well. She was the only one home, and her son had showed up at the door earlier in the day. Apparently Charlie had wanted to surprise his mother. She said it was more like shock than surprise.

Suddenly Charlie put down the paper and simply said, "Hi, Frances" to his former wife.

Frances just said hello back and then introduced her husband to him.

Patricia couldn't help but notice Tom's reaction. Normally he would have stood up and offered to shake hands, but not tonight. Tom simply nodded his head and continued talking with the rest of the group.

Charlie must have felt awkward because he suddenly got up and walked into the kitchen. No one seemed to notice, or didn't care to notice, except Patricia. After a few minutes, she decided to go into the kitchen and speak with her father.

"Well, how is life going for you?" she inquired.

His reply was "Fine, just fine."

"I wouldn't have expected anything less from you. From what I have heard, you're part of the jet set always traveling all around the country, 'living it up.' Do you like that kind of life?" she questioned.

Her father smugly answered her saying, "Absolutely. Look, I've had a great life. I've lived all over and traveled everywhere. I've met the best of people and have been to the best of places, and then some. A life here in Queens wouldn't have satisfied me. Oh no, I lived my life the way I wanted to live it, and I was happy doing it. It's been great! I wouldn't have changed any of it."

His words stung in Patricia's mind. *So he lived the great life, did he? He never even cared or thought about what happened to my mother or me.* Instead of arguing or blasting him, she just replied, "Good for you, Charlie," and with that she turned and walked back into the living room.

A Matter of Survival

When she returned, everyone was getting ready to say good night. Mom wished them well, telling them to come again anytime. She always loved seeing them.

Just as Frances was leaving, she stopped in the doorway and whispered in her mother-in-law's ear. "Thank you so much, Mom. What would I have done without you? I love you very much."

As they left she observed the older woman standing at the door, throwing kisses to them all as she usually did. Patricia leaned over to kiss her grandmother, saying good night and telling her she would stop by during the week and to please tell her aunt she would be calling her tomorrow.

Just as she was about to step outside, her father placed his hand on her shoulder and turned her toward him saying "Look, Patricia, everything I told you before was a lie. I didn't mean it. I know I missed out on a lot and deeply regret it, but there is nothing that can be done now to change the past. I married an angel and threw it all away. I know I made terrible mistakes, and I hope someday you can find it in your heart to forgive me."

Patricia just blankly starred at him and then turned away. She continued down the steps to join the group.

A few months later Patricia learned her father was killed in a car crash while driving from Los Angeles to Las Vegas. She thought, *So that is that,* and felt no sorrow whatsoever.

The cause for his behavioral change many years ago went undiagnosed and the truth about what was wrong with him went with him to his grave.

Forty-Three

A Thanksgiving Not to Be Forgotten

It was now 1974 and Frances continued working at one of the better department stores on the Miracle Mile in Manhasset located on the North Shore of Long Island. Even though she'd told the family she didn't want a job with heavy responsibility, it was apparent her supervisor and management personnel disagreed and quickly delegated additional duties to her. As time went by, Frances once again developed a following of wealthy women who insisted that only Frances take care of them. Before long, the customers not only appreciated the service Frances provided, but it showed in the department's financial figures as well. There was no doubt her sales efforts were partly responsible for this. Often when a particular style of dress arrived at the store, Frances would telephone her customers, telling them about it, and invariably they would come into the store to buy it. Yes, the store manager was glad to have Frances! As it turned out, Frances liked working again.

Patricia had been married for a number of years, and now there was a five-year-old little boy and a year-old baby girl for all of them to love. The holidays seemed to take on a new meaning since there were grandchildren in the picture. Patricia's baby boy was adorable with very blond hair and beautiful blue eyes. The baby girl had beautiful dark curly hair and dark eyes. The children seemed to know how to charm their way into their grandparents' hearts. Although Frances wanted to spend as much time as possible with her daughter and grandchildren, she and Tom decided they should work for a few more years in order to provide for their retirement.

Peter, Wilma, and their girls continued to visit often, and life was going along just fine. Peter was doing very well at his job, and his girls were both excellent students, not only making their parents very proud of them, but they were also the apple of their aunt and uncle's eyes.

Traditionally, it had been arranged that Thanksgiving would take place at Peter and Wilma's home and Christmas would be celebrated at Frances and Tom's home.

Frances and Tom loved entertaining during the holidays, especially Tom. They would go to great lengths to decorate both the outside and inside of their home. The outside looked so festive that people would stop to ask if they'd had it professionally decorated. The holidays were fast approaching. Patricia's baby was now almost two and wasn't quite sure what to make of all the excitement. Their little boy was thrilled with the anticipation that Christmas would soon be coming.

Frances and her sister-in-law would coordinate as to what their contributions would be toward the Thanksgiving dinner. As usual, Wilma had everything beautifully planned, and a fabulous dinner menu would be created.

Frances's specialty was her baking. She would make numerous delicious desserts, not only for the immediate family to enjoy, but also for others who would stop by her brother's house in the evening. Frances loved visiting her brother's home, especially for Thanksgiving, which was now quite imminent.

Wilma continued her preparations for the forthcoming holiday. It had become a yearly tradition for Wilma and one of her closest friends, who lived across the street, to prepare homemade cranberry sauce and other festive treats for their holiday menu. The two women would cook together and prepare much of the food in advance. Days were passing quickly, and it was now the Tuesday before Thanksgiving. The two women worked the entire morning. They had their work down to a science, and even though there was much to do, there was also great pleasure in accomplishing their work. The ladies didn't stop until almost three o'clock.

Since it was the Tuesday before Thanksgiving, Frances had scheduled the necessary baking, which she needed to get accomplished right after work. First, and as usual, she picked up Tom at the train station as he arrived home about six o'clock. Even though she was working a full schedule, she typically had everything well organized. Frances planned a quick dinner, anticipating she could start her baking immediately after it. She, with Tom's help, would start baking some of her specialties.

It was customary that when the family had finished their Thanksgiving dinner, they would be joined by many friends and neighbors. So many desserts were put on the table that it looked as if it was an annex to a bakery.

Because Tom loved the holidays so much, Frances could sense his excitement of the season swiftly coming upon them. Frances had acknowledged long ago, it was because of her husband that she'd also learned to love the holidays as much as he did. Admittedly, this was one of the many reasons she loved him. For his part, Tom never hesitated to pitch in to help his wife. They were both looking forward to being together with family and friends on Thursday afternoon.

As Frances started the baking, she thought how great it was for someone such as herself, who grew up without anyone, to now be so blessed—to have so much. She had an adoring husband, a loving daughter who was happily married, and now two little grandchildren whom she adored. It was wonderful to have everyone around her. She was almost overwhelmed with happiness thinking about her family being together and celebrating at her brother's house. Today the holidays were more than just wonderful to Frances; it was more like filling in the empty spaces of her childhood and taking away the sadness of her early years.

Tonight, as Frances started her preparations for the baking, she started to think back to the days of her childhood in the convent. She could not remember a single Thanksgiving holiday being celebrated in all the years she was there. It brought tears to her eyes again remembering the fright she'd felt when she arrived on that first day. She reflected back, about growing up with the strictness of the nuns. She was always hungry and was forever looking for extra food, but extra food was just not there. *Oh yes, we are all so blessed. Now whenever we get together, it always includes an elaborate feast.*

A Matter of Survival

Tom stopped for a moment and asked, "Fran, what are you thinking about? I'm looking at you, and you seem so deep in thought."

Frances replied, "Tom, I'm so happy that the holidays are upon us, and we will all be together."

"Good," Tom replied. "Now let's get some of this work done."

The two started to work diligently. About a half hour had passed, and already Frances was about to put one of the cakes in the oven when the phone rang. She assumed it was probably Patricia, wanting to ask about one of my recipes. Tom walked over to the phone and answered. After he said hello, Frances saw a look of shock and horror on his face. Frances stopped what she was doing.

"Tom, Tom, what's going on? What's wrong? What's going on?"

He didn't answer his wife; instead she heard him say, "We'll be right there," and hung up the telephone.

"Tom, please answer me," Frances begged.

Tom turned off the oven. At the same time, he reached for his wife's hand and guided her to one of the chairs at the kitchen table. Frances was starting to panic, made obvious by her trembling hands. She saw Tom take a deep breath.

"Fran, I'm afraid it isn't good."

"What, what happened?" She quivered.

"Your brother went across the street to pick up the cranberry sauce that Wilma made earlier today and was hit by a car. We don't know how serious it is, but I think we better get to their house right away."

Frances could think of nothing else but to quickly get redressed and leave their house as fast as possible. She literally threw on a pair of slacks and a sweater and grabbed her handbag and coat, and they were out the door.

The trip from the north shore to south shore of Long Island seemed as if it was taking forever. Tom drove quickly but carefully. They made almost the entire trip without saying a word to each other. As they approached the parkway exit, Frances mumbled, "I hope Peter is okay. I hope he isn't hurt too badly."

Tom didn't answer. As soon as they reached the exit and turned onto the main thoroughfare where Peter lived, they observed numerous police cars, two ambulances, and even a fire truck, all with emergency lights blazing. There was yellow tape strung around on both sides of the street, but it was particularly concentrated in front of her brother's house. Police were directing traffic, requesting drivers to detour to another block. There appeared to be mass confusion and hysteria everywhere. Tom finally spoke.

"Fran, it doesn't look good. You should prepare yourself for the worse."

"Oh no," Frances replied. "Even if he's hurt badly, we'll get him the best doctors. We'll see to it that he gets the best of care."

Tom interrupted her. "Fran, Fran—listen to me. From the looks of the scene ahead, I don't think Peter is alive."

Frances felt like she was going to faint.

"No, no, you're wrong, Tom. He's probably just badly hurt, that's all."

Tom drove right up to the police officers who were diverting traffic, showing his police badge and explaining his wife's relationship. He stepped out of the car, spoke briefly with one of the officers, and returned. He said they were allowed to park nearby and walk to the house. Both Frances and Tom got out of the car simultaneously.

Tom turned toward his wife; holding on to both of her arms, he started, "Fran, the police officer I just spoke to told me your brother was hit head on, and he doesn't know if your brother even had a chance."

There were medical people all around Peter, who was lying in the street. The police were keeping everyone away from the scene. Frances let out a shriek of pain and started to sob profusely, saying, "I must see my sister-in-law. I don't know how she is taking this horrible accident. I must go inside to see her."

There was as much mass confusion and hysteria inside the house as was outside. Patricia and her husband had already arrived as well as other friends and neighbors. There were several policemen inside, trying to bring some order to the utter chaotic state in the home. It was sheer madness. While all this was going on, a doctor from one of the ambulances was observing Wilma's vital signs. Wilma, with tears streaming down her face, seemed to be in a trance and was staring obliviously at all the confusion. Frances, with tears also flowing down her own face, went immediately over to her sister-in-law. Before she could speak, another policeman entered the home and announced the injured party was being taken by ambulance to the hospital.

Tom immediately took control of the situation, stating Wilma and Frances were going with him in his car to the hospital. Patricia and her husband were to follow also. He designated one of the family friends to stay in the house to answer any questions they were able to answer. Since Peter's girls were not home, he asked another friend to retrieve the younger daughter from a local department store where she was working and bring her immediately to the hospital to be with her mother. As the older daughter was taking a course in Miami, he asked someone else to call her and arrange for her to be met at the airport. He said he wasn't sure when they would return, but would be back after seeing what was what at the hospital.

They all arrived together, rushing into the waiting room, and they were immediately escorted into a private room nearby. They had waited only briefly when a priest suddenly entered and asked who the spouse of the victim was. Wilma raised her hand. He spoke softly but very frankly. "I'm sorry to tell you, your husband died on the way to the hospital. He was killed almost instantly. It appears as if he didn't suffer at all."

Wilma put her face in her hands and started crying uncontrollably. Frances stood there just shaking her head and crying.

"No, no, this just can't be true," Frances sobbed. "All the years we were separated, I swore I would never let anything or anyone separate us again, but this is something I couldn't have imagined."

Unfortunately it was true. Frances's brother was gone for good.

Tom took both women home while all the time trying to make sense of what had occurred earlier. It seemed Peter had been hit by a young driver, a girl who had been having an argument with her parents. She apparently darted out of her house, getting behind the wheel of the family car, and went speeding down the busy street where Peter and Wilma lived. She claimed she never saw him, but was shocked when she realized she'd hit someone. Tom thought it kind of reminded him of the old story, "I didn't know the gun was loaded."

By the time Frances and Tom finally arrived back at their home, it was almost five o'clock in the morning. The baking items were still scattered all over the kitchen. The counter was cluttered with ingredients that were not used. The cake batter was still in its pan, waiting to be placed in the oven. In somewhat of a daze, Frances preheated the oven again and placed the cake pan into it.

"Fran, what are you doing? Let it go until later this morning."

Frances simply replied, "No, I won't sleep anyway, so I might as well clean it all up."

Tom nodded his head and then started helping his wife put everything away.

While cleaning up, Frances thought, *When things are going along too good, look out. Something is bound to happen to mess it up.*

So that Thanksgiving, instead of the wonderful tradition of dinner and getting together with family and friends, it turned out they spent the day inside a funeral home.

Forty-Four

APPROACHING THE SUNSET YEARS

After taking a short leave of absence from her job, Frances continued working and on the weekends looked forward to seeing her daughter and two grandchildren. The holidays were never the same again, although having young children involved in their lives made the loss of her brother more bearable. The children were a source of great pleasure to both Tom and her.

The years passed quickly, and Frances and Tom were now looking forward to their planned retirement. Frances was concerned because Tom's health was starting to show some signs of problems. She attributed it to the stress of losing his parents, the circumstances surrounding the loss of his best friend, and the added unforeseen death of her brother. It was taking its toll on him, and now on top of all this, he was told he had the onset of diabetes. However, the doctor told him with proper care and medication, he should be able to continue a long and active life.

Tom had always been the pillar of strength to his family and friends. It was obvious that everyone looked to him for guidance and advice. He was able to take control of each and every situation when he was called upon to do so and perform it well. He was a brilliant conversationalist and had the ability to analyze any situation placed before him. Yes, Tom was a strong man, and everyone looked up to him. He was often referred to as a "man's man." However, his demeanor didn't fool Frances. Even though Tom was a very big and statuesque man, Frances knew inside he was a real softie. He hid it well, except when it came to the people he loved, especially his wife, Patricia, and the grandchildren. Frances knew that family meant everything to Tom.

Realizing retirement was fast approaching, they decided to put their house on the market, and it sold very quickly. As they wanted to stay somewhere near Patricia and her family, they found a large and lovely apartment in Suffolk County in a very pleasant neighborhood.

Since they were now retired, it was no longer possible for them to afford to continue to live in the affluent area where they had spent many years. The good part was there would be no more commuting into the city for Tom and no more selling dresses for Frances. Retirement life was going to be fabulous for them. Future plans would include trips into the city to see shows, travel to places in the country that they'd never had the time to go before, and generally just relaxation. They had all the time in the world now to visit with family, especially their grandchildren. It was going to be a good time for them both.

Patricia and her husband were just as excited for their retirement and decided to plan a surprise party for them, inviting family and close friends to their home. It was a perfect day, not only to celebrate her parents' retirement, but also to gather everyone together.

Frances and Tom settled into the new area with Frances performing her usual decorating magic to quickly make their new place into a home. As they observed their new surroundings, Frances realized the area was not as affluent as their previous home, but then again, it was their home and they were together.

They had been in their new apartment for only one month when suddenly Tom's health took a major turn for the worse. They were almost finished with setting up their new home when Tom decided it would be nice to place outdoor carpeting on their patio. Apparently, kneeling down in this position caused a terrible strain on his toes. The next day his toes became very painful. Frances tried not to panic but when she looked at his toes on both feet, she could see they were swollen and very red. Before she knew it, he was in the hospital. Here was a man with perfect feet, now faced with the fact he had a serious infection in several toes. All this resulted from the simple task of placing carpet on a patio.

A Matter of Survival

No matter how many antibiotics were administered to her husband, either topically or internally, nothing seemed to eliminate the problem. On his right foot, the large toe was not healing. He was in a double room, and other patients would come and go, but Tom was still not to be discharged. Finally, after a month of being in the hospital, the doctor told Tom and Frances that even with all the treatment Tom had received, unfortunately gangrene had set in the large toe, and if they didn't amputate the toe, it would spread up to his ankle and leg. There was no choice.

Over the next few years, unfortunately Tom's health declined dramatically. After the first amputation, there was another, and then another. Both feet started to show signs of ulcerations, and no matter how hard Frances tried to do everything the doctor told her to do to help heal Tom's feet, it was a losing battle. Their plans for a wonderful retirement were shattered.

Patricia and her husband visited often with their children. The children were now young teenagers and through the years had grown to love their grandparents dearly. They were especially welcomed since their visits seemed to pick up Tom's morale quite a bit. As soon as he knew the children would be visiting, Tom wanted the refrigerator stocked with all the foods that he knew were their favorites. He would have Frances go to the store with a shopping list he'd prepared, which included the bologna and liverwurst they liked, pickles, chips, soda, and any other treats he knew the "kids" would enjoy. Invariably there was more food than the grandchildren could consume, so he would have Frances wrap up the leftovers and send them home with the grandkids. It was just one of the many ways he showed his love and affection to them.

On one such visit in the latter part of August, Patricia noticed Tom was not in good spirits. He appeared to be very irritated with Frances, saying that she was constantly "messing things up." She also observed he was impatient with her mother and seemed to be picking at her for the most nonsensical things. This seemed so unlike him.

Patricia, trying to act as a mediator, pleaded with Tom to be patient with her mother. He just shook his head and didn't answer. Privately, she then tried to comfort her mother, attributing Tom's newfound irritation to his pain and discomfort. Frances agreed this was probably the reason for his behavior. Patricia was concerned as she also noticed this additional stress was starting to show on her mother since she was having difficulty in holding onto her thoughts. Yes, there definitely was too much stress on her.

After dinner Frances served one of her homemade chocolate cakes, and the mood of everyone seemed to be getting back to normal. The men were watching a football game on the TV. Patricia noticed Tom appeared to be calmer. The children were playing a game on the living room floor, and Patricia and her mother were finishing up the dishes. It was good to see Tom's mood change for the better. He was now smiling and laughing at the children. Patricia looked at them pleased to see Tom with this improved behavior. She was sure it was because they had come for a visit. Even her mother now seemed to be in a better frame of mind.

Tom carefully got out of his chair and excused himself to use the bathroom. From the kitchen, one could look past the living room into a hallway where the bathroom was located at the end of the hall.

Patricia and her mother were finishing up the last of the dishes when suddenly Tom, coming out of the bathroom, lost his balance and fell to the floor. Patricia grimaced at the sound; not just from the fall itself, but because she could actually hear the breaking of a bone some fifteen to twenty feet away.

"Oh no," she thought. "What's next?"

Frances started to panic and ran toward her husband. Everyone jumped up and went to Tom's aid. Tom was holding his arm, moaning with the pain. Patricia's husband immediately telephoned to summon an ambulance.

Needless to say, Tom did, in fact, break his arm and was now in a great deal more pain then he already had been. The wait and then the assistance given in the emergency room took several hours, and finally, when a cast was set on Tom's arm, they all went back to the apartment. Patricia wanted to help her mother prepare the bed for Tom. As usual, Frances had their bed prettily made with many decorative pillows arranged on it. Patricia was taken aback to watch her mother grab everything off the bed and toss it on the floor. Stressed or not, this was so unlike her. Usually she would have carefully put the pillows away in a very organized manner. Without saying anything, Patricia simply bent down, gathered all the items, and placed them on the bed in the guest bedroom, as her mother would usually have done.

A Matter of Survival

Finally getting Tom into bed, Frances gave him the medicine given to her by the emergency room doctor, and before long he was fast asleep. Frances looked exhausted. Even though it was now close to eleven thirty at night and they had to go to work the next day, Patricia decided to stay a bit longer to help her mother put the final items away in the kitchen. Actually, she wanted to observe how she was handling all this new stress. She seemed to be managing fine, so her family kissed and hugged her tightly and left for their home. It turned out to be a very nerve-racking day.

After two full months, the doctors decided it was time to remove the cast, but the pain seemed to be persistent. At this point the only solution seemed to be to prescribe more drugs to ease his discomfort. Eventually, Tom's arm healed and the pain subsided somewhat, but the combination of drugs took a further toll on his health.

The holidays were fast approaching, and for obvious reasons Frances decided to not put too much emphasis on the usual festivities. Thanksgiving came and went, and the preparations for it at Patricia's home were not nearly as elaborate as in times past.

As far as Christmas was concerned, it was decided that Frances, Tom, Patricia, and her family would eat Christmas dinner out somewhere. Since most restaurants were closed on Christmas Day, they chose a restaurant at one of the better hotels in the area. The hotel and particularly the restaurant were delightfully decorated for the holidays, and Frances was pleased because it seemed to put her family in an especially festive mood. Surprisingly, Tom ate a very good dinner, and as he put it, he couldn't remember the last time he ate so well. Frances recalled at first she had been reluctant to even leave their apartment, Christmas or not, but now she was happy they had agreed to do this. Tom actually looked good, and his spirits had perked up a good deal. *He certainly is enjoying himself,* she thought. *It must be Christmas.* To top it all off, Patricia's husband insisted on picking up the tab, saying it was an extra Christmas bonus for everyone.

Tom's health was failing rapidly, and it became evident that he was consistently losing weight. Even though Frances was diligent about keeping him on a proper diet and the prescribed medications, the diabetes, together with so many other complications, were starting to cause signs of trauma in his body. Frances didn't know where to turn next. She was extremely worried about Tom, and now she realized that she was not doing as well coping with the situation. Instead of Frances driving home on Christmas night, Patricia insisted they spend the night and leave early in the morning.

 The next morning Frances let her husband sleep and quietly got herself dressed, being careful not to wake him. Going downstairs she discovered Patricia was already in the kitchen preparing breakfast. The smell of coffee perking gave Frances a sense of comfort, and as Patricia poured two cups of the hot beverage for them, Frances took her daughter's other hand and told her how much she loved her. Patricia merely smiled and thanked her mother. Putting the coffeepot back down, she then walked over to Frances and placed a kiss on her mother's head, saying, "Mom, I love you too." Frances thought, *Too often we hesitate to tell the ones we love the most that we do in fact love them and couldn't imagine life without them.* She was glad to have expressed her feelings to her daughter.

 After breakfast Frances was anxious to return to their apartment. Since Christmas had fallen on a weekend, she anticipated there would be just a small amount of traffic and wanted to be on their way. Patricia hated seeing her mother and Tom leave, as she sensed everything was becoming too much for the both of them. Crazy as it may sound, somehow, as she watched them drive away, it seemed as if they were exiting out of her life. *Don't be ridiculous,* she said to herself, shaking off the negative feelings. *I really must be getting carried away with worry. On the other hand, it was nice to have us all together this Christmas, and eating out was really not such a bad idea. Maybe we can do it again next year.* With that, Patricia closed the door and, turning around she said out loud, "I better get busy and start straightening up around here."

It was a crisp, cold winter day, and the drive home was an easy one for Frances. Once they reached their apartment, she had Tom stay in the car for a few minutes so that she could unlock the door and place her purse on the entrance table. She went back to give Tom the assistance he needed getting him into their apartment. He decided he did not want to go back to bed, but just wanted to sit in his easy chair. Frances got him comfortable, taking his coat and hat together with the scarf and gloves, and put them away in the closet. After turning on the TV for him and making sure he was contentedly settled in their living room, she went back to the car, retrieving the suitcases, presents, and other parcels of cooked food Patricia had given her mother. Patricia had prepared extra so that her mother wouldn't have to go through the hassle of food shopping and cooking, at least for the next few days.

Frances made numerous trips back and forth from the car to the house, and finally everything was inside. It took Frances a good half hour or better before everything was brought into their apartment. She remembered all too well when it was her husband who would carry in not only the suitcases, but all the other packages. Now everything was left up to her. It was as if there had been a complete transfer of responsibilities between them. Actually, she didn't mind doing this; it was just that she wanted her husband to be well again. She knew he simply didn't have the strength he once had, and she also knew she wasn't as strong as she used to be either. *Getting old is tough,* she said to herself.

As she started putting the packages away, she unexpectedly found herself reflecting back to their earlier years when Tom was a big, strapping man who could accomplish almost anything put before him. He was the one who everyone went to in times of need, and now he was the one in need, and it was just the two of them. He used to be her pillar of strength, and now she had to try and be there for him.

In the late afternoon, Frances prepared something light for them to eat, but she was startled when Tom said he didn't want anything. Just yesterday, he'd eaten so well when they were out. Frances offered to make him some hot tea, but he refused that as well. He said, "Fran, I feel very tired and completely drained. I don't feel well at all."

"Okay," she said. "Let's just get you into bed, and you can watch TV in the bedroom and fall asleep when you want."

It appeared that getting up from the chair was a tremendous effort for Tom, and even though Frances tried to conceal her worry, she was very concerned for her husband. After somewhat of a struggle, she got Tom into the bedroom and helped him get into his pajamas. She made sure he had everything he needed and left the room. She then telephoned her daughter. The two women stayed on the telephone for twenty minutes recounting the day before, and they agreed that in spite of everything, Christmas worked out rather well. Patricia told her mother the children felt it was still a great Christmas as usual, and now they had invited friends over to their house to view their gifts. She confided to her mother that she was tired and anxious for their friends' parents to retrieve their kids. Laughing, she said, "They'll probably be here for another half hour, and when they all leave, we will finally have peace and quiet."

Frances hastily changed the subject, telling her daughter she wasn't too happy with the way Tom looked tonight. She hoped once he got into his own bed and was able to rest properly, he would feel better in the morning. Patricia assured her mother if she was to need them not to hesitate to call. They would be there to help her as soon as they could. Then both mother and daughter said good night to each other and hung up the telephone. Looking at the clock on the kitchen wall, Frances noted it was only nine thirty, but she felt exhausted. She decided not to stay up watching TV. *The sooner I can get into bed, the better off I will be—it was a long hard day,* she said to herself. Once her head touched the pillow, she fell immediately to sleep.

Although she had a restless sleep, Frances did not wake up until almost seven thirty the next morning. She quietly got up and checked on her husband. As she bent over the bed to look at him, she noticed he was awake and appeared to look very flushed.

"How do you feel, Tom?" she asked.

It seemed as if he could hardly speak, but he managed to say he was not feeling well.

After placing her hand on his forehead, Frances immediately went into the bathroom and retrieved the thermometer to take his temperature. "Just lie still," she said as she efficiently placed the instrument in his mouth. She was trying to sound calm and composed, but actually was starting to feel very nervous. Frances did not like the way he looked or even the way he was acting.

Usually in the mornings he had a little more energy. Normally, he would rise as soon as he awoke to shave and take a shower, and then eat the breakfast Frances prepared, but today he wanted to stay in bed. He complained of having chills, which was obvious from the way his body was shaking. She also noticed the pillowcase and sheet were soaked with perspiration. At this point Frances was anxious to read the thermometer and then figure out what to do next for her ailing husband. Frances looked at the thermometer and couldn't believe her eyes. It was reading 102.5 degrees. Frances decided the first thing she had to do was to help him off with his pajama top. After wiping his face and chest down with a cloth she had rinsed in tepid water, she hurriedly patted him dry. Because weakness had overtaken his entire body, he wasn't much help to her. Putting a large clean towel over the sheet, she tucked it under him. Carefully coaxing him to lie down in bed again, she placed an additional blanket over him.

Trying to sound calm, she told Tom she would be right back as she was going to put coffee on the stove. Frances left the bedroom and walked quickly into the kitchen, snatching the telephone from its receiver to call Tom's doctor. When the doctor's service answered, Frances described everything she had observed this morning. She also told the operator she was very frightened and didn't know what else to do for her husband, saying she wasn't even sure if she should give him aspirin. The operator listened to her and then indicated she was to hold on the line.

After what seemed like an endless wait, but was in actuality only a few minutes, the operator came back, telling her the doctor said for Frances to summon an ambulance. He wanted Tom to get into the hospital immediately, and he would meet them there. Frances dialed the number for the local ambulance service, which had been posted by the telephone. Her heart was pounding as she returned to the bedroom to check on her husband again. This time it appeared as if Tom was in some sort of delirium.

Frances thought, *I must stay calm and get a hold of myself. I will be no good to him this way.* Then Frances realized she wasn't even dressed yet. She hastily pulled slacks and a blouse from the closet. Going to her dresser, she retrieved underwear and started to get dressed without delay. She was almost done when the doorbell rang. The ambulance was already there. While still buttoning her blouse, she let the two men in and directed them to her bedroom. With the greatest precision they took Tom's vital signs and asked if he had taken any medication this morning. Frances answered them by shaking her head no and then verbally saying "no" again. She watched the gurney being placed next to the bed, and then both men simultaneously lifted Tom onto it. One of men turned to Frances, instructing her to meet them at the hospital as soon as possible.

Frances grabbed her coat and handbag, and trembling, she locked the front door. It was extremely cold outside, but today Frances was oblivious to the crispness in the air. Normally she would have spent some time warming up the car before taking off, but not today. She gave the gas pedal just a few taps and immediately backed out of the parking space. She followed the ambulance with its lights flashing and siren screaming as it passed through the development and exited onto the busy road ahead. Frances started to pray, *Please God, don't let him be dying. I'm not ready for that just now. I just want to be able to take care of him.* It was all she could do to prevent tears from streaming down her face. *I must get control of myself,* she thought. *I have always been a strong woman, and I must be strong now. I won't be any good to him this way,* and just like that, she took a deep breath and regained control of herself.

Fortunately, the hospital was only a short distance away from where they lived, and within a few minutes, Frances witnessed the two efficient men exit the ambulance and wheel Tom into the emergency room. Frances quickly parked her car in a designated spot and rushed into the building, following the speeding gurney. Tom was taken into one of the rooms while Frances was summoned to stay behind to answer the inevitable questions asked by the admissions staff.

Yes, she was his spouse; yes, they were fully covered with medical insurance; yes, he had many aliments—heart problems, diabetes, et cetera, et cetera, and today he was also having difficulty breathing compounded with a temperature of 102.5 degrees.

The woman at the desk said very little to Frances but wrote down everything discussed with her. Finally, the woman said she could go into the room to stay with her husband, but not before asking, "Would you like us to call anyone for you?"

In her haste Frances hadn't even thought of calling Patricia and gave the clerk her daughter's name and telephone number.

A Matter of Survival

As promised, their doctor was already in the room with Tom and the emergency room resident doctor. Frances observed a bottle and tube hanging from a portable chrome stand next to her husband. She followed the plastic piping with her eyes and realized an IV was already in place in Tom's arm. Both doctors appeared to be examining him very systematically and speaking softly to each other. After about a half hour, Tom's doctor requested Frances to follow him.

He started, "As you are aware, your husband has a very advanced case of diabetes and a rather serious heart condition, and now he has pneumonia, which is why he is running a high fever. We have hooked him up to an IV, which is depositing strong antibiotics into his body. We are admitting him into the intensive care unit. He will have to stay here in the hospital for however long it takes for him to get over the pneumonia."

"He will recover, won't he, Doctor?" the frightened woman asked.

"Frances, let's take one problem at a time for right now, okay?"

One of nurses came over to Frances and guided her to the outside waiting room, saying they were preparing a bed for her husband on an upper floor in the intensive care area, and it might be a while before she would be allowed to see him.

Frances sat in one of the comfortable chairs provided for the long wait. She knew that the onset of pneumonia on top of all the other health problems Tom had was not good. She almost felt angry with herself. She should have realized last night that something was wrong. He didn't act much like his usual self, but then again, here of late she didn't know what he was supposed to act like. *At least now he's getting the proper attention,* she said to herself.

In less than an hour, her daughter and husband appeared in the waiting room and sat down next to Frances.

"Mom, we are here with you so you won't have to face this alone. Please tell us what happed today," Patricia said.

Frances related the entire story from beginning to end, starting with her waking up at seven thirty. "Now all we can do is just wait until Tom is in his room and settled in bed. There is nothing else for us to do."

"I think the first thing we must do is to get you coffee and a little something to eat," Patricia said. Her husband left to go to the hospital cafeteria, where he was able to get something for each of them.

After about an hour and a half, a nurse finally came over to Frances, saying she could go up to see her husband, but they must be very quiet. "He is a very sick man," she stated.

Frances thought, *She's telling me he's a very sick man; I live with him!*

The three took turns sitting in the room with Tom. He looked awful. Patricia asked her husband, "How could anyone change so quickly in just one day?" She couldn't understand how just two days ago he'd seemed to be in such good spirits, had eaten a marvelous dinner, and then *bam!* Everything changed.

Tom was hooked up to not only the IV, but to several other computerized monitors as well, which were making all sorts of weird sounds. Frances tried desperately to comprehend what these machines were, but of course, none of them made sense to her, her daughter, or her son-in-law. Frances leaned over Tom's bed and gently stroked his forehead. She whispered to him that she was nearby and there for him. It seemed to Frances as if it took every bit of strength he had, but he opened his eyes and saw his wife standing beside him. It was only a flicker of recognition, but she knew he was pleased she was there with him. She had gently leaned on the bed, her hand placed near his, when unexpectedly Frances could feel her husband's hand enclosing hers.

Frances whispered to him, "Tom, we are all here for you. You are very sick, but you will come out of this just like all the other times. I love you. We love you very much."

After a very short time, one of the nurses appeared in the doorway, quietly telling them to please leave the room as the patient needed to rest. Frances was sure that even though the nurse was soft-spoken, her husband had heard the request. Admittedly, he looked very tired, so she nodded in agreement.

Before they left, Patricia leaned over, gently kissing the man who had long ago become her father, telling him she loved him and she would be back tomorrow. Then Patricia's husband squeezed his hand and wished him well. Finally Frances approached his bedside and told him how very much she loved him and kissed him again on his forehead. She said she would be back to see him as soon as they let her. The nurse on duty told Frances they would be in touch with her later today and she should not plan to come back to visit until sometime tomorrow—they would let her know when.

As they waited for the elevator, Patricia noticed her mother looked quite ragged. Without saying a word, she thought, *This is the woman who usually sets an example of looking one's best; now she looks disheveled and completely worn out. We are going to have to make sure to take good care of her.*

Patricia said aloud, "I think we will go to your apartment and get you settled in for the rest of the day."

Once they reached the apartment, Frances realized it was almost two o'clock in the afternoon. She couldn't believe it. It seemed as if they had left the apartment only an hour ago. She was now very tired.

Patricia's husband took all the coats and hung them up, allowing his wife to take care of her mother. Patricia had her mother sit down at the kitchen table and immediately put water in a kettle, placing it on the stove.

"Okay, let's see what I can fix for you to eat."

Taking some items out of the refrigerator, Patricia started to prepare a light lunch for the three of them.

"So, Mom," she started. "Now that things have settled down a bit, tell us what happened this morning. Did you notice right away Tom wasn't feeling well? Did he appear to be in pain, or what?"

Patricia turned to her mother and was a little startled to see her with her fingers placed on each side of her temples. "I can't think straight right now." She seemed to be struggling with each and every word.

"Gee, she really must be exhausted," she whispered to her husband.

Placing her hand on her mother's, she said, "Don't worry about it. You did everything right, and Tom's getting good care. Here, I've made a sandwich for you and a nice hot cup of tea. I want you to eat it, and then as soon as you are finished, even though it's early, I want you to get into your nightgown and get into bed. I'll set up the bedroom for you so that you will be comfortable."

As Patricia entered her mother's bedroom, she noticed the bed was still not made and decided to change the sheets. She found clean sheets in the linen closet and a fresh blanket. After putting the pillows in their cases, she puffed them up and placed them carefully against the headboard. Remembering her mother kept a portable snack table behind the guest room door, she set it up and placed it next to her mother's bed. Patricia decided it might be nice to let some of the afternoon light into the room and opened up the blinds to let the room flood with the warm winter sunshine.

Returning to the kitchen, she was pleased to see her mother had eaten the sandwich that she had placed before her earlier.

"Okay, why don't you change and rest in bed for a while? I have everything ready for you," she said to her mother. Patricia turned the stove on again after putting some additional water in the kettle. "Why don't we all have another cup? This way I can keep you company in your room." While quickly placing the small amount of dishes in the dishwasher, Patricia asked her husband to see if he could find something on the living room TV and to just make himself comfortable, because she wanted to spend some additional time with her mother. As usual he was understanding and agreed, telling her to take all the time she needed.

Patricia brought the two cups into the bedroom, placing them on the little table next to her mother's bed.

"Feel a little better now, Mom?" she inquired. Her mother didn't answer but nodded her head. Patricia had just sat back to make herself comfortable in the bedroom chair when the phone rang. Frances immediately picked up the receiver and soon started asking questions, but somehow the questions she was asking didn't make sense. For some reason, the words just weren't coming out right. Looking very frustrated, she handed the telephone to her daughter, saying, "I just can't think straight."

Patricia said it was fine, not to worry, and started speaking into the telephone.

"Yes, yes, I understand. That will be fine. Does he seem any better this afternoon? You have my mother's and my phone numbers, so if you need to call, please don't hesitate." Then, thanking the woman on the other end of the phone, Patricia hung up.

Frances spoke first.

"Patricia, I guess I must be extra tired, because I couldn't think of the right words to say to her."

"No problem, Mom. We know you've been through a lot this afternoon. That was the nurse we met earlier today, and she said Tom was showing some slight improvement and was resting comfortably. They do not want him to have any visitors tonight, but it would be fine for you to visit tomorrow afternoon. She said you could come over about two o'clock. As you know, I have to return to work tomorrow, but I'll come out right after I finish and meet you there."

Frances thanked her daughter, saying she was very pleased she was with her this afternoon.

"Patricia, you are always there when I need you."

Smiling, Patricia replied, "And you were always there when I was little and needed you."

The two women smiled, grateful they had each other.

As Frances was starting to show signs of sleepiness, Patricia rose from the chair and closed the blinds. She made sure the TV was on the station her mother liked and adjusted the volume so it was not too loud. She then took the two empty cups into the kitchen and placed them in the dishwasher. At the same time she suggested to her husband they should get ready to go home soon. She took a glass from the cupboard and a small bottle of water from the refrigerator. All the time she was going through these steps, she felt her heart was sinking, not only for Tom, but for her mother as well. Patricia felt there was something not right with her mother, but she was too tired to try to analyze her feelings right now.

Patricia went back in her mother's room and placed the water and drinking glass on the small table beside the bed. She made sure the telephone was in easy reach. Glancing around the room, Patricia decided all looked good to her and went to retrieve her coat and scarf.

With her coat on, Patricia entered her mother's bedroom to say good night and to tell her to be sure to telephone if she needed them. Frances thanked her again and turned over as if to go to sleep. Patricia turned the small bedside lamp off and left the light on in the bathroom with the door slightly ajar. Even though Frances probably wouldn't hear her, Patricia called softly, saying, "Good night, Mom. I love you."

Patricia locked the front door behind them, and they got into their car.

The trip home took the usual forty-five minutes, and both husband and wife were glad there were no tie-ups on the road this evening. They drove in silence for some time, when Patricia placed her hand on her husband's.

At the same time, she thanked him for his support and for being there for her.

Patricia speaking again said, "You know, hon, I can't place my finger on it exactly, but I'm a little concerned about my mother. I've noticed she's having difficulty when speaking. It's as if she's trying to find the correct words, but can't."

"I'm sure your mother is just exhausted with worry and you shouldn't think about it anymore tonight."

Patricia agreed saying, "I suppose you're right. I'll try not to dwell on it."

She was anxious to get home and get into bed early too, but she knew she still had to prepare her own clothes for work the next day and thought by the time she showered and finished up, it would be much later than she wanted. It had been wonderful to have the long weekend off for Christmas, but it was too bad it had ended so poorly.

⁂

Frances woke several times during night and tried to go back to sleep each time. After a while she gave up and decided to watch TV, changing the channels to find anything that would occupy her mind. She hoped the TV would take the place of the terrible ache inside her since she couldn't stop worrying about her husband. Frances couldn't wait for the night to be over so it would be tomorrow and she could spend some time with her husband.

When Frances opened her eyes again, she looked at the clock and couldn't believe she had slept straight through until eight thirty in the morning. She couldn't remember the last time she'd slept until eight thirty. She rose and flipped the TV channel to the morning news. There were excerpts of people enjoying the Christmas that had just passed, another story about others who were running around seeking after-Christmas bargains, and still another showing the remains of a fire in someone's home on Christmas Day. *Guess we all have our problems,* she thought.

Frances got up and walked into the kitchen. She put some coffee in the electric pot, dropped a piece of bread into the toaster, and sat down at the table. She said out loud, "What am I supposed to do now?"

A Matter of Survival

There really was nothing else for her to do. Normally she would prepare breakfast for her husband and help him with whatever he needed, but today she was alone. She then decided to go back to bed for a while. This was very unusual for her, but she felt completely lost without Tom in their apartment.

She stayed in bed until ten thirty, watching various nonsensical programs, and then the telephone rang. At first she felt as if her heart had stopped, hoping it wasn't bad news. She hesitantly answered it and was relieved it was her daughter. After their brief conversation, Frances decided to get up, take a shower, and get dressed. She felt like a robot, but after dressing she at least felt better about the way she looked. She occupied the rest of the morning by making the bed and doing other miscellaneous chores, which weren't very many. She also decided to prepare some food to take with her today, as she didn't want to come home and then have to go back to the hospital again.

Glancing at her watch, she read it was one fifteen, and even though it was early, she wanted to leave for the hospital. Gathering up her handbag, her sandwich, and a magazine or two, she put on her coat. Frances then looked around and decided it would be best to put on a light or two, knowing she would be returning after dark. *One more thing*, she thought. She tilted the blinds to allow only a little light into the apartment. *Strange, there are so many little things to think about now that he's not with me.*

Frances left the apartment, locked the door, and got into her car. She warmed it up for a few minutes and then backed out of her parking space. One of the neighbors walked over to her just as she was pulling away. She offered to help if needed, and Frances thanked her for her kindness. She didn't want to appear rude, but at the same time she didn't want to get into a lengthy conversation with her. She just wanted to get to the hospital.

Once inside the hospital, Frances went to the desk clerk, saying she knew she was early, but could she please see her husband now. The woman at the desk picked up the phone and spoke to the nurse in the unit.

"Yes, you may go upstairs now, but please see the nurse on duty first."

Frances was relieved the woman allowed her access to the upper floor. As soon as she got off the elevator, the nurse beckoned to her, saying she would let Frances stay in the room with her husband, but to let him rest as much as possible.

Tom looked very ashen. It was as if he was drained of every bit of color he ever had. He was still hooked up to all the complicated-looking machines. Frances took off her coat and sat in a chair next to him. He was sleeping, and she did not want to disturb him. She glanced through the magazines, not paying a bit of attention to what she was looking at. After a short while, maybe fifteen minutes, she heard Tom moan and realized he was aware she was beside him. Frances smiled and, bending over gently, kissed him hello. She spoke softly, telling him what had transpired yesterday and how later they went back to the apartment. She told him Patricia had everything under control for her and that she would also be there to visit him after she got off work. At first he acknowledged her words and seemed pleased, but then he drifted back to sleep.

As she had planned, Frances stayed the entire day with him and only left his side to use the bathroom and to eat her sandwich in the cafeteria. The nurses on duty were extremely kind to her and let her stay in the room with her husband even though it was part of the intensive care unit. At about six thirty Patricia showed up as promised, and then they both sat in the room quietly for about an hour. During the entire time that Patricia was there, Tom did not open his eyes once or acknowledge them in any way. After an hour Patricia suggested they go back to her mother's apartment and get something to eat.

As soon as they arrived, Frances changed into her comfortable nightclothes and sat down in the kitchen. Patricia also changed, glad she had had enough sense to put a change of clothes in the car the night before. It felt good to get out of the work clothes.

"Okay," Patricia said, "let's see what we have to eat." She found cans of tuna in the cupboard and decided to make sandwiches.

The two sat at the table and hardly spoke a word to each other. They were too tired to have even simple conversation. Patricia knew her mother was exhausted, and so was she. They sat with their tea in hand. Patricia told her she would be back the next day and was planning to come out every day while Tom was in the hospital.

A Matter of Survival

"Don't worry, Mom, I will be here for you, and it might also be a good idea if I stayed with you over the weekend."

Frances agreed; she was glad to have the company of her daughter. It was nice to have someone else to share the worry with her. They continued in the same routine for almost two weeks.

New Year's Eve had come and gone without celebration. Not only were the days shorter but they were much colder as well, and then there also was the ever-present threat of snow in the air. Patricia dreaded driving so far out on the Island from where she worked at La Guardia Airport, especially in heavy snow, but so far the only showing of snow was just a light dusting. Without mentioning anything to her mother, she was always glad when she completed the round-trip drive. They would arrive home sometimes as late as ten o'clock. The two women kept up their vigil, hoping by some miracle Tom would recover. After Tom was in the intensive care unit for just over two weeks, Frances and Patricia were informed by his nurse he was going to be moved to one of the regular floors. The news pleased Frances so much that she started making plans for his homecoming. The nurse waited until Frances's excitement subsided, then laying her hand on Frances's, she spoke softly.

"Oh honey, I'm afraid you won't be able to take your husband home. He is a very sick man, and he is going to need specialized care. No matter how you may want to, you will never be able to take care of him. It will be too much for you. Even if you were to try, you would wind up in the hospital, and then what? You certainly wouldn't be any good to him then."

Frances pleaded with her. "There must be a way. I always promised my husband I would never put him in a nursing home."

The nurse didn't answer but shook her head and looked down at the desk.

Frances waited for Tom's transfer to be completed. When he was finally settled into the new room, she noticed all the wires and machines were still attached to his body. The daily schedule continued, only now it was on a different floor of the hospital. Since it was a small hospital, it seemed as if the entire hospital staff recognized Frances when she arrived each day. They were always very cordial and invariably greeted her with an understanding smile. Somehow this seemed like a source of encouragement to Frances. She felt since they knew her so well, her husband would get extra-special care.

Frances went early each day to the hospital to sit beside her husband. Sometimes he was aware of her presence, and other times Frances didn't think he had any awareness at all. When the room was quiet, she would sing a variety of songs softly and caress his face. Frances had a fairly nice voice, and Tom loved when she sang while she was cleaning the house. Sometimes Tom would open his eyes, and he would try to smile at her. Once in a while he would even recognize Patricia's presence in the room, but mostly he was not aware of what was going on around him. Occasionally Frances's sister-in-law and her nieces would visit Tom, but more often than not, he gave no acknowledgement of their presence. Frances thought, *It's so sad; as we grow older, the family we loved so much has dwindled down to so little.*

It was now approaching the end of January, and Frances couldn't believe Tom was still in the hospital. She didn't see any signs of improvement, and the doctor was not too encouraging either. She just kept hoping he was going to get better.

One afternoon during the second week in February, Frances was visiting Tom as usual. She had brought the newspaper with her, and sitting next to his bedside, she tried to read the latest story behind the headlines. The room was very quiet except for the monotonous sounds of the equipment she had become used to hearing. She found herself dozing off a bit. All at once she was awakened by a sounding alarm filling the room with a screeching clatter. Startled by the sound, Frances jumped to her feet and was about to summon the nurse when the nurse came rushing into the room followed by a medical team. They gruffly insisted Frances leave and wait outside. It was obvious Tom was having difficulty breathing. A minute or two later, a doctor arrived, and before Frances knew what was happening, Tom was being whisked away on a gurney. Frances stood there in the hall with her hand over her mouth, not knowing what to do. She wanted to ask questions but was afraid of what the answer might be.

One of the nurses who stayed behind asked Frances to go back into his room with her. She explained that they had to summon the doctor because they were going to perform emergency surgery on her husband. He needed a tracheotomy since he was having extreme difficulty breathing, and this was the only way possible to save him.

The whole situation was becoming too much for Frances. She had to sit down; she felt so weak that she thought she was going to faint. The nurse left the room and returned with a cool cloth for Frances's head and offered her some cold water as well.

"Frances, this is the best thing for your husband right now. There wasn't a choice. He should be down from surgery within a few hours. If you would like to go home, we will call you when he gets back into the room." Frances was grateful to this woman. She hardly knew her, but found she was very much a source of comfort to her.

Frances retrieved her coat from the closet and quickly put it on. She absent-mindedly buttoned it as she walked out of the room. Without saying a word to anyone, she headed straight to the elevator. Once outside she walked to the parking lot, not noticing the coldness in the air. She finally had to face the facts. Her worst fears were becoming a reality. The man she loved so dearly, the man who rescued her from loneliness and despair, her pillar of strength, was now dying. All she had been through had not prepared her for this. She did not want to let him go, not yet, not ever.

Somehow she drove to her apartment. She wasn't even sure how she got there. As soon as she entered, she locked the door behind her and walked to the telephone. Dialing her daughter's number at work, she removed her coat at the same time. When Patricia answered the phone, she immediately sensed the worst.

"What is it, Mom?" she asked.

Frances, relating the ordeal that she had been through that afternoon, asked her daughter not to come until her normal time. She didn't think she would have to be back at the hospital until much later. Frances said it would be better if Patricia met her at the apartment, and they could both head back to the hospital together. Her daughter agreed, and Frances could hear the despair in her voice as well.

By the time Patricia got to the apartment, Frances had still not heard from the nursing staff. Patricia spoke first. "Let's just go over there and see what is going on."

The two women headed out and drove to the hospital without saying a word to each other. When they reached Tom's room, they discovered he still was not there. The floor nurse saw Frances and called to her, and the women walked to the nurses' station. The nurse explained that Tom was still in recovery and was expected to return to his room within the hour.

Later, as Tom was wheeled into the room, Frances gasped at the sight of him. Her daughter held her hand tightly as if to offer some sort of support. Her husband had a tube coming from his throat that was attached to yet another machine. She knew her heart was breaking at the sight.

Tom was awake and very much aware of what had happened to him. It was obvious after several attempts that he was not able to speak to her. Frances gathered all her strength, telling him everything was going to be all right, and that this procedure was only a temporary one, and in a few days, they would probably be removing the tube. Weakly he seemed to dismiss her words with his hand. Frances knew he was always a very smart man and thought, of course, he doesn't believe me. Even though there was no more to be said, the two women stayed with him until visiting hours were over.

Frances and her daughter went home feeling depressed and upset. Patricia telephoned her husband, who said he would come to the hospital the next night.

Bringing their children, Patricia and her husband joined Frances at the hospital, and then later they went back to her apartment. Frances's sister-in-law and her girls came to visit also, and afterward they too went back to stay with Frances for a while. The little family that Frances had left was all together that night, and she appreciated their help and support more than she could possibly express. She was very grateful to have them with her, especially tonight.

As Frances looked at the family surrounding her and offering their support, it took her back to the tragedy when her brother had been suddenly taken from them. She reminisced about how they all had stuck together during that terrible night, a subject that was now rarely discussed among them. It was noticeable that the stress of Tom's worsening condition was beginning to show on Frances. It was becoming evident to everyone. Frances was exhausted and so tired that she couldn't even get her words straight.

A Matter of Survival

Sometimes when she tried to speak, everything came out garbled. Everyone stayed for a little while with Frances, but then decided to leave and let her get some much-needed rest. Thanking them all, Frances excused herself, saying she just wanted to go to bed and try to forget this nightmare.

Tom continued to hang on for almost another two weeks, and then one night at two o'clock in the morning, Frances received the dreaded telephone call—her husband had passed away. *It's too bad,* she thought. *I wish I had been there with him.*

As Frances hung up the telephone, a feeling of frightening isolation and sadness came over her. She never did get used to being alone, attributing the fright to the little girl inside who had been left alone on the gigantic staircase many years before. Tonight was no exception. Only now she knew being alone meant her husband was gone forever. She was thankful to have been there for him, even though she had known in her heart it was the beginning of the end. Now there would be no more visits to the hospital to distract her from the void of the empty apartment. She knew she would miss him terribly. It was all over.

Forty-Five

...Until Death Do You Part

As the funeral Mass and other preparations were made, Frances was thankful she at least had her daughter, who was able to guide her and take over everything in these difficult times. Tom had always been so proud of Patricia, knowing she would be there for her mother. Many times when Frances and he talked, he'd expressed his confidence that Patricia would handle everything just fine. She was her mother's daughter. Ironically, it worked out that Tom's funeral Mass was held on Ash Wednesday, the beginning of Lent, a sad time for all.

Patricia, together with her husband, invited Frances to stay with them for a few weeks until it could be determined what her next step was going to be. Frances was thankful not to be alone. It was decided she should give up the apartment, as it would be too far for them to travel back and forth for frequent visits. All of Frances's possessions, except the very necessary items, were put into storage.

Patricia set up the guest room for her mother, and she seemed to settle in quite well. All the stress she had been through was beginning to subside, and Frances was becoming more and more like her old self. Frances was happy staying at her daughter's home, even though with an additional person, it was somewhat crowded. The two women spent a great deal of time together, and it was good for Frances to unwind this way. While Patricia worked, Frances would help in dinner preparations as well as doing some daily tasks around the house. It made her feel useful. Patricia thought, *I guess this is what is meant by "role reversal." We really do become parents of our parents*, but she didn't mind.

Shortly after Frances began staying at their home, on one Saturday afternoon, Patricia's husband got an idea. He summoned both his wife and mother-in-law, telling them they were all going out shopping together. Patricia inquired, "Why, what is it you want to buy?" He told his wife it was not for either of them, but rather something for her mother.

The two women dressed nicely for their promised adventure. Patricia was trying to figure out just what her husband had in mind, but she couldn't think of anything her mother needed. After driving for a short distance, her husband pulled the car up to one of the better furriers in town.

"Mom, Tom always wanted to buy you a fur coat, and I figure he would want you to still have it. We are going to make sure you get one today."

Frances was ecstatic. She never, ever dreamed she was going to have another fur coat, and now her son-in-law was seeing to it that she would have one. Frances selected a beautiful dark ranch mink stroller coat that looked absolutely stunning on her. Frances was sorry Tom couldn't be with her today, but knew if he were, he would have wanted her to have it. She wore the coat out of the shop and loved wearing it whenever the occasion arose. She was thankful to have such a terrific daughter and son-in-law who were so good to her.

After about a month or so, Frances suggested that she would like to have a place of her own again. She loved her daughter, but with two teenagers in the house (not to mention their friends), she thought her daughter had enough to do just taking care of her own family along with her job. They would go out early on the weekend to visit several areas, hoping to find the perfect place for Frances. Finally they found a lovely apartment in a rather exclusive area just twenty minutes away. It was perfect, and she would be able to keep almost all of her furniture. The new apartment was housed in a lovely complex, and there was a scenic little pond in the back, which her bedroom overlooked. It not only gave her a sense of privacy, but when she wanted to, she could watch the ducks floating nearby. There was also a little patio in the front where Frances could spend her afternoons outside, perhaps reading the paper or just relaxing. It was perfect for Frances, and surprisingly it was affordable, even now that her income had been reduced with Tom's passing.

Frances was excited at the prospect of the new place. The apartment was a first-floor corner unit of a two-story building, and she would be surrounded by several neighbors. She thought the location was perfect, and she didn't get the feeling of being either isolated or alone.

Together the women selected a few pieces of new living room furniture and had Frances's remaining furniture taken out of storage. They also selected cheerful wallpapers for the kitchen and bathroom, and Patricia's husband helped hang it. The new apartment took only two weeks to complete, and it looked fantastic. Patricia was happy her mother had a place of her own again. Once Frances moved into her new home, they decided Patricia would visit several nights after work. It would be much easier to visit each other now that she was going to live so much closer.

Mother and daughter set up a schedule so that Frances could make weekly visits and stay overnight. On these days, Patricia would help Frances run her errands, such as her banking, getting her hair done, grocery shopping, and anything else that she needed to accomplish. Months passed, and everything seemed to be working out nicely for Frances, and Patricia was pleased things were working out so well.

Frances joined the local senior group in her neighborhood and liked being a member. It gave her a sense of involvement, since there was no one to talk to during the day. She also looked forward to Patricia's visits as well as her weekly visit to her daughter's home.

Frances continued to live quietly in this lovely apartment for more than two years, but she became more and more concerned that her speech patterns were unpredictably changing. It was also becoming apparent she was starting to forget ordinary little things. One afternoon while speaking with Patricia on the phone, Frances confessed to her that she must have been very tired that morning because while having breakfast she fell asleep, and when she woke up, she found herself on the kitchen floor. Frances was not alarmed by this, but her daughter was.

Patricia made an appointment to take her mother to a prominent doctor for a thorough checkup, but unfortunately, it would take several weeks to get a date to see him. Undecided as to what to do in the meantime, she

A Matter of Survival

then looked to her aunt, Wilma, for her opinion regarding her mother's health.

As much as she didn't want to admit it, and hesitating to give her opinion, Wilma finally confessed to Patricia she also noticed a problem developing. Silently both women looked at each other with the sad realization that even without a doctor's diagnosis, their worst fear was Frances could very well be developing Alzheimer's disease.

Finally, the day arrived for Frances to see the doctor. It was an extremely cold winter's day, and Patricia had made arrangements to take off from work. She was more than anxious to accompany her mother on this imperative visit. While driving to her mother's apartment, she was more than concerned and very apprehensive as to how today's doctor's visit may conclude. Once Patricia arrived at her mother's apartment, she noticed Frances seemed to be taking the whole matter very lightly. The only thing she seemed to be concerned about was that she should look her best, and that was all. She insisted that she wear her fur coat, and even though it wasn't necessary, Patricia thought, *Funny, I'm so worried about her, and she's acting like she's going out to dinner. Oh well, if it makes her happy, so be it.*

The doctor had been highly recommended by their family physician and specialized in neurological disorders, particularly in the elderly. After giving Frances a very thorough examination including both a complete physical and mental evaluation, he told Patricia he wanted to discuss his findings with her privately. Patricia sensed she was about to be told the worst; she didn't need to be drawn a picture to know that the news was not going to be good.

Patricia directed her mother to sit in the waiting room with the excuse that she needed to take care of the bill. This would give her the necessary time to speak privately with the doctor. As Patricia looked at her, Frances didn't seem the slightest bit concerned.

The doctor indicated with a motion of his hand for Patricia to take a seat in front of his desk. He didn't hesitate to speak, and without wavering he began.

"I'm afraid the outcome of my examination is not good. While there is not a definitive test to prove conclusively that one is developing Alzheimer's disease, all the indications are that your mother has started to progress with the illness. Eventually, she is going to need constant care as the illness will become worse. You should start to think about making alternative arrangements for her, as I do not think she should be living alone much longer."

Patricia's heart sank with the news, the dreaded news she was so afraid to hear.

The doctor continued, saying something to the effect that he wanted to check her mother's progress again in about six months, et cetera, et cetera, but all the while he was speaking, Patricia was unaware of what he actually was saying. She was concentrating only on the word, "Alzheimer," and at the same time asking herself, *How could this happen to her?* Patricia continued to be deep in thought. *Her whole life was so difficult; why couldn't she just go on and enjoy the rest of it?* Suddenly she realized the doctor had stopped speaking as he knew Patricia was no longer paying attention to him. Patricia apologized. She told him this was the news she feared the most and she needed to digest everything that he told her today.

The doctor was very compassionate. He said he understood and he knew his findings were not easy to accept. Patricia asked if there was any medication that she could give her mother. Shaking his head, he told the distressed woman before him that at the present time, there wasn't anything that could stall or stave off the effects of the disease. He was hopeful, however, as scientists were on the verge of discovering something that might help in delaying its effects. The doctor then reached inside his desk and handed Patricia some booklets to read, saying that they might be helpful in answering any questions she may have. Patricia rose from the chair, thanking the doctor for his time. At the same time she noticed her knees seemed weak, and it took all the strength she could muster to walk into the waiting room to retrieve her mother and act as if everything was fine.

Frances looked at her daughter and asked, "Is everything okay?"

"Fine," Patricia said.

Frances continued, "I knew it would be. I kept trying to tell you. I'm just tired. How 'bout we go out to lunch?"

Patricia nodded, saying "Yes, going out for lunch will be fine."

As she started the car, she realized Tom must have known her mother was developing Alzheimer's, and this might have been the reason why he

A Matter of Survival

appeared to be so irritable and impatient with her. He was probably not only worried about his own health but was also facing Frances's failing mental health, and likely wondering how they would ever be able to take care of each other. Patricia thought sadly, *this must be a really big problem as we age.*

It wasn't long after that Patricia and her family decided it was time to move Frances in with them. By this time, Frances's grandson had gotten married, and as such it freed up his room. Patricia and her husband made arrangements to break up the lovely apartment they had so carefully put together and set out to make the vacated room in their home as pleasant as possible for Frances.

As each year passed, it was obvious the disease was progressing. Soon after moving in with her family, Frances joined the senior center in her daughter's neighborhood, where she was able to spend a good portion of the day being supervised. Frances loved the center and looked forward to joining the group, participating in activities every day. Patricia was able to adjust her working hours so that she would arrive home shortly after Frances. At home, little accommodations and adjustments were made to try to make her life a little easier. Unfortunately, after a little over three years, Frances's condition became more and more worrisome to everyone. She started doing things at home that could become dangerous, and Patricia now was faced with hiring someone when the family was not home. Patricia, her husband, and even Frances's granddaughter would spend much of their weekends trying to find a place where Frances could eventually go to live, but nothing seemed satisfactory. They looked all over Long Island and eventually even in Queens, but Patricia found fault with all of them. Then, unexpectedly one day in the spring of the third year of Frances living with her family, they came upon a beautiful new nursing home that had recently opened. The home met all the criteria the family had been seeking, and it appeared that Frances's daughter had run out of excuses not to place her mother. As much as Patricia didn't want to admit it, the time had come to place her mother in a nursing home.

It was a warm and bright Sunday afternoon in June. Patricia, her husband, and her mother were sitting together outside. The three were savoring the long-awaited summer sunshine when Patricia gathered the courage to speak to her mother concerning the illness that was rapidly taking over her mind.

Almost trembling, she started. "Mom, I need to discuss something important with you, and please, when I'm finished, I want you to give me your opinion. You know we all love you and we have tried to do everything possible to keep you comfortable and safe here, but we are getting more and more worried about you. The doctor has told us you need additional supervised care. Care that we are not able to provide for you. It breaks my heart to tell you this, but we have found a beautiful place for you to live. It's a place near the airport, and I will be able to visit you often and take you home for weekend visits. It's brand new, and the people there seem to be very, very nice."

Patricia stopped speaking, surprised to observe her mother's reaction. Frances simply nodded her head affirmatively and said she agreed with them as she, too, knew she was failing. She also knew it was time, and while she didn't want to upset her daughter, she had already accepted the fact that someday soon she was going to have to leave. Patricia's heart broke for her mother. But then Frances took Patricia's hand and expressed her thanks and gratitude for the redemptive power of her daughter's love and devotion. She continued, saying she knew this was the one thing that she could always depend on; it gave her strength, and she felt she was blessed to have the daughter God gave her. Even with all the heartaches and tribulations she had suffered in her life, she knew that life did have meaning.

Patricia was touched by her mother's words. It was astonishing to her that the woman before her could face another awful change in her life and still accept it with such dignity and grace. She certainly was a remarkable lady.

The week passed, and now it was time for Patricia and her husband to accompany Frances to her new home. The three walked slowly together into the lobby of this lovely new facility and were quickly greeted by someone in administration. She requested them to have a seat while the necessary paperwork was gathered as well as a few other details that needed to be completed.

A Matter of Survival

Frances was silent. The three sat solemnly down, and Patricia found she was not able to speak, for if she did, she was sure the tears would start and she would not be able to stop. There were no more words to say. *Strange,* Patricia said to herself. *This whole terrible scenario reminds me of the instance that occurred so many years ago when the time had come to put our dog to sleep.* It was the dog she and her husband had had before they had children and one she dearly loved. This, she recalled, had been one of the worst and most painful moments that had occurred in their life, and now for some strange reason, her feelings in this situation brought it all back. *Funny,* Patricia thought, *I haven't thought about that dreadfully sad time in years.*

The three sat in silence in the lobby waiting area. Patricia sat facing her mother and husband with her back to the entrance. All at once, they were startled as an almost shouting voice behind them yelled, "Frances, Patricia, I can't believe it's you!"

The three quizzically looked up. Both Frances and Patricia could not believe their eyes. It was Frances's oldest and dearest friend from years and years ago: Val, the woman with whom she had worked and lived when Patricia was just a little girl. The two women embraced and hugged each other. They held on to each other for the longest time. To say they were excited was an understatement. They were more than ecstatic to find each other after so many years. The two were laughing and almost crying at the same time. Patricia and her husband were astounded at the scene before them. This sad, sad time was now one of rejoicing and the renewal of an old and very dear friendship.

In the meanwhile, the woman from administration returned to direct the group to meet a nurse on one of the upper floors. As fate would have it, it just happened to be on the same floor where Val's husband was now living. He occupied a room just three rooms away from where Frances was being assigned.

Frances spoke first. "Val, I must go up to see your husband. How is Al? Why is he here? It's been so many years since we have seen each other. We have a lot to catch up with."

Frances stood up, turned toward her daughter, saying "I'm going upstairs with Val to visit her husband. I'll see you later," and with that, the elevator closed behind them.

Arleen Patricia Mercorella

Patricia and her husband looked at each other in disbelief.

"Some coincidence isn't it?" she said.

The two took the next elevator to the upper floor to join the group. After more than a half hour of searching, the panicked administrator thought Frances must have gotten lost. They simply couldn't find their newest resident. All the time while they were searching for her, Frances was sitting with Val and Al in his room laughing and reminiscing about old times. Needless to say, this entire episode made Frances's transition into the home much easier than anticipated. Patricia left with the feeling that somehow Tom had something to do with it!

Frances settled in very nicely into what was now her new home enjoying visits with Val and Al just a few rooms away from hers. Patricia visited often after work and was gratified to see how well her mother adjusted to accepting this last phase of her life.

Epilogue

On July 28, 2014 I received notification from the doctor at the nursing home that Frances suddenly passed away at the age of ninety-seven dying peacefully in her sleep.

She had been living in the nursing home for fifteen years and for the last ten years she sat in her room, unaware of anything around her or any part of her past life. She lived in a world of her own since Alzheimer's disease had completely taken over her mind. So now at last she had crossed the final hurdle of her life.

While writing this book I realized that although Frances had many challenges and obstacles throughout her life, there were the happy times also with the wonderful people she met along the way. From the very beginning when she entered the home there was the young girl, Melody, who befriended Frances helping her adjust to her new environment, then while attending high school she met her classmate, Kay, who became her best friend and later became my godmother. There also was her Uncle Ralph and Aunt Jean who supported her emotionally giving her sound advice during her most difficult times.

I would be remiss if I didn't mention my paternal grandmother who was able to put her own heartache aside and help raise me, often giving wise advice to Frances when she needed it the most. Later as a working woman she met Val, a friendship that she treasured for many years. It was an astonishing and a touching coincidence that Val appeared when Frances was being admitted into the nursing home, making the transition into institutional life easier not only for my mother, but for me as well.

Arleen Patricia Mercorella

While Frances had considerable reluctance to take on the role of a working mother and raise a daughter, she summoned the courage to do so resulting in one of the happiest times when she befriended Mildred and the wonderful years that were spent with her, her daughter, Carolyn, and me. Being reunited with her brother, Peter, brought her much happiness. Of course, there was also, her sister-in-law, Wilma, and her two nieces, Grace and Loretta, who she loved dearly. Most of all there was Tom who gave her a sense of stability. She deeply loved him and appreciated his strength and his love.

Later in her twilight years she was grateful to her son-in-law, Ralph, who helped her cope with the loneliness after losing Tom and welcomed her to live with us. She found much pleasure in her grandchildren as they added so much happiness to her life. It gave her a great deal of enjoyment as they anticipated her chocolate cakes. I can still picture their eyes lighting up with the fact that Grandma would visit and bring them her special homemade treats.

I like to remember all these wonderful people who crossed her path and not dwell on the sadness. Even though a great majority of her life she lived in turmoil, there were times she met someone who would bring a semblance of sanity to her life when she desperately needed it.

One may wonder how it was that she was able to remain so kind and sweet and never became bitter. How did she always manage to find the strength to move on and to overcome the many obstacles she encountered in her life? How? Perhaps it was growing up in the convent that gave her such a strong character, or maybe it was her faith that got her through all the problems she had, or maybe, just maybe it was the special love shared between mother and daughter. Whatever it was, she did it, or then again, maybe it was just a matter of survival.

Made in the USA
Lexington, KY
08 April 2015